essential
BAKING

essential
BAKING

MURDOCH BOOKS

Published in 2011 by Murdoch Books Pty Limited

Murdoch Books Australia
Pier 8/9
23 Hickson Road
Millers Point NSW 2000
Phone: +61 (0) 2 8220 2000
Fax: +61 (0) 2 8220 2558
www.murdochbooks.com.au

Murdoch Books UK Limited
Erico House, 6th Floor
93–99 Upper Richmond Road
Putney, London SW15 2TG
Phone: +44 (0) 20 8785 5995
Fax: +44 (0) 20 8785 5985
www.murdochbooks.co.uk

Publisher: Kylie Walker
Project Editor: Melody Lord
Food Editor: Anneka Manning
Editor: Anna Scobie
Concept Design: Vivien Sung
Designer: Susanne Geppert

Photographers: Jared Fowler, Louise Lister
Stylist: Jane Hann, Cherise Koch
Food preparation: Dixie Eliot, Sharon Kennedy, Lucy Moore, Alan Wilson

Text copyright © Murdoch Books Pty Limited 2011
Based on The essential Baking cookbook, first published by Murdoch Books in 2000.
Recipes developed in the Murdoch Books Test Kitchen.
Design copyright © Murdoch Books Pty Limited 2011

National Library of Australia Cataloguing-in-Publication entry

Title: Essential baking.
ISBN: 978-1-74266-093-6 (pbk.)
Series: Essential.
Notes: Includes index.
Subjects: Baking
Dewey Number: 641.815

A catalogue record for this book is available from the British Library.

Printed by 1010 Printing International Limited, China.
Reprinted 2011.

IMPORTANT: Those who might be at risk from the effects of salmonella poisoning (the elderly, pregnant
women, young children and those suffering from immune deficiency diseases) should consult their doctor
with any concerns about eating raw eggs.

CONVERSION GUIDE: Cooking times may vary depending on the oven you are using. For fan-forced ovens, as a
general rule, set the oven temperature to 20°C (35°F) lower than indicated in the recipe. We have used 20 ml (4 teaspoon)
tablespoon measures. If you are using a 15 ml (3 teaspoon) tablespoon, add an extra teaspoon for each tablespoon
specified. We have used 60 g (Grade 3) eggs in all recipes.

On the cover: lebkuchen, top (page 109); coffee kisses, centre (page 100); jaffa triple-choc brownies, left (page 131);
melting moments, bottom (page 106).

baking
know-how

There are two things you need to know about baking. One — it's a miracle that a pile of flour, some shortening and a good blast of heat can form the base for such a varied and scrumptious array of food. Two — the sum of these raw materials may sometimes prove temperamental, moody and difficult, and may well drive you mad if your first attempts at baking are not as successful as you'd hoped. If this does happen to you, try not to feel discouraged. As well as making sure our recipe methods are clear and informative, we've given a lot of thought to the problems you might encounter along the way, and have put together a series of "what went wrong?" pages to help you with your next baking adventure. It really is worth taking the time to learn the art of baking, and once you've mastered it, you'll be so proud of yourself, you'll wonder why you didn't get started years ago.

contents

what went wrong?

special features

history in the baking

When looking at the history of baking we have to start with bread, which is certainly the basis for other types of baking such as cakes and biscuits. As people became more skilled at baking and leavening techniques, and a greater variety of ingredients became available, these baked goods began to assert their individuality and gradually earned names of their own. So now when we try to define 'baking' in its most general sense, we mean anything that has a flour base and is cooked in an oven. But let's go back to the beginning.

bread

Bread has been an important staple since Stone Age farmers created the first flatbread. A rough porridge was mixed together and spread thinly over hot stones to form a soft pancake-like bread. It truly is an amazing feat that the connection was made between wheat, water and sunshine to give us this most enduring of foods. The next step forward was achieved 5000 years ago in the Bronze Age, when it was discovered that inverting a pot over hot stones forms a primitive but effective oven.

But the honour of mastering the art of yeast fermentation goes to the ancient Egyptians, who observed that if dough was left out in the open for a few hours it would often bubble and smell a little sour. If this sour dough was baked, the resulting bread had a lighter texture and a pleasant yeasty flavour. The downside to this discovery was that it relied on airborne yeast particles, which made it completely unreliable. To overcome this, the Egyptians would simply save a piece of fermented dough from a previous successful batch, and mix it into the new dough. Brilliant!

Bread has always played a telling role in Europe's social history — the bread in your hands would reveal your rank. White bread was regarded as superior and only suitable for the upper classes. These days, wholegrain breads are thought to be a healthy, more nourishing option and so carry a higher price.

cakes

During the medieval period the distinction between bread and cake was hazy, yet both words passed from Anglo-Saxon to English. Size may have been a telling factor, as 'cake' was translated into Latin as 'pastillus', meaning a little cake or pie.

By the 17th century, the haze had lifted and Europe was familiar with the key ingredients for modern cake-making — in particular, chocolate, sugar, vanilla and treacle. Cake hoops and tins also began to emerge at this time.

But it was the technology of the 19th century that brought the greatest breakthrough. Bicarbonate of soda, the chemical raising agent, made a grand entrance in the early 1800s, closely followed by baking powder. This powder replaced yeast (creating further distinctions between the two forms of baking) but still maintained excellent leavening power. A ready supply of white flour, granulated sugar and cheap shortening made the whole cake-baking experience much simpler (and therefore more popular). Another important development at this time was ovens with reliable temperature control. Imagine that!

Cast your eye over any classic movie set in the early to mid 20th century, and you'll quickly see that good cake-baking skills were something any housewife was proud to possess. Homemade cake not only suggested warmth and hospitality, but displayed an air of abundance and comfort. Attitudes have changed significantly since then — we have less time to spend in the kitchen and have become more health-conscious and this, sadly, restricts our intake of these delicious homemade goodies. Unlike bread, cakes are viewed as more of a treat than a staple.

biscuits

The word 'biscuit' is derived from the Latin 'panis biscotus' (which means 'bread twice cooked') because up until the 18th century, the dough was first baked in a hot oven, then transferred to a cooler oven to dry out (much like modern-day biscotti). Since then, however, cooks the world over have taken the basic recipe and run with it, giving us a staggering array of shapes, flavours and textures to choose from, and making a modern definition of the term rather more difficult.

Luckily there are two subcategories most people are familiar with. The 'cracker' is a thin, unsweetened, dry biscuit whose name probably comes from the cracking noise it makes when broken. The earliest biscuits would have been like these, in that they were unsweetened, hard rounds. Taking a sweeter turn, the word 'cookie' comes from the Dutch 'koekje', meaning little cake, and these tend to be richer, softer and quite chewy in texture. The most famous variety would have to be chocolate chip cookies. These were created by Mrs Ruth Wakefield in the 1930s and were originally known as Toll House cookies, named after the inn she ran with her husband. They were an accidental discovery — when she ran out of regular baker's chocolate, she tried using a bar of chocolate, broken into bits, instead. Surprise, surprise, the chocolate held its shape and didn't melt into the cookie dough, and history was made.

pastry

The Romans used a pastry made of flour, oil and water to cover meat and poultry during baking, thus sealing in the juices. The pastry was not meant to be eaten, which is just as well as it was very dry and tough. In medieval Northern Europe, pastry was used for a similar purpose, but there is also evidence during this time of a finer, richer pastry made from fine white flour, butter and sugar that was certainly meant to be eaten.

Specific recipes for pastry began to appear from about the mid 16th century. In those days, pies generally contained savoury fillings — fruit fillings were very much the exception. It was not long, however, before sweet tarts became popular. These generally contained flower petals, which were chopped up and mixed with sweet biscuits, rosewater, cream, eggs and spices to make rich, yellow cream centres.

teatime

Teatime gives us the chance to enjoy all of the baked goodies we have just been discussing — dainty sandwiches, pastries, scones, tea cakes and biscuits — washed down with a perfectly brewed cup of tea. For this delightful custom, we must thank Anna, wife of the seventh Duke of Bedford. In the 19th century, lunch was a very light meal, and dinner was not served until eight o'clock. Not happy with this arrangement, The Duchess of Bedford asked that tea and cakes be served mid-afternoon because, she claimed, she had 'a sinking feeling'. She invited friends to join her and in no time it became the fashionable thing to do!

Our star rating:

When we test recipes, we rate them for ease of preparation. The following cookery ratings are used in this book:

✼   A single star indicates a recipe that is simple and generally quick to make, perfect for beginners.

✼✼   Two stars indicate the need for a little more care or a little more time.

✼✼✼   Three stars indicate special dishes that need more investment in time, care and patience, but the results are worth it. Even beginners can make these dishes as long as the recipe is followed carefully.

glossary

Understanding the terms used in recipes for baking will help you cook with confidence, as will knowing the function of common ingredients.

bake blind means to partially or totally cook a pastry case before filling it. This prevents the pastry going soggy. Pastry should be partially cooked when it is going to be filled with an uncooked mixture (such as egg in a quiche), or fully cooked for fresh fruit flans. The uncooked pastry is lined with baking paper or foil and, to prevent it rising, it is filled with dried beans, uncooked rice or special-purpose baking beads.

baking powder is a leavener used to aerate cakes, bread and buns. It is a mixture of bicarbonate of soda (baking soda), cream of tartar (an acid) and usually cornflour/cornstarch (to absorb moisture). As a substitute, you can use a mixture of three parts cream of tartar and one part baking soda.

batter is an uncooked mixture of flour, liquid and sometimes a leavener such as baking powder. It can be a thick, spooning consistency as with cake batter, or thin, pouring consistency such as the batter made for pancakes, crepes and pikelets.

beat means to briskly combine ingredients, usually using electric beaters but sometimes a wooden spoon, to introduce a little air into a mixture to make it smooth and light. Beating also helps to create a finer texture for cakes, biscuits and other baked products.

bicarbonate of soda, or baking soda, is both a component of baking powder and a leavener in its own right, one that gets its leavening power with the aid of acid in yoghurt, sour cream, crème fraîche, molasses or buttermilk. It is best to work quickly with the mixture after it has been activated and to get the batter in the oven as soon as possible.

biscuit base or crumb crust is crushed bought biscuits combined with melted butter and sometimes spices. The mixture is pressed onto the base and/or sides of a cake or tart tin. It can be baked or unbaked and is mostly used as a base for cheesecakes and slices.

bread dough is a mixture of flour, liquid, leaven (yeast) and, sometimes, other flavouring and enriching ingredients. The dough should be pliable enough to knead with your hands on a floured surface until it is smooth, elastic and not sticky. Kneading by hand usually takes about 10 minutes. The dough is fully kneaded when it springs back after a finger is indented into the dough. The dough will be smooth, elastic and not sticky and will often have small air bubbles on the surface.

butter is produced when the fat content of cream is separated from the liquid (the buttermilk). When cream is churned, the fat globules combine and become solid, forming butter. Butter is the most commonly used fat for making cakes as it creams well and has an acceptable flavour. Salted butter has two per cent salt added. Originally salt was added as a preservative, but today it is included for taste. We specify unsalted butter (also known as sweet butter) for use in baking biscuits, slices, cakes and sweet pastries.

buttermilk is traditionally the liquid that is left after cream is churned into butter. Today, it is made by adding a culture to skim milk and leaving the mixture for up to 24 hours to sour and thicken. It has a tangy flavour. Because of its acidic content it is used to activate a raising agent, such as bicarbonate of soda (baking soda), especially when making quick breads and scones.

chocolate is made from components extracted from cocoa beans, which grow in pods on the cacao tree. The beans are roasted, then shelled, leaving the nibs which are ground to produce chocolate liquor (bitter chocolate). This forms the base for all chocolate products. The liquor is either pressed to extract cocoa butter and cocoa powder, or blended with varying amounts of cocoa butter and flavouring to produce different chocolates. Couverture chocolate is considered the best. It has a good flavour and glossy finish that is suitable for cake decoration.

cinnamon is the dried aromatic bark from the laurel family of trees native to Asia. The paper-thin inner bark is rolled and dried to form quills or sticks. The sticks are used as a flavour infusion in syrups and poached fruits. Ground cinnamon adds flavour to cakes, puddings, biscuits and yeast breads.

cinnamon sugar is used to decorate cakes, before or after baking, and to flavour buttered toast. Caster (superfine) sugar and ground cinnamon are combined in a proportion of four parts sugar to one part (or more, to taste) cinnamon.

cloves are the strongly scented flower buds of the clove tree, which are sun-dried until hard. They contain essential oils and are used whole or ground in baking. The flavour marries especially well with apple.

cocoa is ground into a powder from the dry solids left when the cocoa butter (the fat) is removed from cocoa beans. It is used extensively in baking. Cocoa is usually sifted in with the dry ingredients so it is distributed evenly. Sweetened cocoa powder is sold as drinking chocolate. Dutch cocoa, available from delicatessens, is considered to be the best flavoured cocoa for baking. It is rich, dark in colour and unsweetened.

cookie is an American term for biscuit. It was originally a small, dry flat cake that was twice baked so that it would be crisp and would keep for longer. Today, the terms 'cookie' and 'biscuit' cover a wide range of baked goods from crispy to chewy. The basic ingredients usually include flour, butter, eggs and sugar. Other flavours such as chocolate, nuts and dried fruit can be added.

copha, or white vegetable shortening, is made from purified coconut oil that is processed into a white solid. Copha is generally used in making uncooked confections and slices or bar cookies.

corn syrup is a liquid form of sugar refined from corn. A variety of corn syrups are produced, from light, which is less sweet, to dark, which is a caramel colour and has flavour added. Corn syrup adds flavour to baked products and is available at speciality shops and delicatessens.

cornflour or cornstarch is a fine white powder made from maize or corn (gluten-free) or from wheat (labelled as wheaten cornflour). It is used in small quantities in baking, such as in sponges and shortbread, to produce a lighter texture. It is also used to thicken sauces and fillings because it forms a gel when heated. Cornflour is usually mixed to a paste with a small amount of cold liquid before being added to the remaining liquid.

cream is the fat globules that rise to the top of unhomogenised milk. The old method of collecting cream was to leave the unrefrigerated milk to stand until the cream separated to the required amount. Today, the separation process is done by using centrifugal force. The fat content determines the type of cream. Cream is used extensively in baking, either as part of the mixture or whipped to decorate. In order to be whipped successfully, cream must have a fat content of at least 30 per cent. If the fat content is higher than this, a lighter foam results when the cream is whipped.

cream of tartar is a component of baking powder. It activates bicarbonate of soda (baking soda) to act as a raising agent when combined. It is sometimes used to help stabilise the beating of egg whites, as in meringue.

cream together means to beat one or more ingredients, usually butter and sugar, until the combined mixture is light and fluffy. Electric beaters or a wooden spoon can be used. The creaming process dissolves the sugar and softens the butter, resulting in a light texture in the baked product.

crème fraîche is a naturally soured cream with a nutty, slightly sour taste. You can make your own crème fraîche by mixing a little sour cream or yoghurt into cream and leaving the mixture in the refrigerator for up to 24 hours to sour. It makes an interesting flavour to accompany sweet desserts, especially tarts. It is available at delicatessens.

dust means to cover lightly, usually referring to icing sugar or cocoa powder that is sifted over the top of a cake or pie for presentation.

eggs in baking are used to enrich and also add flavour, moisture, nutritive value and yellow colour. They have three main functional properties in cooking — coagulation, emulsification and foaming ability. To maintain freshness, eggs should be refrigerated. Bring them back to room temperature before using them in baking.

egg whites increase in volume when whisked, due to the entrapment of air. There are four stages in the whisking of whites. The first is the large bubble stage where the foam is frothy and unstable. The soft peak stage is where the whites form a glossy mass and just hold their shape (to fold into creams and cake mixtures). The next stage is medium peaks, where the foam is very white and glossy, the peaks are soft and the tip falls a little (used for soufflés, mousses and ice creams). The final stage is stiff peaks, where the bubbles are very fine and the peaks hold their shape (as in meringue). To successfully whisk by hand or beat using electric beaters, make sure all utensils are spotlessly clean and free of fat and that the bowl is deep enough to hold the volume of whisked whites. Egg whites also act as leaveners, adding volume and texture to soufflés, flourless cakes and sponge cakes. The whisked whites are gently folded into the mixture just before baking. When cooked, the air is trapped and the mixture expands and coagulates.

essences are concentrated flavourings that enhance the taste of food. Vanilla essence is used extensively in the baking of cakes and biscuits. Almond essence is also used to boost chopped or ground almond flavour in cakes. An extract is a stronger, purer concentration.

evaporated milk is tinned milk with most of its water removed. After opening, it should be refrigerated and used within a couple of days. Diluted, it can be used as milk. Undiluted, it can replace cream. It is used to enrich sauces and moisten food. With the addition of lemon juice, chilled evaporated milk will whip to form a stable foam. Sometimes it is used to make ice cream.

fat or shortening contributes flavour, colour and shortness (tenderness) to shortcrust pastries, cakes and biscuits, and flakiness to layered pastries, such as flaky and puff. Butter, margarine and lard (or a combination) are all suitable for baking. Shredded suet is used in traditional baked pie crusts including steak and kidney pie. Oils may be used in one-bowl or quick-mix cake mixtures such as carrot cake, resulting in a heavier texture. A little oil or butter is added to bread dough for flavour and tenderness. Fat can be creamed with sugar, rubbed into the dry ingredients, melted and mixed into the dry ingredients or kneaded into bread doughs.

flour provides the basic structure of bread, cakes, batters and pastry. The process of manufacturing the whole grain where the grain is converted into a variety of flours is called milling. Wheat flour is the most versatile of all the flours. Roller milling produces white flours and most wholemeal (whole-wheat) flours. Some flours are produced by stone milling. Other non-wheat cereals are milled and used in cooking, for example cornflour (cornstarch), polenta (cornmeal), potato flour, rice flour and rye flour. Unlike wheat flour, some lack, or have lower levels of, the protein gluten, which gives the strength, elasticity and structure necessary for baking. However, they are useful for people who are intolerant to wheat products. Bread doughs made with non- or low-gluten flours do not have the elasticity of dough made with wheat-based flour so the bread will have a dense texture.

Plain white flour, also known as all-purpose flour, has a medium protein content of about 10 per cent. Most baked goods use this flour. Self-raising flour has the same protein qualities as plain flour, but has baking powder added to it. You can make self-raising flour by adding 2 teaspoons baking powder to 125 g (4½ oz/1 cup) plain flour and then sifting thoroughly several times. Wholemeal flours are coarsely milled or finely ground and can be used instead of plain white flour. If you do use wholemeal, the baked product will have a denser crumb and less volume.

Bread flour is produced from hard wheat with a higher protein (gluten) content, about 12 per cent, than plain flour. It is smoother in texture and is used to ensure that the dough is elastic and strong so that the bread has structure, strength and elasticity. It is available in supermarkets and health food stores. Sometimes it is called strong flour. It can be used for general baking.

frangipane is creamed butter and sugar with eggs, ground almonds and a liqueur. It is used as filling in a pastry or tart case.

galettes are open fruit tarts. They have a thin pastry base topped with raw sliced or halved fruit that is sprinkled with sugar, then dotted with butter and baked. Galettes are usually made with puff pastry, either homemade or bought, cut into individual rounds or squares, topped with the fruit and sugar and baked. They can also be made with filo, shortcrust pastry or a yeasted dough. Dried fruit and nuts can be used as a topping if preferred.

gelatin is extracted from collagen, the connective tissue present in the bones and cartilage of animals. Gelatin is a setting agent available in powdered form and as sheets or leaves: 3 teaspoons powdered gelatin is equivalent to 6 sheets, which will set 500 ml (17 fl oz/2 cups) of liquid to a light jelly. To dissolve gelatin sheets, soften them in a bowl of cold water for 5 minutes, then remove and squeeze well. Next, dissolve them in warm to hot liquid. To dissolve powdered gelatin, sprinkle the powder over water in a small, heatproof bowl. Sit the bowl in a larger bowl of hot water and leave to dissolve. Agar-agar is a substitute suitable for vegetarian people. Follow the instructions on the packet.

ginger is the rhizome or root of the ginger plant, and is native to South-East Asia. It is available fresh or dried (ground). Fresh ginger should be bought while plump and firm with a pale outer skin. The outer skin is peeled away and the flesh is finely grated just before use. The powder is used in baking to flavour cakes, biscuits, puddings and gingerbread. Crystallised ginger is used in cakes, desserts and as decoration. The flavour is pungent, sweet and spicy.

glacé fruit is fruit that is preserved in sugar. The fruit, usually citrus or pineapple slices, or cherries, is cooked in a strong syrup solution until the fruit is impregnated by the sugar. Cherries are often coloured with various food dyes.

glaze is a liquid — such as milk, sugar syrup, melted butter, softened and sieved jam, beaten whole egg, egg yolk and water, or egg white — that is brushed onto food, often before baking but sometimes after, to give colour and shine.

gluten, a protein found in wheat flour, is the muscular, elastic substance that strengthens the cellular structure of the bread dough. Without gluten, bread is flat and heavy. Gluten flour or powder is sometimes added to bread dough for an improved volume, structure and texture. Non-wheat flours, notably rye, oat, barley and corn, don't have the same gluten content. If volume is wanted, these flours require added gluten in the form of gluten flour or the addition of wheat flour. Breads made without the addition of gluten are heavy and dense as in German rye bread, corn breads and oatcakes. Gluten flour or powder is available at health food shops and some supermarkets.

golden syrup is a by-product of sugar refining. It is a thick, sticky syrup with a deep golden colour and distinctive flavour. It is used in the baking of gingerbread, tarts and some breads to give flavour and moisture. It can be substituted for treacle in baked goods.

icing sugar, also known as pure icing sugar or confectioners' sugar, is powdered white sugar that is used in the making of icings, including buttercreams, glacé and royal, and fondants, to decorate cakes. It should always be sifted before use to remove lumps and obtain a smooth finish.

Icing sugar mixture is icing sugar to which a small amount of starch is added to prevent lumping during storage. It is used in the making of icings such as buttercreams and glacé, but is not suitable for royal icing as it won't set hard.

jams are traditionally made from whole fruit that has been cooked to a pulp with sugar until it jells or sets. Jam heated and strained through a sieve, then brushed over a cake or sweet bread, makes an attractive finish. Small amounts of jam or marmalade blended into a cake mixture add extra flavour and moisture.

knead means to work a bread dough with your hands on a flat, floured surface. The dough is rhythmically pushed, stretched and folded in order to develop the gluten in the flour. It takes about 10 minutes of kneading for the gluten to be fully developed.

knock back is a term for when bread dough is punched down (literally, one punch) after its first rising. This allows the bubbles of carbon dioxide to be expelled, preventing the gluten walls from stretching and collapsing. The dough is then ready to be shaped and left to rise a second time.

lard is purified fat from pork. It is sold in solid form in packets and can be refrigerated for weeks. It is traditionally used in pastry-making. Lard is a good shortening (tenderising) agent but lacks flavour and colour, so a blend of butter and lard will produce the most tender pastry with more flavour.

leavened is a term describing baked products such as breads and cakes that contain a raising agent, usually yeast or baking powder, to increase the volume of the goods.

malt extract is produced from grain, in a process that converts grain starch to a sugar called maltose. The resulting powder or syrup is used widely in baking, brewing and distilling. It retains moisture, thus giving malted breads their distinctive flavour and moist texture. It also aids in the rising of bread dough. It is a nutritious addition to breads, puddings and cakes. The powdered form is used in drinks.

maple syrup is a light-brown syrup processed from sap of the maple tree. It has a distinctive flavour and is often used as a topping for pancakes and waffles. It is also used in baking cakes and biscuits and to flavour icings and ice creams. Maple syrup is available at most supermarkets.

marzipan is a mixture of almond paste (meal), egg white and icing sugar. It is mainly used, rolled out thinly, to cover fruit cakes before they are finished with a layer of royal icing. Marzipan can also be tinted with food dyes and shaped to resemble fruits or animals, to decorate cakes.

meringue is stabilised egg-white foam and dissolved sugar crystals, brought about by whisking. The quantity of sugar required per egg white in order to form a stable meringue varies from 50–75 g (1¾–2¾ oz). There are three types of meringue. Swiss meringue produces an externally crisp and dry texture, usually with a dry centre. It is suitable for piping, pie toppings and pavlovas. The standard proportion is 50–60 g (1¾–2¼ oz) sugar for each egg white.

Soft and creamy in texture, Italian meringue is more stable than the Swiss and is used as a cake frosting, for Baked alaska, and sometimes in ice creams and whipped cream (crème chantilly). The basic proportion is 50–60 g (1¾–2¼ oz) sugar per egg white — a sugar syrup is made first and then slowly poured onto the beaten white.

Meringue cuite (cooked) is a very firm, dry meringue mostly used by pastry cooks in the making of meringue baskets and meringue decorations that can be stored for a time. 75 g (2¾ oz) icing sugar to one egg white is used for this.

Meringues need to be baked at a very low temperature, preferably in an electric oven, as they need to dry out and maintain their white colour.

mixed peel, or mixed candied citrus peel, is a mixture of chopped citrus fruit peel preserved in sugar and glucose syrup. It is mainly used in fruit cakes, mince pies and some puddings.

mixed spice, or pumpkin pie spice, is a blend of ground spices, usually allspice, cinnamon, nutmeg, cloves and ginger. It adds a lightly spicy flavour to cooked fruit, such as apples, and also to cakes, fruit cakes, puddings and biscuits.

nutmeg is the dried kernel or seed of the fruit of an evergreen tree native to South-East Asia. The seed has a lacy husk called mace. Mace is used in flakes (blades) or powdered form and added to savoury dishes such as pickles and instead of nutmeg in sweet dishes. The nutmeg kernel is grated whole or used in powder form to flavour cakes and desserts. Freshly grated nutmeg has a much better flavour. Grate on the fine holes of a grater, or use a special nutmeg grater.

nuts are formed after a tree or plant has flowered. They are the hardened and dried fruit encased in tough shells that have to be cracked to open (such as macadamias and chestnuts). However, the term 'nut' is also used to describe any seed or fruit with an edible kernel in a hard or brittle shell (almonds, walnuts and coconuts). Nuts are used extensively in baking. They are an important source of food and oil in all cuisines. Because of their high fat content it is advisable to refrigerate nuts in an airtight container to prevent them turning rancid.

oils are similar to fats, but differ in their physical state. Oils are liquid at room temperature, whereas fats are solid. Animal fats (saturated fats) that are used in baking include butter, cream, ghee, lard and suet. Vegetable oils (polyunsaturated and monounsaturated fats) include fruit oils (such as olive oil), nut oils (such as walnut or hazelnut oil), seed oils (such as sesame or sunflower oil), pulse oils (such as soybean oil) and cereal oils (such as corn oil). All of them are used in one form or the other for the baking of cakes, biscuits, desserts, puddings and breads. Oils enhance the flavour and level of moistness, as well as the keeping qualities in baked products.

organic ingredients have generally been produced without the use of pesticides, insecticides, herbicides, fungicides or artificial fertilisers. Increasingly, ingredients that are commonly used in baking, such as flour, butter and eggs, are being produced organically and made more generally available. These products can be substituted in recipes and this decision is entirely personal.

powdered milk is milk from which most of the moisture has been removed. The resulting milk powder can be stored in airtight tins or foil bags for up to a year. It is reconstituted to milk by adding water, or can be used in its powder form to enrich baked products, especially bread doughs. Powdered milks are made from both full-fat and non-fat (skim) milk.

proving (also called the second rise) describes the process of the bread dough being knocked back, then shaped and left to rise on its baking tray until it has doubled in bulk, before baking. Test by gently pressing a finger into the dough and if the imprint remains, the dough is proved and ready for baking.

ribbon stage is when eggs and sugar are beaten, either using electric beaters or a hand whisk, until the sugar has dissolved and the egg becomes pale and firm with very small bubbles. The beaters or whisk will leave a raised mark on top of the mixture when the ribbon stage is reached. The term is used when sponge cakes are being made. The result of the beating is a very light aerated cake. Usually only small amounts of flour and perhaps ground nuts are gently folded into the mixture before baking.

salt is used as a seasoning, preservative and flavour enhancer. Salt improves the balance of flavours in sweet baking goods and most recipes will include some. The flavour of bread is greatly improved with the addition of salt. Iodised salt, often used as table salt, has a trace element of iodine added. Sea salt is made by extracting sea salt by natural means. Rock salt is mined from under the ground.

suet is the fat that surrounds the kidneys of beef cattle. Before use, suet needs to be skinned and cleaned, then grated or shredded. It is often used in dried-fruit puddings. Fresh suet can be bought from a butcher. Dried, shredded suet can generally be found at supermarkets. Butter can be used instead.

sugar is the common name for sucrose, the simplest form of carbohydrate. Sugars are found in virtually all plants, including many fruits and vegetables. There are several types of sugar. The most widely used is white sugar (granulated, caster, cubed and icing sugar). It is usually manufactured from sugar cane or sugar beet and is used extensively in baking and general use. In baking, sugar is important as it adds flavour, taste and moisture, and has a tenderising effect.

Coloured sugars, also made from sugar cane, include brown sugar (also called soft brown sugar), a golden-brown refined sugar used in baked goods. These sugars add colour and flavour and help create a moist texture, especially in cakes. Brown sugar is also available as dark brown sugar. The colour in these sugars comes from the molasses content.

Raw sugar, coarse straw-coloured crystals, is also produced from sugar cane. It can be substituted for white sugar to add texture, but is difficult to dissolve.

Demerara sugar is a coarse crystal, amber in colour and similar to raw sugar, also used in baking, especially crumble topping.

treacle is a blend of concentrated refinery syrups and extract molasses. It is used in baking to give a distinctive colour and flavour. It also adds moistness and keeping qualities to a baked product. Golden syrup can be substituted for treacle when used in baking.

vanilla is extracted from the pods of a climbing orchid plant native to South America. The pods or beans are dried and cured. For use in cooking, the pod is split open and infused with the food to allow for maximum flavour. The pod can be washed, dried and re-used. Vanilla is also available as pure essence or extract, which has a concentrated flavour and is widely used in baking.

vanilla sugar is made by placing a vanilla pod or bean in a jar of caster (superfine) sugar and leaving it to stand so the flavour is absorbed into the sugar. This is a good method of storing a vanilla pod, as it flavours the sugar and also prevents the pod drying out. For a flavour boost in baking, use vanilla sugar instead of regular caster sugar.

whisk means to combine and incorporate air into either whole eggs, egg whites, egg yolks (sometimes with sugar) or cream until it thickens to the desired consistency — foamy, soft peaks, medium peaks or stiff (firm) peaks. Use either a balloon whisk or an electric beater with a whisk attachment.

yeast is a biological (naturally occurring) raising agent. Fresh (compressed) yeast, available from bakeries, needs to be blended with water to form a smooth cream, then added to any remaining liquid and left to foam before being added to the dry ingredients. Dried yeast, available in sachets from supermarkets, can be added to liquid or mixed straight into the dry ingredients.

For fermentation of the yeast to take place, it needs the right conditions of food (sugar), warmth (26–29°C) and moisture (liquid).

zest, or rind, is the outside peel of any citrus fruit. It contains all the essential oils and therefore the flavour. Be careful when removing it that you do not include the bitter white pith beneath. If the fruit has a wax coating, wash it off in hot water before removing the zest. Finely grated or shredded zest is used to flavour cakes, biscuits, syrups and doughs. It can also be thinly peeled from the fruit, leaving the white pith behind, then finely shredded with a small, sharp knife.

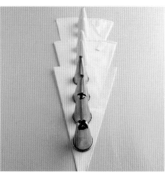
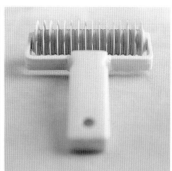
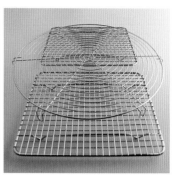

basic utensils

When you investigate the secrets of baking at home, you will need to invest in some basic utensils. If you buy good-quality ones, you will find they last longer.

wooden spoons
Useful for beating, mixing and stirring, as they do not conduct heat or scratch non-stick surfaces. Choose spoons with hard, close-grained wood for durability.

metal spoons
Large metal spoons are best for folding in dry ingredients, or combining one mixture with another without losing too much air.

piping bags and nozzles
Piping (icing) bags of different sizes accommodate small metal or plastic nozzles with various shaped openings. The bags should be washed thoroughly after use and then dried inside-out to prevent odours developing.

lattice cutters
For topping pies and tarts, these simplify cutting a lattice pattern into rolled-out pastry. They are usually made from plastic so they will not mark work surfaces.

cooling racks
These footed metal grids enable air to circulate around food during cooling.

dough scrapers
These are used to divide, separate and scrape dough on a work surface. They are used mainly for pastry and bread doughs.

graters
Graters with perforations of different sizes are designed for specific functions, from grating cheese to citrus zest. Nutmeg graters are small and concave, often with a compartment for the whole spice.

rolling pins
These should be large enough to roll out a full sheet of pastry, ensuring a smooth surface. Good-quality rolling pins are made from hard wood with a close grain and very smooth finish. Wood is preferable to ceramic and marble as its surface collects and holds a fine layer of flour to help prevent the pastry from sticking.

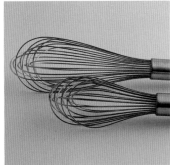

flour sieves and dredgers
These are ideal for incorporating air into flour or dusting flour onto work surfaces. They can also be used when decorating or dusting with icing sugar or cocoa.

baking beads
Small reusable ceramic or metal beads used when blind-baking pastry. Uncooked rice or dried beans can be substituted.

whisks
Whisks incorporate air into ingredients and remove lumps. Balloon whisks are loops of stainless steel joined by a handle. There are larger ones for whisking egg whites and smaller ones for batters and sauces.

apple corers
These cylindrical blades fit neatly around the core of an apple to remove it without damaging the whole fruit.

citrus zesters
Zesters have a row of holes with sharp edges running across the top. When they are drawn down firmly across a citrus fruit, they peel off the zest or rind in long, thin shreds.

pastry brushes
Made with nylon or natural bristles, pastry brushes can be flat or round and are used for glazing. Care should be taken when using nylon bristles with very hot liquids as the bristles may melt. Brushes should be washed and dried thoroughly before storage and it is a good idea to keep separate brushes to use for oil and melted butter.

pastry wheels
These are wooden, metal or plastic wheels used for cutting fluted edges on pastry.

cutters
These come in a variety of shapes and sizes, ranging from plain and fluted rounds to hearts and gingerbread people. Metal cutters have a better edge than plastic, but need to be dried and stored carefully as they can easily rust or be bent out of shape.

measuring cups and spoons
All spoon and cup measures in this book are level, not heaped. Dry ingredients should be levelled off with a knife. The recipes in this book use 20 ml (4 teaspoon) tablespoon measures. If you are using a 15 ml (3 teaspoon) tablespoon, add an extra teaspoon for each tablespoon specified.

sifters
Hand sifters are used to aerate lumpy flour and are useful for sifting small amounts of flour to a light consistency.

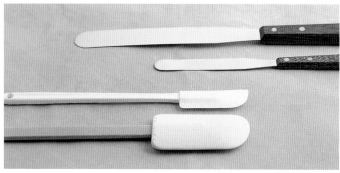  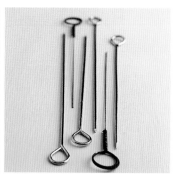

palette knives

These are available in various sizes and degrees of flexibility. The blade is thin and flat with a rounded end and is useful for transferring flat items such as biscuits and for spreading decorative icings.

spatulas

These are useful for scraping a bowl completely clean and getting residue out of blender and food processor bowls. Rubber spatulas are more flexible than plastic ones, but do tend to absorb colour and flavour so keep separate ones for sweet and savoury use.

scales

Essential for weighing ingredients, kitchen scales vary from balance scales to digital display and most of them provide both metric and imperial weights.

metal skewers

Long and thin with a sharp, pointed edge, these are useful for testing to see whether a cake is cooked through.

paring knives

With a short blade, these are handy all-purpose knives. They are perfect for cutting fruit, as well as trimming pastry and making small incisions.

serrated knives

These are best for slicing through bread and cakes neatly and evenly.

electric mixers

These can be hand-held or stand on the benchtop. They make creaming mixtures, mixing batters and whisking whites much easier than by hand.

mixing bowls

Stainless-steel bowls are durable and are good conductors of heat and cold. Heatproof bowls are essential for slow heating over a water bath. Glass and ceramic bowls need to be sufficiently heavy to sit firmly in place while ingredients are combined.

oven thermometers

These are designed to stand or hang in the oven. When baking, it is essential to check the oven's temperature is accurate.

citrus juicers

These are available in glass, ceramic, plastic and wood, as well as electric.

bakeware

Bakeware should respond quickly and evenly to the oven temperature. Shiny metal bakeware will deflect heat and prevent scorching, whereas dark, matt, non-stick bakeware will absorb and hold heat and may need a slightly lower cooking temperature or a little less cooking time. Baking trays should be solid so they don't buckle.

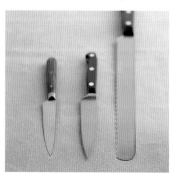   

bread tins

cake and slab tins

baking trays, slice tins and loaf (bar) tins

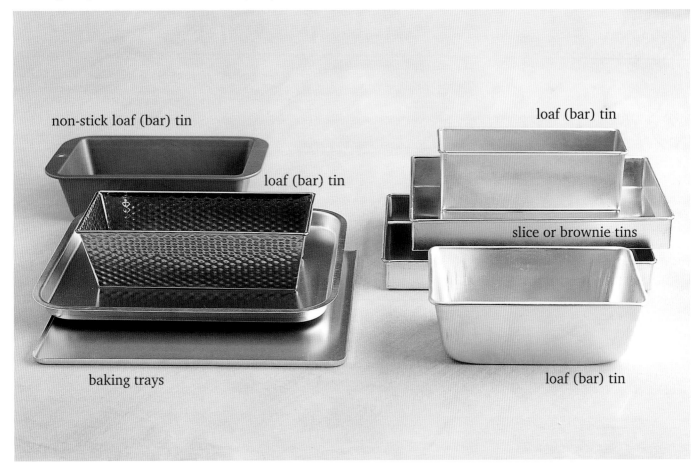

non-stick loaf (bar) tin

loaf (bar) tin

loaf (bar) tin

slice or brownie tins

baking trays

loaf (bar) tin

speciality cake tins

angel food tin

deep, fluted ring tin

round spring-form tins

charlotte tin

nut-roll tin

savarin tin

kugelhopf or bundt tins

tube or ring tin

muffin and small cake tins

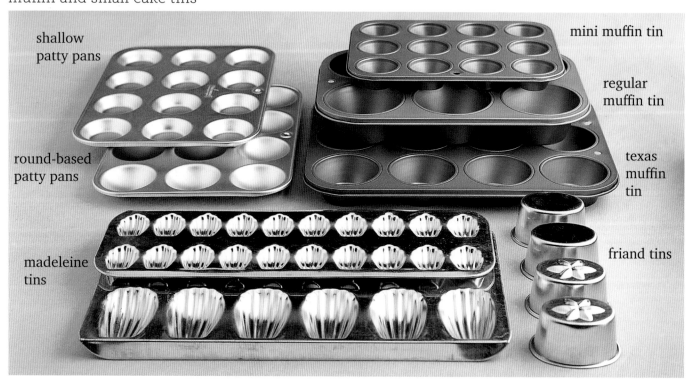

shallow patty pans

mini muffin tin

regular muffin tin

round-based patty pans

texas muffin tin

madeleine tins

friand tins

round cake tins

deep tins

shallow or sandwich tins

fluted tart tins (with removable bases)

general baking tips

- Read the recipe through and take note of any soaking, standing and overnight refrigeration times, and make sure you have the necessary equipment.
- Always follow one set of measurements — metric or imperial, or cups. We have included cup measurements for ingredients such as flour, sugar and liquids, and weights for everything else.
- Electronic scales have a digital display and can be programmed for metric and imperial weights. They are the most accurate way of measuring by weight.
- If you don't have exactly the right size tin, it may not matter. A 1 cm (½ inch) difference will not ruin a pie or tart — you may just have a little too much, or not quite enough, filling and the pastry will be a bit thinner or thicker. However, a difference of more than 2 cm (¾ inch) may change things too much, so use your judgement.
- Ovens do not all behave in the same way. Fan-forced ovens will cook more quickly and can be used to cook more than one thing at a time as they have a more overall heat.
- Not all ovens are accurate so use an oven thermometer placed in the centre of the oven to check the temperature.
- Pastry that needs a quick exposure to heat to set it is best cooked near the oven element, whereas dishes cooked in a water bath should be placed away from the element.
- Glass heatproof bowls are useful for whisking egg whites and melting chocolate. Stainless-steel bowls also work well for these functions, as well as heating up and cooling down quickly when required. A large ceramic bowl is invaluable for mixing large quantities.
- Buy a good-quality food processor with a bowl large enough to cope with large quantities. A spice grinder will take care of any small quantities.
- Blenders should have a good motor and blades that sit both up and down in the goblet, otherwise small amounts will simply go round and round.
- A kitchen timer is essential for accurate timing and to prevent burning food.
- Baking paper or parchment should be non-stick to be most effective. Greaseproof paper is not non-stick but is useful for making piping (icing) bags.
- Many recipes can be varied by substituting or adding your favourite flavours. Again, use your judgement.

teatime

A warming fireside, a squashily comfortable armchair, perhaps a little sprinkle of rain outside. The kettle whistles noisily in the kitchen and everyone's spirits brighten — it's time for tea. The tradition of teatime conjures up a cosy, safe and reassuring feeling and is an excellent opportunity to indulge in some of your favourite comfort foods. Light-as-air scones with homemade strawberry jam and clotted cream, muffins, friands, wonderfully old-fashioned cream buns and madeleines . . . mmmm, lovely. Pour yourself a nice cup of tea, crook your little finger daintily as you drink, and enjoy the moment.

scone secrets

Scones are so easy, it is quicker to make them than go out and buy them. For perfect scones, handle them quickly and lightly, and bake in a hot oven.

light and easy

All scones are made according to the same principles: add the wet ingredients to the dry and mix the dough as briefly and lightly as possible. Because the moisture content of flour varies, you may not need all the liquid stated in your recipe. The amount of liquid the flour absorbs can also change according to the room temperature and even the altitude. Although our recipe uses self-raising flour, some people prefer to use plain (all-purpose) flour and add more raising agents such as baking powder. Salt is added to enhance the flavour of all scones, even sweet ones, and the taste is not noticeable.

making perfect scones

Follow these simple directions to achieve a good batch of high, light and golden scones. Remember that unlike bread, which requires vigorous kneading, scone dough just needs quick, light handling. To make 10 to 12 scones, you will need 310 g (11 oz/2½ cups) self-raising flour, 1 teaspoon baking powder, a pinch of salt, 40 g (1½ oz) unsalted butter, chilled and cut into small cubes, and 250 ml (9 fl oz/1 cup) milk. Assemble all the ingredients as well as a large bowl, a flat-bladed metal spatula or knife for mixing, a round scone or biscuit cutter, a pastry brush and a baking tray. You will also need a clean tea towel (dish towel) to wrap the cooked scones.

Before you begin mixing, preheat the oven to 220°C (425°F/ Gas 7) and lightly grease the baking tray or line it with baking paper. Sift the flour, baking powder and salt into a bowl. Sifting aerates the dry ingredients and helps achieve lighter scones. Many bakers sift the flour twice. Rub in the butter briefly and lightly with your fingertips until the mixture is crumbly and resembles fine breadcrumbs. Mixing in 1 tablespoon of sugar at this stage will lessen any floury taste. Make a well in the centre. Pour in almost all the milk and mix with a flat-bladed knife, using a cutting action, until the dough comes together in clumps. Rotate the bowl as you work. Add the remaining milk if the mixture seems too dry. Handle the mixture with great care and a very light hand. If you are heavy-handed and mix too much, or knead, your scones will be tough. The dough should feel slightly wet and sticky.

With floured hands, gently gather the dough together, lift onto a lightly floured surface and pat into a smooth ball. Do not knead. Pat or lightly roll the dough out to 2 cm (¾ inch) thick. Don't pat it out too thinly or the scones will not be a good height. Using a floured 6 cm (2½ inch) scone cutter, cut into rounds. Gather the scraps and, without handling too much, press out and cut more rounds. Place close together on the baking tray and lightly brush the tops with milk. Bake in the top half of the oven for 12–15 minutes, or until the scones are risen, golden and cooked through.

It is important to bake scones at a high temperature, otherwise the raising agents will not work. If you aren't sure the scones are cooked, split one open. If it is still doughy in the centre, cook for a few more minutes. For soft scones, wrap them in a dry tea towel (dish towel) while they are hot. For scones with a crisp top, transfer to a wire rack to cool slightly before wrapping. Serve the scones warm or at room temperature, with butter or jam and whipped or clotted cream. Scones contain little fat so they dry out quickly — they're best eaten soon after baking. Scones can be frozen successfully, which is an excellent idea for any leftovers.

CORNWALL COLLEGE
LEARNING CENTRE

breadcrumbs. Stir in the sultanas. Make a well in the centre of the dry ingredients.

2 Add almost all the milk and mix with a flat-bladed knife, using a cutting action, until the dough comes together in clumps. Add the remaining milk if necessary. With floured hands, gently gather the dough together, lift out onto a lightly floured surface and pat into a smooth ball. Do not knead or the scones will be tough.

3 Pat the dough out to 2 cm (¾ inch) thick. Using a floured 5 cm (2 inch) scone cutter, cut into rounds. Gather the trimmings and without over-handling, press out as before and cut more rounds. Place close together on the tray and brush with the extra milk. Bake for 12–15 minutes, or until risen and golden brown. Serve the scones warm or at room temperature.

cheese scones

✳

Preparation time: **15 minutes**
Cooking time: **15 minutes**
Makes **12**

250 g (9 oz/2 cups) self-raising flour
1 teaspoon baking powder
½ teaspoon dry mustard
30 g (1 oz) butter, chilled and cubed
25 g (1 oz/¼ cup) freshly grated
   parmesan cheese
90 g (3¼ oz/¾ cup) finely grated
   cheddar cheese
250 ml (9 fl oz/1 cup) milk

1 Preheat the oven to 220°C (425°F/ Gas 7). Lightly grease a baking tray or line with baking paper. Sift the flour, baking powder, mustard and a pinch of salt into a bowl. Using your fingertips, rub in the butter until the mixture resembles fine breadcrumbs. Stir in the parmesan and 60 g (2¼ oz/½ cup) of the cheddar, making sure they don't clump together. Make a well in the centre.

2 Add almost all the milk and mix with a flat-bladed knife, using a cutting action, until the dough comes together in clumps.

sultana scones

sultana scones

✳

Preparation time: **10 minutes**
Cooking time: **15 minutes**
Makes **12**

250 g (9 oz/2 cups) self-raising flour
1 teaspoon baking powder
30 g (1 oz) unsalted butter,
   chilled and cubed

60 g (2¼ oz/½ cup) sultanas
   (golden raisins)
250 ml (9 fl oz/1 cup) milk, plus extra,
   to glaze

1 Preheat the oven to 220°C (425°F/ Gas 7). Lightly grease a baking tray or line with baking paper. Sift the flour, baking powder and a pinch of salt into a bowl. Using your fingertips, rub in the butter until the mixture resembles fine

Add the remaining milk if necessary. With floured hands, gently gather the dough together, lift out onto a lightly floured surface and pat into a smooth ball. Do not knead or the scones will be tough.

3 Pat the dough out to 2 cm (¾ inch) thick. Using a floured 5 cm (2 inch) scone cutter, cut into rounds. Gather the trimmings and, without over-handling, press out as before and cut more rounds. Place the rounds close together on the tray and sprinkle with the remaining cheese. Bake for 12–15 minutes, or until risen and golden brown. Serve the scones warm or at room temperature.

pumpkin and sage scones

Preparation time: **10 minutes**
Cooking time: **20 minutes**
Makes **8**

250 g (9 oz/2 cups) self-raising flour
250 g (9 oz/1 cup) cooked and puréed
  pumpkin (winter squash)
20 g (¾ oz) butter, chilled
1 tablespoon chopped sage
a little milk

1 Preheat the oven to 180°C (350°F/ Gas 4). Lightly grease a baking tray or line with baking paper. Sift the flour into a bowl with a pinch of salt. Using your fingertips, rub the pumpkin and butter into the flour, then add the sage.

2 Bring the mixture together with a little milk and turn it out onto the tray. Shape the mixture into a round and roll it out to about 3 cm (1¼ inches) thick. Gently mark or cut the scone into eight segments and bake for 15–20 minutes, or until lightly browned and cooked through.

cheese scones

muffins

Wonderfully simple, muffins can be plain, sweet or savoury. Once you have mastered the basic muffin recipe, you can start experimenting with different flavour combinations.

perfect muffins

To make 12 muffins, you will need 310 g (11 oz/2½ cups) self-raising flour, 125 g (4½ oz/½ cup) caster (superfine) sugar, 375 ml (13 fl oz/1½ cups) milk, 2 lightly beaten eggs, 1 teaspoon natural vanilla extract and 150 g (5½ oz) unsalted butter, melted and cooled. We used the medium size (100 ml/3½ fl oz) American-style tins, but mini and Texan sizes are also available. Most muffin tins have non-stick surfaces, but we still advise greasing the holes or lining with paper cases, especially for sweet muffins as the sugar can make them sticky.

Assemble your ingredients and utensils and preheat the oven to 200°C (400°F/Gas 6). Sift the flour into a bowl to aerate it and ensure a light muffin. Add the sugar to the bowl and stir through the flour. Make a well in the centre. In a jug, mix together the milk, eggs and vanilla. Pour the liquid into the well in the flour and add the cooled butter. Melted butter doesn't always combine well with other liquids so it is often added separately. Fold the mixture gently with a metal spoon until just combined. Be careful not to overmix or the muffins will become tough and rubbery. The mixture should still be slightly lumpy.

Divide the mixture evenly among the holes using two metal spoons — fill each hole to about three-quarters full. Try to use the hole size specified in the recipe, because if you use a different size the cooking time changes. The larger the hole, the longer the baking time.

Muffins can be frozen for up to 3 months. Thaw, wrap in foil and reheat in a 180°C (350°F/Gas 4) oven for 8 minutes.

cooking

Bake the muffins for 20–25 minutes, or until they are risen, golden and come away slightly from the sides of the holes.

Test them by pressing lightly with your fingertips — they should feel firm and spring back. Or insert a skewer into the centre — if it comes out clean, they are ready. Most muffins should be left in the tin for a few minutes once out of the oven, but not for too long or the bases will become soggy. Transfer to a wire rack and eat warm or allow to cool.

simple variations

The basic recipe can be adapted to add many flavours. You can use the same tin size, but the muffin holes will be quite full.

choc chip

Add 260 g (9¼ oz/1½ cups) chocolate chips to the sifted flour. Replace the caster (superfine) sugar with 95 g (3¼ oz/½ cup) soft brown sugar.

blueberry

Add 300 g (10½ oz) blueberries to the sifted flour. If fresh blueberries are unavailable, frozen ones can be used. Add them while still frozen to avoid streaking the batter.

banana

Add an extra 60 g (2¼ oz/¼ cup) caster (superfine) sugar and ½ teaspoon mixed (pumpkin pie) spice to the sifted flour and 240 g (8½ oz/1 cup) mashed ripe banana (about 2 bananas) to the cooled butter. Reduce the milk to 250 ml (9 fl oz/1 cup).

pecan

Replace the caster (superfine) sugar with 140 g (5 oz/¾ cup) soft brown sugar. Add 90 g (3¼ oz/¾ cup) chopped pecans to the sifted flour.

apple cinnamon muffins and chocolate muffins

apple cinnamon muffins

❋

Preparation time: 15 minutes
Cooking time: 25 minutes
Makes 12

400 g (14 oz) tin pie apple, drained
310 g (11 oz/2½ cups) self-raising flour
2 teaspoons ground cinnamon
125 g (4½ oz/⅔ cup) soft brown sugar
350 ml (12 fl oz) milk
2 eggs
1 teaspoon natural vanilla extract
150 g (5½ oz) unsalted butter, melted and cooled
60 g (2¼ oz/½ cup) walnuts, finely chopped

1 Preheat the oven to 200°C (400°F/ Gas 6). Lightly grease a 12-hole medium muffin tin or line with paper cases. Place the pie apple in a small bowl and break up with a knife.
2 Sift the flour and cinnamon into a bowl and add the sugar. Make a well in the centre. Whisk together the milk, eggs and vanilla in a jug and pour into the well. Add the melted butter.
3 Fold the mixture gently with a metal spoon until just combined. Add the pie apple and gently stir through. Do not overmix — the mixture should still be slightly lumpy.
4 Fill each muffin hole with the mixture (these muffins don't rise as much as some) and sprinkle with walnuts. Bake for 20–25 minutes, or until or until golden and a skewer inserted into the centre of a muffin comes out clean. Allow to cool for a couple of minutes, then loosen with a flat-bladed knife and transfer to a wire rack. Serve warm or at room temperature.

NOTE: Completely cool the melted butter before adding it. It doesn't always combine well with other liquids so it is often added separately.

flavouring muffins

Using buttermilk instead of milk in muffins results in a softer texture and a good crust. It also adds to the flavour. To achieve the same effect, you can sour your own milk by adding a few drops of lemon juice or vinegar, just until it curdles the milk, or you can use milk that has gone slightly sour. Muffins can also be iced with a simple icing (frosting), made by combining 125 g (4½ oz/1 cup) sifted icing (confectioners') sugar with 10 g (¼ oz) softened butter and about 1 tablespoon hot water to form a smooth paste. Flavour it with vanilla or finely grated citrus zest. For a chocolate-flavoured icing, add 1 tablespoon unsweetened cocoa powder to the sifted icing sugar. Use a small metal spatula to spread the icing over the muffins.

chocolate muffins

Preparation time: 15 minutes
Cooking time: 25 minutes
Makes 12

310 g (11 oz/2½ cups) self-raising flour
40 g (1½ oz/⅓ cup) unsweetened
    cocoa powder
½ teaspoon bicarbonate of soda
    (baking soda)
180 g (6¼ oz/⅔ cup) caster (superfine)
    sugar
375 ml (13 fl oz/1½ cups) buttermilk
2 eggs
150 g (5½ oz) unsalted butter,
    melted and cooled

1   Preheat the oven to 200°C (400°F/
Gas 6). Lightly grease a 12-hole medium
muffin tin or line with paper cases. Sift
the flour, cocoa and bicarbonate of soda
into a bowl and add the sugar. Make a
well in the centre.
2   In a jug, whisk the buttermilk and eggs
together and pour into the well. Add the
butter and fold gently with a metal spoon
until just combined. Do not overmix —
the mixture should still be lumpy.
3   Divide the mixture evenly among
the muffin holes — fill each hole about
three-quarters full. Bake for 20–25
minutes, or until golden and a skewer
inserted into the centre of a muffin comes
out clean. Allow to cool for a couple of
minutes, then loosen with a flat-bladed
knife and transfer to a wire rack. Serve
warm or at room temperature.

NOTE: Muffins are most delicious if eaten
on the day they are made and served
warm. If you want to store muffins for a
couple of days, let them cool completely,
then store them in an airtight container
at room temperature. Muffins are also
suitable for freezing.

orange poppy seed muffins

Preparation time: 15 minutes
Cooking time: 30 minutes
Makes 12

310 g (11 oz/2½ cups) self-raising flour
40 g (1½ oz/¼ cup) poppy seeds
80 g (2¾ oz/⅓ cup) caster (superfine)
    sugar
125 g (4½ oz) unsalted butter
315 g (11¼ oz/1 cup) orange marmalade
250 ml (9 fl oz/1 cup) milk
2 eggs
1 tablespoon finely grated orange zest

1   Preheat the oven to 200°C (400°F/
Gas 6). Lightly grease a 12-hole medium
muffin tin or line with paper cases. Sift
the flour into a bowl. Stir in the poppy
seeds and sugar, and make a well in the
centre. Put the butter and 210 g (7½ oz/
⅔ cup) of the marmalade in a small
saucepan and stir over low heat until the
butter has melted and the ingredients are
combined. Cool slightly.
2   Whisk together the milk, eggs and
orange zest and pour into the well. Add
the butter and marmalade. Fold gently
with a metal spoon until just combined.
Do not overmix — the batter should still
be slightly lumpy.
3   Divide the mixture evenly among
the muffin holes — fill each hole about
three-quarters full. Bake for 20–25
minutes, or until golden and a skewer
inserted into the centre of a muffin
comes out clean.
4   Heat the remaining marmalade and
push it through a fine sieve. Brush
generously over the warm muffins. Leave
them to cool in the tin for a few minutes.
Gently loosen with a flat-bladed knife
before turning out onto a wire rack. Serve
warm or at room temperature.

NOTE: A variation of this muffin can be
made using lime marmalade and finely
grated lemon zest.

eggs

Eggs quickly lose their quality
so it is important to store them
correctly. Check the use-by date
when you buy them and look
to make sure none of the eggs
are broken. Store eggs in their
cartons to protect them. They
are commercially packed with
the pointed end down to prevent
damage to the air cell and to
keep the yolk centred. Eggs
should be refrigerated as this
slows down moisture loss. For
every day that an egg is left out
of the refrigerator, as much as
four days in quality can be lost.

friand tins

Friands are small oval-shaped cakes baked in special-purpose oval tins called friand tins or barquette moulds. Sometimes the same mixture is baked in a rectangular tin and is then named Financier, meaning 'gold ingot', which the shape resembles. Both are very popular in cafés and come in a variety of flavours. The tins can be purchased from kitchenware shops. Traditional friands are made with almond meal.

hazelnut and chocolate friands

Preparation time: 20 minutes
Cooking time: 40 minutes
Makes 12

200 g (7 oz) hazelnuts
185 g (6½ oz) unsalted butter
6 egg whites
155 g (5½ oz/1¼ cups) plain (all-purpose) flour
30 g (1 oz/¼ cup) unsweetened cocoa powder
250 g (9 oz/2 cups) icing (confectioners') sugar, plus extra, to dust

1 Preheat the oven to 200°C (400°F/ Gas 6). Lightly grease a 12-hole friand tin.
2 Spread the hazelnuts out on a baking tray and bake for 8–10 minutes, or until aromatic (take care not to burn them). Wrap in a clean tea towel (dish towel) and rub vigorously to loosen the skins. Discard the skins. Cool, then process in a food processor until finely ground.
3 Melt the butter in a small saucepan over medium heat, then cook for 3–4 minutes or until deep golden. Strain to remove any residue (the colour will deepen on standing). Remove from the heat and set aside to cool to lukewarm.
4 Place the egg whites in a clean, dry bowl and lightly whisk until frothy but not firm. Sift the flour, cocoa and icing sugar into a large bowl and stir in the ground hazelnuts. Make a well in the centre, add the egg whites and butter and mix gently until just combined.
5 Divide the mixture evenly among the friand holes — fill each hole to about three-quarters full. Place the tin on a baking tray and bake in the centre of the oven for 20–25 minutes, or until a skewer inserted into the centre of a friand comes out clean. Leave to cool in the tin for 5 minutes before turning out onto a wire rack to cool completely. Dust with icing sugar before serving.

almond friands

✳ ✳

Preparation time: 10 minutes
Cooking time: 20 minutes
Makes 10

160 g (5¾ oz) unsalted butter
90 g (3¼ oz/1 cup) flaked almonds
40 g (1½ oz/⅓ cup) plain (all-purpose) flour
165 g (5¾ oz/1⅓ cups) icing
   (confectioners') sugar, plus extra,
   to dust
5 egg whites

1 Preheat the oven to 210°C (415°F/ Gas 6–7). Lightly grease 10 holes in a 12-hole friand tin. Melt the butter in a small saucepan over medium heat. Cook for 3–4 minutes, or until deep golden. Strain to remove any residue (the colour will deepen on standing). Remove from the heat and set aside to cool to lukewarm.
2 Put the almonds in a food processor and process until finely ground. Transfer to a bowl and sift the flour and icing sugar into the same bowl.
3 Put the egg whites in a separate bowl and lightly whisk with a fork until just combined. Add the butter to the flour mixture along with the egg whites. Mix gently with a metal spoon until all the ingredients are just combined.
4 Divide the mixture evenly among the 10 friand holes — fill each hole to about three-quarters full. Put the tin on a baking tray and bake in the centre of the oven for 10 minutes, then reduce the oven to 180°C (350°F/Gas 4) and bake for a further 5 minutes, or until a skewer inserted into the centre of a friand comes out clean. Leave to cool in the tin for 5 minutes before turning out onto a wire rack to cool completely. Dust with icing sugar before serving.

NOTE: These friands will keep well for up to 3 days in an airtight container. To make berry friands, make the mixture as above and put a fresh or frozen raspberry or blueberry on the top of each friand before placing in the oven. To make lemon friands, add 2 teaspoons finely grated lemon zest to the flour and sugar mixture and proceed as above.

what went wrong: muffins

perfect The texture of the muffin is even with a nicely risen centre and good golden colouring. If a skewer is inserted into the centre, it will come out clean. The muffin has started to come away from the side of the holes. Muffins need to be cooked in a preheated 200°C (400°F/ Gas 6) oven so the batter will set and peak correctly as it has here.

overflowing mixture Make sure you use the size of muffin tin suggested in the recipe. Do not fill the muffin holes more than three-quarters full. This leaves room for the batter to rise.

too peaked The crust is too coloured and too peaked. This is caused by mixing too much or an oven that is too hot. The muffins have a tough, rubbery texture and uneven shapes. Make sure all the dry ingredients are evenly distributed by sifting and mixing them, including the raising agent, before adding the wet ingredients. The mixture should be slightly lumpy, so do not over-mix.

undercooked The finished muffin is moist in the centre with insufficient peaking. The muffin is not properly coloured and didn't shrink away from the tin. The oven was probably not sufficiently preheated or not hot enough, or the cooking may have been too short.

poorly risen The muffin texture is too heavy and dense. This can be caused by insufficient raising agent or a missing ingredient. To avoid leaving out any vital ingredient, check that you have all the ingredients assembled and correctly weighed out before you start.

more about muffins

If you like the idea of having freshly baked muffins for breakfast but don't want to start the day making a mess in the kitchen, you can make a muffin mixture, then spoon it into the muffin tin and refrigerate it overnight, ready for baking the following day. Uncooked mixture for the plainer muffins such as chocolate or blueberry, or those without fillings, can be frozen in paper-lined muffin tins for up to a month. When you want to cook them, simply remove from the freezer and bake in a preheated 200°C (400°F/ Gas 6) oven for 25–30 minutes, or until golden and a skewer inserted in the centre comes out clean.

what went wrong: friands

perfect The friand is nicely domed and has a moist, even texture and a good golden colour. The batter has shrunk from the side of the tin.

undercooked The friand is a pale colour and has a wet, buttery and dense texture. The oven was not hot enough. Make sure you cook friands in an oven that has been preheated to 210°C (415°F/Gas 6–7).

overcooked The friand has a badly cracked top and the top and base are over-coloured. The friand is dark and crusty around the edges. The oven was too hot, or the cooking time was too long.

what went wrong: scones

perfect The scone is evenly risen, has a soft crust and soft inside texture and is light golden. The dough should not be overworked, but just lightly mixed with a flat-bladed knife until combined.

poorly risen If the scone texture feels heavy and dense, the dough may have been either too dry or too wet, or the dough may have been mixed or worked too much.

overcooked The scone has a dark crust and a dry texture. Either the cooking time was too long or the oven temperature was too hot.

swedish tea ring

✹ ✹ ✹

Preparation time: 35 minutes
  + 1 hour 45 minutes proving time
Cooking time: 25 minutes
Serves 10-12

2 teaspoons dried yeast
170 ml (5½ fl oz/⅔ cup) milk
60 g (2¼ oz) unsalted butter, softened
2 tablespoons caster (superfine) sugar
375 g (13 oz/3 cups) plain (all-purpose)
  flour
1 egg, lightly beaten
1 egg yolk, extra

FILLING
30 g (1 oz) unsalted butter
1 tablespoon caster (superfine) sugar
100 g (3½ oz) roughly ground blanched
  almonds
95 g (3¼ oz/½ cup) mixed dried fruit
105 g (3½ oz/½ cup) glacé cherries,
  halved

ICING
125 g (4½ oz/1 cup) icing (confectioners')
  sugar
1–2 tablespoons milk
2 drops natural almond extract

1 Lightly grease a baking tray or line with baking paper. Dissolve the yeast in 2 tablespoons warm water in a bowl. Leave in a warm, draught-free place for 10 minutes, or until bubbles appear on the surface. The mixture should be frothy and slightly increased in volume. If your yeast doesn't foam, it is dead, so you will have to discard it and start again. Heat the milk, butter, sugar and ½ teaspoon salt in a saucepan until lukewarm.
2 Sift 250 g (9 oz/2 cups) of the flour into a large bowl. Add the yeast and milk mixtures, and beaten egg, and mix to a smooth batter. Add enough of the remaining flour to make a soft dough. Turn onto a lightly floured surface and knead for 10 minutes, or until smooth and elastic. Place in a large, lightly oiled bowl and brush the top with oil. Cover with

plastic wrap or a damp tea towel (dish towel) and leave in a warm, draught-free place for 1 hour, or until well risen.
3 Meanwhile, to make the filling, cream the butter and sugar using electric beaters until light and fluffy, then mix in the almonds, mixed dried fruit and cherries.
4 Knock back the dough and knead for 1 minute. Roll the dough out to a 25 x 45 cm (10 x 17¾ inch) rectangle. Spread the filling over the dough, leaving a 2 cm (¾ inch) border. Roll up and form into a ring, then place on the tray with the seam underneath. Mix the egg yolk with 1 tablespoon water and use a little to seal the ends together. Snip with scissors

from the outside edge at 4 cm (1½ inch) intervals, cutting about two-thirds of the way in. Turn the cut pieces on the side and flatten slightly, giving a petal-like appearance. Cover with plastic wrap and leave in a warm, draught-free place for 45 minutes, or until well risen.
5 Preheat the oven to 180°C (350°F/ Gas 4). Brush the tea ring with some of the egg yolk and water and bake for 20–25 minutes, or until firm and golden. Cover with foil if the tea ring is browning too much. Remove and cool.
6 To make the icing (frosting), combine the ingredients until smooth. Drizzle over the cooled tea ring and allow to set.

date and walnut rolls

✽ ✽

Preparation time: 25 minutes
Cooking time: 1 hour 10 minutes
Serves 12

90 g (3¼ oz/¾ cup) self-raising flour
90 g (3¼ oz/¾ cup) plain (all-purpose) flour
½ teaspoon bicarbonate of soda (baking soda)
1 teaspoon mixed (pumpkin pie) spice
125 g (4½ oz/1 cup) chopped walnuts
100 g (3½ oz) unsalted butter, chopped
140 g (5 oz/¾ cup) soft brown sugar
240 g (8½ oz/1½ cups) chopped stoned dates
1 egg, lightly beaten

1 Preheat the oven to 180°C (350°F/ Gas 4). Lightly grease two 8 x 17 cm (3¼ x 6½ inch) nut roll tins and their lids. Sift the flours, bicarbonate of soda and spice into a large bowl, then stir in the walnuts. Make a well in the centre.
2 Combine the butter, sugar, dates and 125 ml (4 fl oz/½ cup) water in a saucepan. Stir constantly over low heat until the butter has melted and the sugar has dissolved. Remove from the heat and set aside to cool slightly. Add the butter mixture and egg to the flour and stir well.
3 Spoon the mixture evenly into the prepared tins. Bake, with the tins upright on a baking tray, for 1 hour, or until a skewer inserted into the centre of the loaves comes out clean. Leave in the tins, with the lids on, for 10 minutes before turning out onto a wire rack to cool. Serve in slices spread with butter.

banana bread

✽ ✽

Preparation time: 20 minutes
Cooking time: 45 minutes
Serves 10

250 g (9 oz/2 cups) plain (all-purpose) flour
2 teaspoons baking powder
1 teaspoon mixed (pumpkin pie) spice
150 g (5½ oz) unsalted butter, softened
185 g (6½ oz/1 cup) soft brown sugar
2 eggs, lightly beaten
235 g (8½ oz/1 cup) mashed ripe bananas (about 2 bananas)
icing (confectioners') sugar, to dust

1 Preheat the oven to 180°C (350°F/ Gas 4). Grease and line the base of a 13 x 23 cm (5 x 9 inch) loaf (bar) tin. Sift together the flour, baking powder, mixed spice and ¼ teaspoon salt into a bowl.
2 Cream the butter and sugar in a large bowl using electric beaters until soft. Add the egg gradually, beating thoroughly after each addition. Mix in the banana. Gradually add the sifted dry ingredients and mix until smooth.
3 Spoon the mixture into the tin and bake for 35–45 minutes, or until a skewer inserted into the centre of the loaf comes out clean. Cool in the tin for 10 minutes before turning out onto a wire rack. Serve warm or at room temperature, dusted with icing sugar.

banana bread

cream buns

Preparation time: 40 minutes
  + 1 hour 15 minutes proving time
Cooking time: 20 minutes
Makes 12

2 teaspoons dried yeast
2 tablespoons sugar
350 ml (12 fl oz) milk, warmed
435 g (15½ oz/3½ cups) plain (all-purpose) flour
60 g (2¼ oz) unsalted butter, melted and cooled
160 g (5¾ oz/½ cup) strawberry jam
310 ml (10¾ fl oz/1¼ cups) pouring (whipping) cream
1 tablespoon icing (confectioners') sugar, sifted, plus 2 tablespoons, extra, to dust

1 Put the yeast, 1 teaspoon of the sugar and the milk in a small bowl. Leave in a warm, draught-free place for 10 minutes, or until bubbles appear on the surface. The mixture should be frothy and slightly increased in volume. If your yeast doesn't foam, it is dead, so you will have to discard it and start again.

2 Sift the flour into a large bowl and stir in ½ teaspoon salt and the remaining sugar. Make a well in the centre and pour in the milk mixture and butter. Mix to a dough, first using a wooden spoon and then using your hands. Turn the dough out onto a lightly floured surface and knead for 10 minutes, or until it is smooth and elastic. Place in a lightly oiled bowl, cover with plastic wrap, and leave in a warm, draught-free place for 1 hour, or until well risen.

3 Knock back the dough and turn onto a lightly floured surface, then knead for 2 minutes or until smooth. Divide into 12 pieces. Knead one portion at a time for 30 seconds on a lightly floured surface and then shape into a ball.

4 Preheat the oven to 210°C (415°F/ Gas 6–7). Lightly grease two baking trays, dust lightly with flour and shake off any excess. Place balls of dough, evenly spaced, on the trays. Set aside, covered with plastic wrap, in a warm, draught-free place for 15 minutes, or until well risen.

5 Bake for 20 minutes or until well browned and cooked. Set aside for 5 minutes before transferring to a wire rack to cool completely. Using a serrated knife, make a cut into the centre of each bun, to a depth of 5 cm (2 inches), from the top towards the base.

6 Spoon some jam into the cut on each bun. Using electric beaters, whisk the cream and icing sugar in a small bowl until firm peaks form. Spoon into a piping (icing) bag and pipe the whipped cream into the buns. Dust the tops with the extra icing sugar.

finger buns

Preparation time: 45 minutes
  + 1 hour proving time
Cooking time: 15 minutes
Makes 12

500 g (1 lb 2 oz/4 cups) plain (all-purpose) flour
35 g (1¼ oz/⅓ cup) milk powder
1 tablespoon dried yeast
115 g (4 oz/½ cup) caster (superfine) sugar
60 g (2¼ oz/½ cup) sultanas (golden raisins)
60 g (2¼ oz) unsalted butter, melted
1 egg, lightly beaten
1 egg yolk, extra, to glaze

GLACÉ ICING
155 g (5½ oz/1¼ cups) icing (confectioners') sugar
20 g (¾ oz) unsalted butter, melted
pink food colouring

yeast

Yeast is available dried or fresh (compressed). Small amounts of fresh yeast can be bought from some health food stores and bakeries but the most convenient yeast is the dried granules readily available from the supermarket. It is packed in foil sachets and keeps for a long time. It is very reliable so can be added directly into the dry ingredients, or added to some liquid in the traditional way and left until it froths. The latter method is always used for fresh yeast to check that it is still alive.

1   Mix 375 g (13 oz/3 cups) of the flour with the milk powder, yeast, sugar, sultanas and ½ teaspoon salt in a large bowl. Make a well in the centre. Combine the butter, egg and 250 ml (9 fl oz/ 1 cup) warm water and add all at once to the flour. Stir for 2 minutes, or until well combined. Add enough of the remaining flour to make a soft dough.

2   Turn out onto a lightly floured surface. Knead for 10 minutes, or until smooth and elastic, adding more flour if necessary.

Place in a large lightly oiled bowl and brush with oil. Cover with plastic wrap and leave in a warm, draught-free place for 1 hour, or until well risen.

3   Lightly grease two large baking trays. Preheat the oven to 180°C (350°F/ Gas 4). Knock back the dough and knead for 1 minute. Divide into 12 even pieces. Shape each into a 15 cm (6 inch) long oval and place on the trays, leaving 5 cm (2 inches) between each to allow for spreading. Cover with plastic wrap and

set aside in a warm, draught-free place for 20–25 minutes, or until well risen.

4   Combine the extra egg yolk with 1½ teaspoons water and brush over the dough. Bake for 12–15 minutes, or until firm and golden. Transfer the buns to a wire rack to cool.

5   To make the icing (frosting), stir the icing sugar, 2–3 teaspoons water and the melted butter together in a bowl until smooth. Mix in the food colouring, spread over the tops of the buns and allow to set.

butterfly cakes

Preparation time: **20 minutes**
Cooking time: **20 minutes**
Makes **12**

120 g (4¼ oz) unsalted butter, softened
145 g (5½ oz/⅔ cup) caster (superfine)
    sugar
185 g (6½ oz/1½ cups) self-raising flour
125 ml (4 fl oz/½ cup) milk
2 teaspoons natural vanilla extract
2 eggs
125 ml (4 fl oz/½ cup) pouring (whipping)
    cream
105 g (3½ oz/⅓ cup) strawberry jam
icing (confectioners') sugar, to dust

1 Preheat the oven to 180°C (350°F/
Gas 4). Line a 12-hole patty pan tin with
paper cases.
2 Put the butter, sugar, flour, milk, vanilla
and eggs in a bowl and beat using electric
beaters on low speed for 2 minutes, or
until well mixed. Increase the speed and
beat for 2 minutes, until smooth and pale.
3 Divide the mixture evenly among the
paper cases and bake for 20 minutes, or
until a skewer inserted into the centre of
a cake comes out clean. Transfer to a wire
rack to cool.
4 Whip the cream to soft peaks. Using
a small sharp knife, cut shallow rounds
from the top of each cake. Cut these in
half. Spoon a little cream into the cavity
in each cake, then top with a little jam.
Position the two halves of the cake tops in
the jam in each cake to resemble butterfly
wings. Dust the cakes with icing sugar
before serving.

NOTE: To make iced (frosted) cupcakes,
don't cut off the tops. Mix 60 g (2¼ oz/
½ cup) sifted icing (confectioners') sugar,
1 teaspoon softened unsalted butter and
½ teaspoon natural vanilla extract with
up to 3 teaspoons hot water to form
a smooth paste, then spread over the
cooled cupcakes.

butter

Butter is made by churning
cream until it solidifies.
Unsalted butter is also known
as sweet butter and is used in
baking and desserts as it has a
good flavour. Cultured butter,
also called Danish butter, can
be used for sweet baking. It has
a bacteria added to give extra
flavour and interest. Prior to
refrigeration, salt was added to
butter to help preserve it, but
today salt is added for taste
only. Butter should always
be covered, or well wrapped,
and stored in the refrigerator
because it very readily takes on
other flavours. It freezes well.

rock cakes

Preparation time: 15 minutes
Cooking time: 15 minutes
Makes about 20

250 g (9 oz/2 cups) self-raising flour
90 g (3¼ oz) unsalted butter, chilled and cubed
125 g (4½ oz/½ cup) caster (superfine) sugar
95 g (3¼ oz/½ cup) mixed dried fruit
½ teaspoon ground ginger
1 egg
60 ml (2 fl oz/¼ cup) milk

1 Preheat the oven to 200°C (400°F/ Gas 6). Grease two baking trays. Sift the flour into a large bowl and rub in the butter with your fingertips until the mixture resembles fine breadcrumbs. Stir in the sugar, fruit and ginger.
2 Whisk the egg and milk together. Mix into the dry ingredients. Drop heaps of mixture, about 3 tablespoons at a time, onto the trays. Bake for 10–15 minutes, or until golden. Cool on a wire rack.

orange cupcakes

Preparation time: 15 minutes
Cooking time: 20 minutes
Makes 12

120 g (4¼ oz) unsalted butter, softened
145 g (5½ oz/⅔ cup) caster (superfine) sugar
185 g (6½ oz/1½ cups) self-raising flour
125 ml (4 fl oz/½ cup) orange juice
2 teaspoons natural vanilla extract
2 eggs
3 tablespoons finely grated orange zest
shredded orange zest, to decorate (optional)

ICING
60 g (2¼ oz) unsalted butter, softened
90 g (3¼ oz/¾ cup) icing (confectioners') sugar
1 tablespoon orange juice

1 Preheat the oven to 180°C (350°F/ Gas 4). Line a 12-hole patty pan tin with paper cases.
2 Place the butter, sugar, flour, orange juice, vanilla and eggs in a bowl and beat using electric beaters on low speed for 2 minutes, or until well mixed. Increase the speed and beat for 2 minutes, or until smooth and pale. Stir in the orange zest.
3 Divide the mixture among the cases and bake for 20 minutes, or until a skewer inserted into the centre of a cake comes out clean. Transfer to a wire rack to cool.

4 To make the icing (frosting), beat the butter in a bowl using electric beaters until pale. Beat in half the icing sugar, all the orange juice, then the remaining icing sugar. Spread over the cakes, then decorate if desired.

orange cupcakes

chelsea buns

✳ ✳

Preparation time: 25 minutes
  + 1 hour 30 minutes proving time
Cooking time: 20 minutes
Makes 8 buns

2 teaspoons dried yeast
1 teaspoon sugar
310 g (11 oz/2½ cups) plain (all-purpose)
  flour, sifted
125 ml (4 fl oz/½ cup) milk, warmed
185 g (6½ oz) unsalted butter, cubed
1 tablespoon sugar, extra
2 teaspoons finely grated lemon zest
1 teaspoon mixed (pumpkin pie) spice
1 egg, lightly beaten
45 g (1¾ oz/¼ cup) soft brown sugar
185 g (6½ oz/1 cup) mixed dried fruit
1 tablespoon milk, extra, to glaze
2 tablespoons sugar, extra, to glaze

GLACÉ ICING
60 g (2¼ oz/½ cup) icing (confectioners')
  sugar
1–2 tablespoons milk

1 Combine the yeast, sugar and
1 tablespoon of the flour. Add the milk
and mix until smooth. Leave in a warm,
draught-free place for 10 minutes, or
until bubbles appear on the surface. The
mixture should be frothy and slightly
increased in volume. If your yeast doesn't
foam, it is dead, so you'll need to start
again. Place the remaining flour in a bowl
and rub in 125 g (4½ oz) of butter with
your fingertips. Stir in the extra sugar,
lemon zest and half the mixed spice.
Make a well in the centre, add the yeast
mixture and egg and mix. Gather together
and turn onto a lightly floured surface.
2 Knead for 2 minutes, or until smooth,
then shape into a ball. Place in a large,

lightly oiled bowl, cover with plastic wrap
and set aside in a warm place for 1 hour,
or until well risen. Knock back the dough
and knead for 2 minutes, or until smooth.
3 Preheat the oven to 210°C (415°F/
Gas 6–7). Lightly grease a baking tray.
Beat the remaining butter with the brown
sugar in a small bowl using electric
beaters until light and creamy. Roll the
dough out to a 25 x 40 cm (10 x 16 inch)
rectangle. Spread the butter mixture all
over the dough to within 2 cm (¾ inch)
of the edge of one of the longer sides.
Spread with the combined fruit and
remaining spice. Roll the dough from the
long side, firmly and evenly, to enclose
the fruit. Use a sharp knife to cut the roll
into eight slices about 5 cm (2 inch) thick.
Put the slices, close together and seams
inwards, on the tray. Flatten slightly.
4 Set aside, covered with plastic wrap,
in a warm, draught-free place for

Spread the creamed butter and
sugar all over the dough, leaving a
small border along one long edge.

Put the slices, close together and
seams inwards, on the tray.

30 minutes, or until well risen. Bake for 20 minutes, or until brown and cooked. When almost ready, stir the extra milk and sugar in a saucepan over low heat until the sugar dissolves and mixture is almost boiling. Brush over the hot buns. Cool.
5 To make the icing (frosting), mix the icing sugar and milk, stir until smooth, then drizzle over the cooled buns.

madeleines

❋

Preparation time: **20 minutes**
Cooking time: **15 minutes**
Makes **12**

125 g (4½ oz/1 cup) plain (all-purpose) flour
2 eggs
170 g (5¾ oz/¾ cup) caster (superfine) sugar
185 g (6½ oz) unsalted butter, melted and cooled
1 teaspoon finely grated orange zest
2 tablespoons icing (confectioners') sugar, to dust

1 Preheat the oven to 180°C (350°F/ Gas 4). Grease a 12-hole madeleine tin or shallow patty pan. Lightly dust the tin with flour and shake off any excess.
2 Sift the flour three times onto baking paper. Combine the eggs and sugar in a heatproof bowl. Place over a saucepan of simmering water, making sure the base of the bowl does not touch the water, and whisk using electric beaters until very thick and pale yellow. Remove the bowl from the saucepan and continue to beat the mixture until it has cooled slightly and increased in volume.
3 Add the sifted flour, butter and orange zest to the bowl and fold in quickly and lightly with a metal spoon until just combined. Spoon the mixture carefully into the madeleine holes and bake for 10–12 minutes, or until lightly golden. Carefully remove from the tin and transfer to a wire rack to cool. Dust with icing sugar before serving. Madeleines are best eaten on the day of baking.

Place the bowl over simmering water and whisk the mixture until very thick and pale yellow.

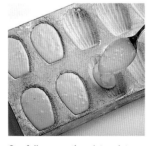

Carefully spoon the mixture into the lightly greased and floured madeleine holes.

eccles cakes

These spicy currant pastries originated in the British town of Eccles in Lancashire. They were traditionally made for the Eccles Wakes festival days and are still a favourite today. The puff pastry round is rolled thinly so the enclosed filling will show through when the pastry is cooked. They can be made with shortcrust pastry but whichever pastry is used, they are always sprinkled with sugar before baking and are best eaten warm straight from the oven.

eccles cakes

eccles cakes

Preparation time: **20 minutes**
Cooking time: **20 minutes**
Makes **about 27**

150 g (5½ oz/1 cup) currants
95 g (3¼ oz/½ cup) mixed peel (mixed candied citrus peel)
1 tablespoon brandy
1 tablespoon sugar, plus 2 teaspoons, extra, to sprinkle
½ teaspoon ground cinnamon
500 g (1 lb 2 oz) block ready-made puff pastry, thawed
1 egg white

1 Preheat the oven to 210°C (415°F/ Gas 6–7). Lightly grease two baking trays. Combine the currants, peel, brandy, sugar and cinnamon in a bowl. Divide the pastry into three portions and roll each portion out to a thickness of 3 mm (⅛ inch). Using an 8 cm (3¼ inch) scone cutter, cut nine circles from each sheet of pastry. (Any remaining pastry can be frozen.)
2 Place 2 level teaspoons of filling on each circle. Bring the edges up together and pinch to seal. Turn them seam-side down and roll out to 1 cm (½ inch) thick ovals. Place on the trays. Brush with egg white and sprinkle with extra sugar. Make three slashes across each cake. Bake for 15–20 minutes, until golden. Serve warm.

lamingtons

✳ ✳

Preparation time: 50 minutes
Cooking time: 1 hour
Makes 16

150 g (5½ oz) self-raising flour
75 g (2½ oz) plain (all-purpose) flour
125 g (4½ oz) unsalted butter, softened
145 g (5 oz/⅔ cup) caster (superfine) sugar
3 eggs
60 ml (2 fl oz/¼ cup) milk
1 teaspoon natural vanilla extract
185 ml (6 fl oz/¾ cup) thick (double/heavy) cream
270 g (9½ oz/3 cups) desiccated coconut

ICING
500 g (1 lb 2 oz/4 cups) icing (confectioners') sugar
40 g (1½ oz/⅓ cup) unsweetened cocoa powder
30 g (1 oz) unsalted butter, cubed
125 ml (4 fl oz/½ cup) boiling water

1 Preheat the oven to 180°C (350°F/ Gas 4). Lightly grease a 20 cm (8 inch) square cake tin and line with baking paper.
2 Sift the flours into a medium bowl. Add the butter, sugar, eggs, milk and vanilla. Using electric beaters, beat on low speed until the ingredients are just combined. Increase the speed to high and beat for 3 minutes, or until free of lumps, pale in colour and increased in volume. Spoon the mixture into the tin and smooth the surface. Bake for 35–40 minutes, or until a skewer inserted into the centre of the cake comes out clean. Leave in the tin for 5 minutes before turning out onto a wire rack to cool.
3 Using a serrated knife, trim the top of the cake to level it, if necessary. Trim the crusts from the sides, then carefully cut the cake in half horizontally. Using electric beaters, whisk the cream in a medium bowl until stiff peaks form. Place the first layer of cake on a board and spread it evenly with the cream. Place the remaining cake layer on top. Cut the filled cake into 16 even squares.

4 To make the icing (frosting), sift the icing sugar and cocoa into a large bowl. Add the butter to the boiling water and stir until it melts. Add to the icing sugar mixture and stir until smooth. Place 90 g (3¼ oz/1 cup) of the coconut on a sheet of baking paper or a plate. Using two forks, dip a piece of cake in the chocolate icing, then hold the cake over a bowl and allow the excess to drain. (Add a little more boiling water to the icing if it is too thick.) Roll the cake in coconut to coat

evenly, then place on a wire rack. Repeat with the remaining cake, adding the remaining coconut as needed.

NOTE: If you cook the cake a day ahead, it will be easier to cut and won't crumble as much when coating in the chocolate icing. Lamingtons are not necessarily filled with cream, so if you prefer, you can ice unfilled squares of cake.

Using a serrated knife, carefully cut the filled cake into 16 squares.

Use two forks to dip each piece of cake in the icing.

Roll the iced cake in coconut to coat, then place on a wire rack.

cakes

Have you ever stopped to consider how much importance we place on cakes? They seem to pop up in almost every aspect of our lives. For example, we promote a diet rich in fruit and vegetables with orange poppy seed cake and carrot cake, not to mention myriad dried fruit cakes and banana cake. Hummingbird and mud cakes suggest an avid interest in nature, while the sponge cake clearly displays a healthy attitude towards cleanliness. Madeira cake, upside-down cake and swiss rolls? Well, perhaps they show a fondness for 'relaxation'.

preparing tins

You'll find the preparation of cake tins varies according to the type of cake you are baking. Below we explain how to line different tins and make a collar.

greasing, lining and dusting with flour

To grease a tin, apply melted unsalted butter or oil evenly and not too thickly, using a pastry brush. Vegetable sprays can be used. Greaseproof paper and non-stick baking paper are both excellent for lining cake tins. If you use greaseproof, it will need to be greased, but non-stick baking paper does not need greasing. Let the greased tin or paper dry a little before dusting with plain (all-purpose) flour. Turn the tin to evenly coat the base and sides, then shake off any excess. Bundt and kugelhopf tins need to be greased and lightly floured.

lining round tins

Place the tin on a sheet of baking paper, draw around it and cut out as marked. Cut a strip of baking paper the same length as the tin's circumference and about 3 cm (1¼ inches) deeper than the height. Fold down a cuff about 2 cm (¾ inch) deep on one edge. Cut the folded cuff diagonally at 2 cm (¾ inch) intervals. Grease the tin. Place the baking paper strip in the tin with the folded side on the base. The cut strip will act like pleats and sit on the base. Press the baking paper into the base and side. Place the round of paper on the base over the pleats.

lining square tins

Place the tin on a sheet of baking paper, draw around it, then cut out as marked. Cut a strip of baking paper the same length as the outside of the tin and about 1 cm (½ inch) deeper than the height. Grease the tin. Place the square of paper in the base and press the strip onto the sides of the tin.

lining swiss roll tins

Place the tin on a sheet of baking paper and draw around it.

Measure the depth of the tin, add 2 cm (¾ inch), then measure that distance from the drawn line and cut at that distance all around. Crease the paper along the drawn lines, then cut a diagonal line from each outside corner to the nearest drawn corner. Lightly grease the tin. Press the paper into the tin.

butter cakes and chocolate cakes

You can usually get away with only lining the base, but it's safest to line the base and sides.

sponge cakes

Grease the tin, line the base and dust the whole tin with flour.

rich fruit cakes

Tins need to have the base and sides lined with a double thickness of paper, but it is generally not necessary to grease the paper. Lining fruit cake tins is fully explained on pages 84–85.

making a collar

Lightly grease the tin, then cut a strip of baking paper long enough to fit around the outside and wide enough to extend 5 cm (2 inches) above the top. Fold down a cuff, about 2 cm (¾ inch) deep, along the length of the strip. Make diagonal cuts up to the fold line about 1 cm (½ inch) apart. Fit the collar around the inside edge of the tin, with the cuts in the base, pressing the cuts out at right angles so they sit flat. Cut a piece of paper to fit in the base, using the tin as a guide, and then place it in the tin.

A collar extends a cake's height and gives extra protection during cooking. As a general rule, a single layer of baking paper is enough for a collar on an average-sized cake. Larger cakes and fruit cakes need two layers of paper for the collar and base.

butter cakes

If you follow our helpful hints, you will have no trouble making a moist and more-ish butter cake that can be dressed up or down to suit any occasion.

equipment

It is crucial to use the correct-sized tin. For this basic butter cake you will need a 20 cm (8 inch) round cake tin. Lightly grease the base and side with melted unsalted butter or oil, using a pastry brush to apply an even, not too thick, layer. Line the tin (pages 48–49) with baking paper or greaseproof paper, then brush the paper evenly with melted unsalted butter or oil.

It is also essential to have a set of standard measuring cups and spoons and accurate kitchen scales. You'll also need a small and large bowl, metal spoon, large sieve, rubber spatula and electric mixer. If the quantities are not too great, adequate results can be obtained using a hand-held electric beater or mixing by hand, but the mixing time increases considerably.

The butter, eggs and liquid should be at room temperature. The butter should be malleable, not melted or very soft.

oven

An accurate oven temperature is vital, so it is a good idea to invest in an oven thermometer. All of the recipes in this book have all been tested in a conventional (not fan-forced) oven.

butter cake

You will need 185 g (6½ oz/1½ cups) self-raising flour, 60 g (2¼ oz/½ cup) plain (all-purpose) flour, 185 g (6½ oz) unsalted butter, chopped and softened, 185 g (6½ oz/¾ cup) caster (superfine) sugar, 3 lightly beaten eggs, 1 teaspoon natural vanilla extract and 60 ml (2 fl oz/¼ cup) milk. When you have assembled all the ingredients and the utensils you need, preheat your oven to 180°C (350°F/Gas 4).

This cake is made using the creaming method, the most frequently used technique in cake-making. The first step is to sift the flours to aerate and separate the particles. Cream the butter and sugar in a bowl using electric beaters at medium speed until light and fluffy. The mixture will almost double in volume and should have no trace of the sugar granules. Scrape the side of the bowl with a spatula several times during the creaming process to make sure the butter and sugar are well incorporated. This initial creaming process can take up to 8 minutes.

With the beaters still running, gradually add the egg, a little at a time, beating thoroughly after each addition. Add the vanilla and beat well to combine.

Transfer the mixture to a large bowl. Using a large metal spoon, gently fold in the sifted flours and the milk. Stir until just combined and almost smooth. Take care with this final stage, mixing the ingredients lightly and evenly. Overly enthusiastic beating can undo all your previous good work and produce a heavy, coarse-textured cake.

Next, gently spoon or pour the mixture into the tin, spread out evenly and smooth the surface. Check the oven temperature. For best results when baking a cake, position an oven rack in the lower third of the oven so the top of the cake is in the middle of the oven. Centre the cake tin on the oven rack and bake for 45 minutes. The cake is cooked when it begins to shrink from the side of the tin and is lightly golden. If gently pressed with a finger, it should spring back into shape. As a final check, insert a fine skewer into the centre — it should come out clean, without any moisture. Avoid opening the oven door until the cake is at least two-thirds of the way through baking.

A cake is quite fragile when removed from the oven, so leave it in the tin for 10 minutes before turning out onto a wire rack to cool. If the cake is stuck, gently run a flat-bladed knife around the side of the tin to release it. Remove the paper immediately.

what went wrong: butter cakes

perfect The texture is light, moist and even, with a golden-brown crust. When a skewer is inserted into the centre of the cake, it comes out clean. The cake springs back when pressed lightly with a fingertip.

overcooked The top of the cake is very dark and the texture of the cake crumb is quite dry. The cooking time may have been too long or the oven may have been too hot. It's also possible that the cake was placed too high in the oven.

undercooked and sunken The centre is sunken and when a skewer is inserted into the cake, it comes out sticky. The cake has a soggy, dense texture. The cooking time may have been too short or the oven temperature too low. Too little flour or too much butter may have been used. The oven door may have been opened during the early stages of cooking.

undermixed The top crust has a mottled effect and the texture of the cake is rough with visible pockets of flour and raising agents. The mixture has not been beaten enough or the flour has not been sifted. The ingredients may not have been mixed until properly combined.

what went wrong: fruit cakes

perfect The crust of the cake is an even, deep golden brown. When a skewer is inserted into the centre of the cake, it comes out clean. The texture of the cake is moist and the fruit is evenly distributed.

overcooked The oven temperature may have been too high or the cooking time too long. The mixture might have had too little fat or too much raising agent. Too much sugar may cause a dark crust. If the cake is colouring too quickly and the oven temperature is correct, the top can be protected by covering with foil or a double layer of baking paper.

undercooked and sunken The baking time may have been too short or the oven temperature may have been too low. There might be too much fruit or too little raising agent. The cake may have been placed too low in the oven.

fruit sunken When cut, a dense layer of fruit is visible at the base of the cake. This may be caused by the oven temperature being too low, too little raising agent being used, or the batter not being mixed well enough. Careful mixing is very important to combine the many ingredients.

chocolate cake

Preparation time: 25 minutes
Cooking time: 50 minutes
Serves 8-10

125 g (4½ oz) unsalted butter, softened
115 g (4 oz/½ cup) caster (superfine) sugar
40 g (1½ oz/⅓ cup) icing (confectioners') sugar, sifted
2 eggs, lightly beaten
1 teaspoon natural vanilla extract
80 g (2¾ oz/¼ cup) blackberry jam
155 g (5½ oz/1¼ cups) self-raising flour
60 g (2¼ oz/½ cup) unsweetened cocoa powder
1 teaspoon bicarbonate of soda (baking soda)
250 ml (9 fl oz/1 cup) milk

CHOCOLATE ICING
50 g (1¾ oz) dark chocolate, finely chopped
25 g (1 oz) unsalted butter
3 teaspoons pouring (whipping) cream
30 g (1 oz/¼ cup) icing (confectioners') sugar, sifted

1 Preheat the oven to 180°C (350°F/Gas 4). Lightly grease a 20 cm (8 inch) square cake tin and line with baking paper.
2 Cream the butter and sugars in a small bowl using electric beaters until light and fluffy. Add the eggs gradually, beating thoroughly after each addition. Beat in the vanilla and jam. Transfer to a large bowl. Using a metal spoon, gently fold in the combined sifted flour, cocoa and bicarbonate of soda alternately with the milk. Stir until the mixture is just combined and almost smooth.

3 Pour into the tin and smooth the surface. Bake for 45 minutes, or until a skewer inserted into the centre of the cake comes out clean. Leave in the tin for 15 minutes before turning out onto a wire rack to cool completely.
4 To make the icing (frosting), stir the ingredients in a small saucepan over low heat until smooth and glossy. Spread over the top of the cake with a flat-bladed knife.

cinnamon teacake

Preparation time: 25 minutes
Cooking time: 30 minutes
Serves 8-10

60 g (2¼ oz) unsalted butter, softened
125 g (4½ oz/½ cup) caster (superfine) sugar
1 egg, lightly beaten
1 teaspoon natural vanilla extract
90 g (3¼ oz/¾ cup) self-raising flour
30 g (1 oz/¼ cup) plain (all-purpose) flour
125 ml (4 fl oz/½ cup) milk

TOPPING
20 g (¾ oz) unsalted butter, melted
1 tablespoon caster (superfine) sugar
1 teaspoon ground cinnamon

1 Preheat the oven to 180°C (350°F/Gas 4). Grease a shallow 20 cm (8 inch) round cake tin and line the base with baking paper.
2 Cream the butter and sugar in a small bowl using electric beaters until light and fluffy. Gradually add the egg, beating thoroughly after each addition. Beat in the vanilla, then transfer to a large bowl. Using a large metal spoon, fold in the sifted flours alternately with the milk. Stir until smooth. Spoon into the tin and bake for 30 minutes, or until a skewer inserted into the centre comes out clean. Leave in the tin for 5 minutes before turning out onto a wire rack.
3 To make the topping, brush the warm cake with the butter and sprinkle with the combined sugar and cinnamon.

chocolate cake

ginger cake

Preparation time: 30 minutes
Cooking time: 1 hour 5 minutes
Serves 8-10

125 g (4½ oz) unsalted butter
175 g (6 oz/½ cup) black treacle or molasses
175 g (6 oz/½ cup) golden syrup or dark
    corn syrup
185 g (6½ oz/1½ cups) plain (all-purpose)
    flour
125 g (4½ oz/1 cup) self-raising flour
1 teaspoon bicarbonate of soda
    (baking soda)
3 teaspoons ground ginger
1 teaspoon mixed (pumpkin pie) spice
¼ teaspoon ground cinnamon
165 g (5¾ oz/¾ cup) firmly packed soft
    brown sugar
250 ml (9 fl oz/1 cup) milk
2 eggs, lightly beaten
glacé ginger, to decorate (optional)

LEMON AND GINGER ICING
250 g (9 oz/2 cups) icing (confectioners')
    sugar
1 teaspoon ground ginger
30 g (1 oz) unsalted butter, melted
3 teaspoons milk
3 teaspoons lemon juice
1 teaspoon finely grated lemon zest

1 Preheat the oven to 180°C (350°F/
Gas 4). Lightly grease a deep 20 cm
(8 inch) square cake tin and line the base
with baking paper. Combine the butter,
treacle and golden syrup in a saucepan
and stir over low heat until the butter has
melted. Remove from the heat.
2 Sift the flours, bicarbonate of soda and
spices into a large bowl, add the sugar
and stir until well combined. Make a well
in the centre. Add the butter mixture to
the well, then pour in the combined milk
and egg. Stir with a wooden spoon until
the mixture is smooth and well combined.
3 Pour into the tin and smooth the
surface. Bake for 45–60 minutes, or until a
skewer inserted into the centre of the cake
comes out clean. Leave the cake in the tin

for 20 minutes before turning out onto
a wire rack to cool.
4 To make the icing (frosting), sift the
icing sugar into a small heatproof bowl
and stir in the ginger, melted butter, milk,
lemon juice and zest until the mixture
forms a smooth paste. Stand the bowl
over a saucepan of simmering water,
making sure the base of the bowl does
not touch the water. Stir until smooth and
glossy, then remove from the heat. Spread
over the cake with a flat-bladed knife.
Decorate with glacé ginger, if desired.

NOTE: This delicious ginger cake can be
served the day it is baked, but it is best
served 2 or 3 days after baking so the
flavours have time to develop. It will
store well for up to a week in an airtight
container, or can be frozen, un-iced, for
up to 3 months. It can also be served
un-iced and lightly dusted with sifted
icing (confectioners') sugar.

citrus zest

The rind from any citrus fruit, including oranges, lemons and limes, is also known as the zest. It contains essential oils that impart an intense flavour. The zest is removed with a fine grater or zester. Remove the coloured area only, as the white pith just under the rind has a bitter flavour. You can also extract the citrus oils by rubbing a sugar cube firmly over the fruit until the sugar cube becomes moist and coloured with the oils.

orange cake

Preparation time: **15 minutes**
Cooking time: **50 minutes**
Serves 8-10

250 g (9 oz/2 cups) self-raising flour
40 g (1½ oz/⅓ cup) custard powder or instant vanilla pudding mix
310 g (11 oz/1⅓ cups) caster (superfine) sugar
80 g (2¾ oz) unsalted butter, softened

3 eggs
2 teaspoons finely grated orange zest
250 ml (9 fl oz/1 cup) orange juice

ORANGE BUTTERCREAM
90 g (3¼ oz/¾ cup) icing (confectioners') sugar
125 g (4½ oz) unsalted butter, softened
1 tablespoon orange juice
1 teaspoon finely grated orange zest

1 Preheat the oven to 180°C (350°F/ Gas 4). Lightly grease the base and side of a 23 cm (9 inch) round cake tin and line the base with baking paper.

2 Sift the flour and custard powder into a large bowl and add the sugar, butter, eggs, orange zest and juice. Beat using electric beaters for 4 minutes, or until the mixture is smooth.

3 Spoon the mixture into the tin and smooth the surface. Bake for 50 minutes, or until a skewer inserted into the centre of the cake comes out clean. Leave in the tin for 5 minutes before turning out onto a wire rack to cool completely.

4 To make the buttercream, beat all the ingredients in a small bowl using electric beaters until smooth and creamy. Spread evenly over the cake.

NOTE: To make a cream cheese topping for this cake, mix 125 g (4½ oz/½ cup) softened cream cheese with 2 tablespoons icing (confectioners') sugar, then spread over the top of the cake.

carrot cake

☀

Preparation time: 40 minutes
Cooking time: 1 hour 30 minutes
Serves 8–10

125 g (4½ oz/1 cup) self-raising flour
125 g (4½ oz/1 cup) plain (all-purpose) flour
2 teaspoons ground cinnamon
1 teaspoon ground ginger
½ teaspoon freshly grated nutmeg, plus extra, to sprinkle
1 teaspoon bicarbonate of soda (baking soda)
250 ml (9 fl oz/1 cup) vegetable oil
185 g (6½ oz/1 cup) soft brown sugar
4 eggs
175 g (6 oz/½ cup) golden syrup or dark corn syrup
390 g (13¾ oz/2½ cups) grated carrot
60 g (2¼ oz/½ cup) chopped pecans

LEMON ICING
175 g (6 oz) cream cheese, softened
60 g (2¼ oz) unsalted butter, softened

185 g (6½ oz/1½ cups) icing (confectioners') sugar
1 teaspoon natural vanilla extract
1–2 teaspoons lemon juice

1 Preheat the oven to 160°C (315°F/ Gas 2–3). Lightly grease a 23 cm (9 inch) round cake tin and line with baking paper. Sift the flours, cinnamon, ginger, nutmeg and bicarbonate of soda into a large bowl and make a well in the centre.

2 Whisk together the oil, sugar, eggs and golden syrup until combined. Add this mixture to the well in the flour and gradually stir with a metal spoon until smooth. Stir in the carrot and nuts, then spoon into the tin and smooth the surface.

3 Bake for 1½ hours, or until a skewer inserted into the centre of the cake comes out clean. Leave the cake in the tin for at least 15 minutes before turning out onto a wire rack to cool completely.

4 To make the icing (frosting), beat the cream cheese and butter using electric beaters until smooth. Gradually add the icing sugar alternately with the vanilla and lemon juice, beating until light and creamy. Spread the icing over the cake using a flat-bladed knife. Sprinkle with freshly grated nutmeg.

bananas

Native to South-East Asia, bananas are now grown in many other places that have a warm climate. There are many varieties but the most common are Cavendish and Lady Finger. Bananas can be purchased green and will slowly ripen. If you need to hurry up the ripening process, place green bananas in a brown paper bag with a ripe banana or apple. For baking purposes a very ripe, or even an over-ripe banana, is very useful. An over-ripe banana adds an intense banana flavour to baked cakes, muffins and ice cream.

banana cake

Preparation time: 20 minutes
Cooking time: 1 hour
Serves 8

125 g (4½ oz) unsalted butter, softened
115 g (4 oz/½ cup) caster (superfine) sugar
2 eggs, lightly beaten
1 teaspoon natural vanilla extract
4 very ripe medium bananas, mashed
1 teaspoon bicarbonate of soda (baking soda)
125 ml (4 fl oz/½ cup) milk
250 g (9 oz/2 cups) self-raising flour, sifted
½ teaspoon mixed (pumpkin pie) spice
15 g (½ oz/¼ cup) flaked coconut, toasted, to decorate

BUTTER FROSTING
125 g (4½ oz) unsalted butter, softened
90 g (3¼ oz/¾ cup) icing (confectioners') sugar
1 tablespoon lemon juice

1 Preheat the oven to 180°C (350°F/ Gas 4). Lightly grease a 20 cm (8 inch) round cake tin and line the base with baking paper. Cream the butter and sugar in a small bowl using electric beaters until light and creamy. Add the egg gradually, beating thoroughly after each addition.
2 Beat in the vanilla and banana until combined. Transfer to a large bowl. Dissolve the bicarbonate of soda in the milk. Using a metal spoon, gently fold the flour and spice alternately with the milk into the banana mixture. Stir until just combined and the mixture is smooth.
3 Spoon the mixture into the tin and smooth the surface. Bake for 1 hour, or until a skewer inserted into the centre of the cake comes out clean. Leave the cake in the tin for 10 minutes before turning out onto a wire rack to cool completely.
4 To make the frosting, beat the butter, icing sugar and lemon juice using electric beaters until smooth and creamy. Spread over the cake using a flat-bladed knife and sprinkle with the coconut.

madeira cake

This rich butter cake was very popular in Victorian England. It was often served with a glass of Madeira, hence the name. It is a moist, tender cake due to the high butter content. Often, citrus rind is added, or a slice of candied citrus peel is placed on top, but usually it is kept fairly plain so as not to mask its delicious buttery flavour.

madeira cake

Preparation time: 20 minutes
Cooking time: 50 minutes
Serves 8

185 g (6½ oz) unsalted butter, softened
170 g (5¾ oz/¾ cup) caster (superfine) sugar
3 eggs, lightly beaten
2 teaspoons finely grated orange or lemon zest

95 g (3¼ oz/¾ cup) self-raising flour, sifted
95 g (3¼ oz/¾ cup) plain (all-purpose) flour, sifted
2 tablespoons milk

1 Preheat the oven to 160°C (315°F/ Gas 2–3). Lightly grease a 10 x 20 cm (4 x 8 inch) loaf (bar) tin and line with baking paper.
2 Cream the butter and sugar in a small bowl using electric beaters until light and fluffy. Add the egg gradually, beating thoroughly after each addition. Add the zest and beat until combined. Transfer to a large bowl. Using a metal spoon, fold in the flours and milk. Stir until smooth.
3 Spoon the mixture into the tin and smooth the surface. Bake for 45 minutes, or until a skewer inserted into the centre of the cake comes out clean. Cool the cake in the tin for 10 minutes before turning out onto a wire rack to cool completely.

NOTE: This cake keeps well in an airtight container for up to a week.

2 tablespoons oil
125 ml (4 fl oz/½ cup) buttermilk

CHOCOLATE ICING
150 g (5½ oz) unsalted butter, chopped
150 g (5½ oz) dark chocolate, chopped

1 Preheat the oven to 160°C (315°F/ Gas 2–3). Lightly grease a deep 24 cm (9½ inch) round cake tin and line with baking paper, extending at least 5 cm (2 inches) above the top edge.
2 Put the butter, chocolate and coffee granules in a saucepan with 185 ml (6 fl oz/¾ cup) hot water and stir over low heat until smooth. Remove from heat.
3 Sift the flours, cocoa and bicarbonate of soda into a large bowl. Stir in the sugar and make a well in the centre. Add the combined egg, oil and buttermilk and slowly stir until combined. Gradually stir in the butter mixture.
4 Pour the mixture into the tin. Bake for 1¾ hours. Test the centre with a skewer — it may be slightly wet. Remove the cake from the oven. If the top looks raw, bake for another 5–10 minutes, then remove. Leave in the tin until completely cooled, then turn out.
5 For the icing (frosting), combine the butter and chocolate in a saucepan and stir over low heat until melted. Remove and cool slightly. Pour over the cake.

NOTE: Keep this cake in an airtight container in the refrigerator for up to 3 weeks or store in a cool, dry place for up to a week. It can be frozen, un-iced, for up to 2 months.

chocolate mud cake

Preparation time: 30 minutes
Cooking time: 2 hours
Serves 10–12

250 g (9 oz) unsalted butter
250 g (9 oz) dark chocolate, chopped
2 tablespoons instant coffee granules

150 g (5½ oz) self-raising flour
150 g (5½ oz/1¼ cups) plain (all-purpose) flour
60 g (2¼ oz/½ cup) unsweetened cocoa powder
½ teaspoon bicarbonate of soda (baking soda)
550 g (1 lb 4 oz/2¼ cups) caster (superfine) sugar
4 eggs, lightly beaten

apple and spice teacake

Preparation time: 30 minutes
Cooking time: 1 hour
Serves 8

180 g (6¼ oz) unsalted butter, softened
95 g (3¼ oz/½ cup) soft brown sugar

2 teaspoons finely grated lemon zest
3 eggs, lightly beaten
125 g (4½ oz/1 cup) self-raising flour
75 g (2¾ oz/½ cup) plain (all-purpose)
 wholemeal (whole-wheat) flour
½ teaspoon ground cinnamon
125 ml (4 fl oz/½ cup) milk
400 g (14 oz) tin pie apple, drained
¼ teaspoon mixed (pumpkin pie) spice
1 tablespoon soft brown sugar, extra
25 g (1 oz/¼ cup) flaked almonds

1 Preheat the oven to 180°C (350°F/ Gas 4). Grease the base and side of a 20 cm (8 inch) spring-form cake tin, and line the base with baking paper.

2 Cream the butter and sugar in a small bowl using electric beaters until light and fluffy. Beat in the lemon zest. Add the egg gradually, beating thoroughly after each addition. Transfer the mixture to a large bowl. Using a metal spoon, fold in the sifted flours and cinnamon alternately with the milk. Stir until just combined and almost smooth.

3 Spoon half of the mixture into the tin and top with three-quarters of the pie apple, then the remaining cake mixture.

Press the remaining pie apple around the edge of the top.

4 Combine the mixed spice, extra sugar and flaked almonds and sprinkle over the cake. Bake for 1 hour, or until a skewer inserted into the centre of the cake comes out clean. Leave in the tin for 15 minutes before removing the side and transferring to a wire rack to cool.

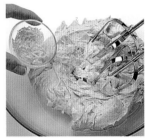

Cream the butter and sugar, then beat in the lemon zest.

Spoon apple onto half the cake mixture, then top with the remaining mixture.

The cake is cooked when a skewer inserted into the centre comes out clean.

pound cake

pound cake

Preparation time: 25 minutes
Cooking time: 1 hour
Serves 8

375 g (13 oz) unsalted butter, softened
345 g (12 oz/1½ cups) caster (superfine)
  sugar
1 teaspoon natural vanilla extract
6 eggs, lightly beaten
375 g (13 oz/3 cups) plain (all-purpose)
  flour, sifted
1 teaspoon baking powder
60 ml (2 fl oz/¼ cup) milk
icing (confectioners') sugar, to dust

1 Preheat the oven to 180°C (350°F/
Gas 4). Lightly grease a 22 cm (8½ inch)
round cake tin and line the base with
baking paper.
2 Cream the butter and sugar in a small
bowl using electric beaters until light and
fluffy. Beat in the vanilla, then add the
egg gradually, beating thoroughly after
each addition. Transfer to a large bowl.
Using a large metal spoon, fold in the
sifted flour and baking powder alternately
with the milk. Stir until the mixture is just
combined and almost smooth.
3 Spoon the mixture into the tin and
smooth the surface. Bake for 1 hour, or
until a skewer inserted into the centre of
the cake comes out clean. Leave in the tin
for 10 minutes before turning out onto
a wire rack to cool. Lightly dust the top
with icing sugar just before serving.

lemon cake with crunchy topping

Preparation time: 25 minutes
Cooking time: 1 hour 20 minutes
Serves 8–10

250 g (9 oz) unsalted butter, softened
200 g (7 oz) caster (superfine) sugar
2 teaspoons finely grated lemon zest

4 eggs, lightly beaten
250 g (9 oz/2 cups) self-raising flour
1 teaspoon baking powder
2 tablespoons lemon juice

TOPPING
125 g (4½ oz/½ cup) sugar
60 ml (2 fl oz/¼ cup) lemon juice

1 Preheat the oven to 170°C (325°F/
Gas 3). Lightly grease a 22 cm (8½ inch)
square cake tin and line the base with
baking paper.
2 Cream the butter and caster sugar in
a small bowl using electric beaters until
the mixture is light and fluffy. Beat in the
lemon zest, then add the egg gradually,
beating thoroughly after each addition.
Transfer the mixture to a large bowl.

3 Using a large metal spoon, fold in the
combined sifted flour, baking powder
and ¼ teaspoon salt, as well as the
lemon juice. Stir until the mixture is just
combined and almost smooth.
4 Spoon the mixture into the tin and
smooth the surface. Bake for 1 hour
20 minutes, or until a skewer inserted
into the centre of the cake comes out
clean. Remove from the heat and turn
out onto a wire rack.
5 For the topping, mix together the sugar
and lemon juice (do not dissolve the
sugar), and quickly brush over the top
of the warm cake. Leave to cool.

lemon cake with crunchy topping

pound cake

This fine-textured buttery cake, dating back to
the 18th century, is traditionally made in a loaf
(bar) tin and was originally based on pound
(pre-metric) measures of one pound each of
butter, sugar, eggs and flour. The butter and
sugar are well creamed before beating in the eggs
and folding in the flour. Vanilla or grated citrus
zest is added for extra flavour. Ground almonds
and dried fruit such as sultanas (golden raisins)
are sometimes added but this is not traditional.

sour cream

Traditionally, sour cream was non-pasteurised cream skimmed from the top of the milk and left at room temperature until it has soured due to the natural bacteria present. Today, however, the process is more controlled as the cream, by law, has to be pasteurised. A special culture is added and results in a slightly soured and thick cream. Sour cream has a tenderising effect when used in baking, resulting in a soft-crumbed cake.

sour cream coffee cake

Preparation time: 25 minutes
Cooking time: 40 minutes
Makes about 20 pieces

125 g (4½ oz) unsalted butter, softened
250 g (9 oz/1 cup) caster (superfine) sugar
3 eggs, lightly beaten
1 teaspoon natural vanilla extract
1 tablespoon instant coffee granules
90 g (3¼ oz/¾ cup) plain (all-purpose) flour
60 g (2¼ oz/½ cup) self-raising flour
90 g (3¼ oz/⅓ cup) sour cream

COFFEE ICING
1 tablespoon instant coffee granules
250 g (9 oz/2 cups) icing (confectioners') sugar
40 g (1½ oz) unsalted butter, melted

1   Preheat the oven to 160°C (315°F/ Gas 2–3). Lightly grease a shallow 28 x 18 cm (11¼ x 7 inch) cake tin and line with baking paper.

2 Cream the butter and caster sugar in a small bowl using electric beaters until light and fluffy. Add the egg gradually, beating thoroughly after each addition. Dissolve the vanilla and coffee granules in 1 tablespoon warm water and beat into the mixture until combined. Transfer to a large bowl. Using a large metal spoon, fold in the sifted flours alternately with the sour cream. Stir until the mixture is just combined and almost smooth.

3 Spoon the mixture into the tin and smooth the surface. Bake for 30–40 minutes, or until a skewer inserted into the centre of the cake comes out clean. Leave the cake in the tin for 5 minutes before turning out onto a wire rack to cool completely.

4 For the icing (frosting), dissolve the coffee granules in 1–2 tablespoons warm water in a small bowl. Add the icing sugar and butter, mix until well combined, then spread over the cooled cake.

lemon coconut cake

✳

Preparation time: 20 minutes
Cooking time: 40 minutes
Serves 8–10

185 g (6½ oz/1½ cups) self-raising flour
45 g (1¾ oz/½ cup) desiccated coconut
1 tablespoon finely grated lemon zest
230 g (8 oz/1 cup) caster (superfine)
   sugar
125 g (4½ oz) unsalted butter, melted
2 eggs
250 ml (9 fl oz/1 cup) milk
thin strips of lemon zest, to decorate

COCONUT ICING
185 g (6½ oz/1½ cups) icing
   (confectioners') sugar, sifted
90 g (3¼ oz/1 cup) desiccated coconut
½ teaspoon finely grated lemon zest
60 ml (2 fl oz/¼ cup) lemon juice

1 Preheat the oven to 180°C (350°F/ Gas 4). Lightly grease a deep 20 cm (8 inch) round cake tin and line with

baking paper. Sift the flour into a large bowl and add the coconut, lemon zest, caster sugar, butter, eggs and milk. Stir, using a wooden spoon, until smooth.

2 Pour the mixture into the tin and smooth the surface. Bake the cake for 40 minutes, or until a skewer inserted into the centre of the cake comes out clean. Leave the cake in the tin for

5 minutes before turning out onto a wire rack to cool completely.

3 To make the icing (frosting), combine the icing sugar and coconut in a bowl, then add the lemon zest and enough lemon juice to make a stiff but spreadable icing. Spread over the cooled cake and use a fork to rough it up a little, if desired. Decorate with lemon zest.

coconut

This fruit of tropical coconut palms contains a milky drinkable liquid surrounded by soft white flesh or 'meat'. The latter is often used in baking, confectionery and sweet meats. It can be used freshly grated or dried as desiccated or shredded coconut. If dried, it can be lightly toasted and used to decorate cakes. Coconut milk and cream are liquid extracted from the flesh and can also be used in baking. The cream is the oily surface that forms on the milk when it has separated after chilling. The milk and cream are available in tins.

orange poppy seed cake

125 g (4½ oz/1 cup) icing (confectioners')
  sugar, sifted
1 teaspoon lemon juice or natural
  vanilla extract

1 Preheat the oven to 180°C (350°F/
Gas 4). Lightly grease a deep 20 cm
(8 inch) round cake tin and line with
baking paper. Sift the flour into a bowl
and add the almonds and poppy seeds.
Make a well in the centre.
2 Place the butter, caster sugar, jam,
orange zest and juice in a saucepan. Stir
over low heat until the butter has melted
and the mixture is smooth. Gradually add
the butter mixture to the dry ingredients,
stirring with a whisk until smooth. Add
the egg and whisk until combined.
3 Pour the mixture into the tin and bake
for 50–60 minutes, or until a skewer
inserted into the centre of the cake comes
out clean. Leave in the tin for 15 minutes
before turning onto a wire rack to cool.
4 To make the icing (frosting), beat the
butter and cream cheese until smooth.
Gradually add the icing sugar and lemon
juice or vanilla and beat until thick and
creamy. Spread over the cooled cake.
Decorate with orange zest, if desired.

lumberjack cake

Preparation time: **30 minutes**
Cooking time: **1 hour 15 minutes**
Serves **8**

200 g (7 oz) fresh dates, stoned and
  chopped
1 teaspoon bicarbonate of soda
  (baking soda)
125 g (4½ oz) unsalted butter,
  softened
230 g (8 oz/1 cup) caster (superfine)
  sugar
1 egg
1 teaspoon natural vanilla extract
2 granny smith apples, peeled, cored and
  grated
125 g (4½ oz/1 cup) plain (all-purpose)
  flour

orange poppy
seed cake

Preparation time: **30 minutes**
Cooking time: **1 hour**
Serves **8–10**

185 g (6½ oz/1½ cups) self-raising flour
35 g (1¼ oz/⅓ cup) ground almonds
40 g (1½ oz/¼ cup) poppy seeds
185 g (6½ oz) unsalted butter

145 g (5½ oz/⅔ cup) caster (superfine)
  sugar
80 g (2¾ oz/¼ cup) apricot jam or
  marmalade
2–3 teaspoons finely grated orange zest
80 ml (2½ fl oz/⅓ cup) orange juice
3 eggs, lightly beaten
orange zest, to decorate (optional)

CREAM CHEESE ICING
100 g (3½ oz) unsalted butter,
  softened
100 g (3½ oz) cream cheese, softened

60 g (2¼ oz/½ cup) self-raising flour
icing (confectioners') sugar (optional),
   to dust

TOPPING
75 g (2¾ oz) unsalted butter
95 g (3¼ oz/½ cup) soft brown sugar
80 ml (2½ fl oz/⅓ cup) milk
60 g (2¼ oz/1 cup) shredded coconut

1 Preheat the oven to 180°C (350°F/
Gas 4). Grease a 20 cm (8 inch) round
spring-form cake tin and line the base
with baking paper.

2 Put the dates in a small saucepan with
250 ml (9 fl oz/1 cup) water and bring to
the boil. Stir in the bicarbonate of soda,
remove from the heat and set aside.
3 Cream the butter and caster sugar
using electric beaters until light and
fluffy. Add the egg and vanilla and beat
until combined. Stir in the lukewarm
date mixture and the apple, then fold in
the sifted flours until just combined and
almost smooth. Spoon into the tin and
smooth the surface. Bake for 40 minutes.
4 To make the topping, combine the
butter, brown sugar, milk and coconut

in a small saucepan and stir over low
heat until the butter has melted and the
ingredients are well combined.
5 Remove the cake from the oven and
carefully spread the topping over the
cake. Return the cake to the oven for
20–30 minutes, or until the topping is
golden and a skewer inserted into the
centre of the cake comes out clean.
6 Remove from the oven and leave
the cake in the tin to cool completely,
then remove from the tin and place on
a serving plate. The cake can be dusted
with icing sugar just before serving.

Cream the butter and sugar
together until light and fluffy.

Fold the flours into the date and
apple mixture until almost smooth.

Gently spread the topping over the
hot cake, then return to the oven.

hummingbird cake

Preparation time: **30 minutes**
Cooking time: **1 hour**
Serves **8–10**

2 ripe bananas, mashed
130 g (4½ oz/½ cup) drained and crushed
    tinned pineapple (see Note)
285 g (10¼ oz/1¼ cups) caster (superfine)
    sugar
210 g (7½ oz/1⅔ cups) self-raising flour
2 teaspoons ground cinnamon or mixed
    (pumpkin pie) spice
170 ml (5½ fl oz/⅔ cup) vegetable oil
60 ml (2 fl oz/¼ cup) pineapple juice
2 eggs

LEMON ICING
60 g (2¼ oz) unsalted butter, softened
125 g (4½ oz/½ cup) cream cheese,
    softened
185 g (6½ oz/1½ cups) icing
    (confectioners') sugar
1–2 teaspoons lemon juice

1 Preheat the oven to 180°C (350°F/
Gas 4). Lightly grease a 20 cm (8 inch)
square cake tin and line with baking
paper. Place the banana, pineapple and
caster sugar in a large bowl. Add the
sifted flour and cinnamon or mixed spice.
Stir with a wooden spoon until combined.
2 Whisk together the oil, pineapple juice
and eggs. Pour over the banana mixture
and stir until combined and smooth.

3 Spoon into the tin and smooth the
surface. Bake for 1 hour, or until a skewer
inserted into the centre of the cake comes
out clean. Leave in the tin for 15 minutes
before turning out onto a wire rack to cool.
4 To make the icing (frosting), beat the
butter and cream cheese using electric
beaters until smooth. Gradually add the
icing sugar alternately with the lemon
juice. Beat until thick and creamy.
5 Spread the icing thickly over the top
of the cooled cake, or thinly over the
top and side.

NOTE: If you are unable to buy crushed
pineapple, use pineapple rings or pieces
chopped very finely. Buy it in natural juice
rather than syrup and reserve the juice
when draining to use in the recipe.

seed cake

Preparation time: **20 minutes**
Cooking time: **50 minutes**
Serves **6–8**

125 g (4½ oz) unsalted butter, softened
115 g (4 oz/½ cup) caster (superfine) sugar
3 eggs, lightly beaten
3 teaspoons caraway seeds
155 g (5½ oz/1¼ cups) self-raising flour
2 tablespoons milk
icing (confectioners') sugar (optional),
    to dust

1 Preheat the oven to 180°C (350°F/
Gas 4). Lightly grease an 18 cm (7 inch)
round cake tin and line the base with
baking paper.
2 Cream the butter and sugar in a small
bowl using electric beaters until light
and fluffy. Gradually add the egg, beating
thoroughly after each addition.
3 Transfer the mixture to a large bowl.
Using a metal spoon, fold in the caraway
seeds and sifted flour alternately with
the milk. Stir until the mixture is just
combined and almost smooth.
4 Spoon the mixture into the tin, smooth
the surface and bake for 50 minutes, or

hummingbird cake

glacé cherries

To help prevent glacé cherries from sinking to the base of a cake during cooking, remove the syrup by rinsing the cherries under cold water, then pat dry and toss in a little flour before stirring into the cake batter. It is also a good idea to cut each cherry in half.

cherry cake

until a skewer inserted into the centre of the cake comes out clean. Leave the cake in the tin for 20 minutes before turning onto a wire rack to cool completely. Serve plain or dusted with sifted icing sugar.

NOTE: Seed cake is a traditional English cake made to celebrate the end of the spring crop sowing. It will keep for up to a week in an airtight container, or can be frozen for up to 3 months.

cherry cake

Preparation time: **30 minutes**
Cooking time: **40 minutes**
Serves **8–10**

210 g (7½ oz/1 cup) glacé cherries
85 g (3 oz/⅔ cup) plain (all-purpose) flour
90 g (3¼ oz) unsalted butter, softened
160 g (5¾ oz/⅔ cup) caster (superfine) sugar
2 eggs, lightly beaten
1 teaspoon natural vanilla extract
125 g (4½ oz/1 cup) self-raising flour
80 ml (2½ fl oz/⅓ cup) milk

ICING
125 g (4½ oz/1 cup) icing (confectioners') sugar
20 g (¾ oz) unsalted butter
pink food colouring

1 Preheat the oven to 180°C (350°F/ Gas 4). Grease a 20 cm (8 inch) kugelhopf tin. Dust with flour, then shake off any excess. Rinse and dry the glacé cherries and cut each in half. Toss the cherries in a little of the flour to coat lightly.
2 Cream the butter and sugar using electric beaters until light and fluffy.

Add the egg gradually, beating thoroughly after each addition. Beat in the vanilla. Use a large metal spoon to fold in the sifted flours alternately with the milk. Stir in the cherries.
3 Spoon the mixture into the tin and smooth the surface. Bake for 35 minutes, or until a skewer inserted into the centre of the cake comes out clean. Leave in the tin for 10 minutes before turning out onto a wire rack to cool completely.
4 To make the icing (frosting), combine the sifted icing sugar and butter with 1–2 tablespoons water in a small heatproof bowl. Stand the bowl over a saucepan of simmering water, making sure that the base of the bowl does not touch the water. Stir the mixture until the butter has melted and the icing is glossy and smooth. Stir in a couple of drops of food colouring. Drizzle over the cake, allowing it to run down the sides.

orange and lemon syrup cake

✹ ✹ ✹

Preparation time: 40 minutes
Cooking time: 1 hour 5 minutes
Serves 10–12

BUTTER CAKE
185 g (6½ oz/1½ cups) self-raising flour
60 g (2¼ oz/½ cup) plain (all-purpose) flour
185 g (6½ oz) unsalted butter, softened
170 g (5¾ oz/¾ cup) caster (superfine) sugar
3 eggs, lightly beaten
1 teaspoon natural vanilla extract
1 teaspoon finely grated orange zest
60 ml (2 fl oz/¼ cup) milk

SYRUP
2 oranges
2 lemons
520 g (1 lb 2¾ oz) caster (superfine) sugar

1 Preheat the oven to 180°C (350°F/ Gas 4). Lightly grease a 20 cm (8 inch) kugelhopf tin. Dust lightly with flour.
2 Sift the flours into a bowl. Cream the butter and sugar in a small bowl using electric beaters until light and fluffy. Add the egg gradually, a little at a time, beating thoroughly after each addition. Add the vanilla and beat well to combine. Transfer the mixture to a large bowl and, using a large metal spoon, gently fold in the sifted flour, orange zest and milk. Stir until just combined and almost smooth. Spoon the mixture into the tin and cook for 1 hour 5 minutes, or until a skewer inserted into the centre of the cake comes out clean.
3 Meanwhile, make the syrup. Cut the oranges and lemons into thin slices. Place 250 g (9 oz) of the sugar in a heavy-based frying pan with 80 ml (2½ fl oz/⅓ cup) water. Stir over low heat until the sugar has completely dissolved.
4 Bring to the boil, then reduce the heat and simmer. Add a quarter of the sliced fruit to the syrup and simmer for 5–10 minutes, or until translucent and toffee-like. Lift out the fruit using tongs and cool on a wire rack. Add an extra 90 g (3¼ oz) of the sugar to the syrup and stir gently to dissolve — the juice from the fruit breaks down the syrup and the fruit won't candy properly unless you add the sugar. Repeat with the remaining sliced fruit, adding 90 g (3¼ oz) of the sugar to the syrup before cooking each batch.
5 When all the fruit has been candied, turn the warm cake out onto a wire rack over a tray and pour the hot syrup over, allowing it to soak in — if the syrup is too thick, thin it with a little orange juice. Put the cake on a serving plate. When the fruit slices are firm, arrange on top of the cake (cut and twist some of the slices).

NOTE: Serve within a few hours of decorating. You can also bake this cake in a 20 cm (8 inch) round tin. The candied fruit can be kept between baking paper in an airtight container for up to 2 days.

semolina lemon syrup cake

✷

Preparation time: 20 minutes
Cooking time: 1 hour
Makes about 20 pieces

125 g (4½ oz) unsalted butter, softened
185 g (6½ oz/¾ cup) caster (superfine)
    sugar
2 teaspoons finely grated lemon zest
3 eggs
185 g (6½ oz/1½ cups) semolina
125 g (4½ oz/1 cup) self-raising flour
125 ml (4 fl oz/½ cup) milk
80 g (2¾ oz/½ cup) blanched almonds,
    toasted and finely chopped
blanched flaked almonds, to decorate

SYRUP
625 g (1 lb 6 oz/2½ cups) sugar
2 tablespoons lemon juice

1 Preheat the oven to 170°C (325°F/
Gas 3). Lightly grease a shallow 18 x 28
cm (7 x 11¼ inch) cake tin.
2 To make the syrup, dissolve the sugar
in 750 ml (26 fl oz/3 cups) water in a
saucepan over high heat. Add the lemon
juice and bring to the boil, then reduce
the heat and simmer for 20 minutes.
Remove from the heat and allow to cool.
3 Meanwhile, cream the butter, caster
sugar and zest using electric beaters until
light and fluffy. Add the eggs one at a
time, beating well after each addition.
4 Sift together the semolina and
flour and fold into the butter mixture
alternately with the milk. Mix in the
chopped almonds, then spread the
mixture into the tin and arrange rows of
flaked almonds on top.
5 Bake the cake for 35–40 minutes, or
until it is golden and shrinks slightly from
the sides of the tin. Prick the surface with
a fine skewer, then pour the cooled syrup
over the hot cake. When the cake has
cooled, cut it into squares or diamonds.

sugar syrup

Sugar syrup is made by stirring sugar and water in a saucepan over low heat, without boiling, until the sugar is completely dissolved. After this, the heat is increased and the syrup is allowed to boil rapidly to form a concentrated syrup. There are several stages a sugar syrup goes through, from a soft, sticky ball to a hard-crack stage, before finally turning into a caramel syrup. Each stage is used for different purposes, from a simple syrup used to poach fresh fruit, to making crème caramel, confectionery and spun sugar.

classic sponge

❋

Preparation time: **20 minutes**
Cooking time: **25 minutes**
Serves **8**

75 g (2¾ oz) plain (all-purpose) flour
150 g (5½ oz) self-raising flour
6 eggs
220 g (7¾ oz) caster (superfine) sugar
2 tablespoons boiling water
160 g (5¾ oz/½ cup) strawberry jam
250 ml (9 fl oz/1 cup) pouring (whipping)
   cream
icing (confectioners') sugar, to dust

1 Preheat the oven to 180°C (350°F/Gas 4). Lightly grease two 22 cm (8½ inch) sandwich tins or shallow round cake tins and line the bases with baking paper. Dust with a little flour, shaking off excess.
2 Sift the flours together three times onto paper. Whisk the eggs in a large bowl using electric beaters for 7 minutes, until thick and pale. Gradually add the sugar, whisking thoroughly after each addition. Use a large metal spoon to quickly and gently fold in the flours and water.
3 Spread the mixture evenly into the tins and bake for 25 minutes, or until the sponges are lightly golden and shrink slightly from the sides of the tins, and a skewer inserted into the centres of the cakes comes out clean. Leave the sponges in their tins for 5 minutes before turning out onto wire racks to cool.
4 Spread jam over one of the sponges. Beat the cream in a small bowl until stiff, then spoon into a piping (icing) bag and pipe rosettes over the jam. Place the other sponge on top. Dust with icing sugar.

NOTE: The secret to making a perfect sponge lies in the folding technique. A beating action, or using a wooden spoon, will cause loss of volume in the egg mixture and result in a flat, heavy cake. Unfilled sponge cakes can be frozen, separately, for up to 1 month. Thaw at room temperature for about 1 hour. Once filled, serve immediately.

cream

Cream is used extensively in baking, as part of the baking mixture or whipped to use as a filling or decoration. It adds richness, moistness and flavour to the finished product. Cream needs at least 30 per cent fat to be whipped successfully. When whipping cream, have the cream cold, straight from the fridge. Ideally, pour it into a cold metal bowl and whisk over a basin of cold water (iced water in hot weather). Whisk until stiff but take care not to overwhisk or it will curdle. You can flavour whipped cream with a teaspoon each of icing (confectioners') sugar and natural vanilla extract.

genoise sponge

✳

Preparation time: **25 minutes**
Cooking time: **35 minutes**
Serves **10–12**

290 g (10¼ oz/2⅓ cups) plain
   (all-purpose) flour
8 eggs
220 g (7¾ oz) caster (superfine) sugar
100 g (3½ oz) unsalted butter, melted
   and cooled
whipped cream and passionfruit icing
   (page 128), to serve

1 Preheat the oven to 180°C (350°F/ Gas 4). Lightly grease two shallow 22 cm (8½ inch) round cake tins with melted butter. Line the bases with baking paper, then grease the paper and dust with a little flour, shaking off any excess.

2 Sift the flour three times onto paper. Mix the eggs and sugar in a large heatproof bowl. Place the bowl over a pan of simmering water, making sure the base does not touch the water, and whisk using electric beaters on high speed for 8 minutes, until the mixture is very thick and pale. Remove from the heat and whisk for 3 minutes.

3 Using a large metal spoon, fold in the butter and flour quickly and lightly until the mixture is just combined.

4 Spread the mixture evenly into the tins. Bake for 18–20 minutes, or until lightly golden and shrunk slightly from the side of the tins, and a skewer inserted in the centres of the cakes comes out clean. Leave in the tins for 5 minutes before turning out onto a wire rack to cool. Sandwich the cooled cakes with cream and top with passionfruit icing (frosting).

NOTE: You can also use a 25 cm (10 inch) Genoise cake tin. Cook for 25 minutes.

genoise sponge

The Genoise sponge is traditionally made in a tin with sloping sides and served dusted with icing sugar. However, it is often baked to be used for a decorated gâteau or celebration cake, in which case it is generally baked in two sandwich tins. In this case, you can ensure you have exactly half the mixture in each tin by weighing each tin first, then dividing the mixture between the tins before weighing the tins again to make sure they are equal in weight.

swiss roll

❈

Preparation time: **25 minutes**
Cooking time: **12 minutes**
Serves **10**

90 g (3¼ oz/¾ cup) self-raising flour
3 eggs, lightly beaten
155 g (5½ oz/½ cup) caster (superfine)
  sugar
icing (confectioners') sugar, to sprinkle
160 g (5¾ oz/½ cup) strawberry jam,
  beaten

1 Preheat the oven to 190°C (375°F/ Gas 5). Lightly grease a shallow 25 x 30 cm (10 x 12 inch) swiss roll (jelly roll) tin. Line the base with baking paper, extending over the two long sides.
2 Sift the flour three times onto a sheet of paper. Whisk the eggs using electric beaters in a small bowl for 5 minutes, or until thick and pale. Add the caster sugar gradually, beating constantly until the mixture is very thick and glossy. Transfer to a large bowl. Using a metal spoon, fold in the flour quickly and lightly. Spread the mixture into the tin and smooth the surface.

3 Bake the cake for 10–12 minutes, or until lightly golden and a skewer inserted into the centre comes out clean.
4 Meanwhile, place a clean tea towel (dish towel) on a work surface, cover with baking paper and sprinkle well with icing sugar. Turn the cooked cake out immediately onto the icing sugar. Using the tea towel as a guide, carefully roll up the cake, along with the paper, from a short side. Stand the rolled cake on a wire rack for 5 minutes, then carefully unroll and allow the cake to cool to room temperature. Spread with the jam and re-roll. Trim the ends with a knife and cut into slices to serve.

chocolate swiss roll

❈ ❈

Preparation time: **55 minutes**
Cooking time: **12 minutes**
Serves **8**

3 eggs
125 g (4½ oz/½ cup) caster (superfine)
  sugar
30 g (1 oz/¼ cup) plain (all-purpose)
  flour
2 tablespoons unsweetened cocoa powder
250 ml (9 fl oz/1 cup) pouring (whipping)
  cream
1 tablespoon icing (confectioners') sugar,
  plus extra, to dust
½ teaspoon natural vanilla extract

1 Preheat the oven to 200°C (400°F/ Gas 6). Lightly grease a shallow 25 x 30 cm (10 x 12 inch) swiss roll (jelly roll) tin. Line the base with baking paper, extending over the two long sides.
2 Whisk the eggs and 90 g (3¼ oz/ ⅓ cup) of the caster sugar in a small bowl using electric beaters until very thick and pale. Using a metal spoon, gently fold in the combined sifted flour and cocoa.
3 Spread the mixture into the tin, smooth the surface and bake for 10–12 minutes, or until the cake is just set.
4 Meanwhile, place a clean tea towel (dish towel) on a work surface, cover

swiss roll

Add the sugar gradually to the eggs, beating until thick and glossy.

Bake the cake until lightly golden on top and springy to touch.

Roll up the cake with baking paper, using the tea towel as a guide.

with baking paper and sprinkle the paper with the remaining caster sugar. Turn the cooked cake out onto the sugar. Using the tea towel as a guide, carefully roll up the cake, along with the paper, from the short side. Stand the rolled cake on a wire rack for 5 minutes, then carefully unroll and allow the cake to cool to room temperature. Trim the ends with a knife.

5 Whisk the cream, icing sugar and vanilla until stiff peaks form. Spread the cream over the cooled cake, leaving a 1 cm (½ inch) border all around. Re-roll the cake, using the paper as a guide. Place the roll, seam-side down, on a tray. Refrigerate, covered, for 30 minutes. Lightly dust the top with icing sugar before cutting into slices to serve.

honey cream roll

Preparation time: **40 minutes**
Cooking time: **12 minutes**
Serves **8–10**

90 g (3¼ oz/¾ cup) self-raising flour
2 teaspoons mixed (pumpkin pie) spice
3 eggs
125 g (4½ oz/⅔ cup) soft brown sugar
icing (confectioners') sugar, to sprinkle

HONEY CREAM
125 g (4½ oz) unsalted butter,
  softened
40 g (1½ oz/⅓ cup) icing (confectioners')
  sugar
2 tablespoons honey

1 Preheat the oven to 190°C (375°F/Gas 5). Lightly grease a shallow 25 x 30 cm (10 x 12 inch) swiss roll (jelly roll) tin and line the base with baking paper, extending over the two long sides.
2 Sift the flour and mixed spice together three times onto a sheet of paper. Whisk the eggs in a large bowl using electric beaters for 5 minutes, or until thick and pale. Add the brown sugar gradually, whisking constantly until the sugar has dissolved and the mixture is very thick

and glossy. Using a metal spoon, fold in the flour quickly and lightly. Spread into the tin and smooth the surface. Bake for 10–12 minutes, or until the cake is lightly golden and springy to touch, and a skewer inserted into the centre comes out clean.
3 Meanwhile, place a clean tea towel (dish towel) on a work surface, cover with baking paper and sprinkle the paper with icing sugar. Turn the cooked cake out

onto the icing sugar. Using the tea towel as a guide, carefully roll up the cake, along with the paper, from the short side. Leave on a wire rack until cool.
4 To make the honey cream, beat all the ingredients in a bowl using electric beaters until light and creamy and the sugar has dissolved. Unroll the cake, spread with the honey cream and re-roll. Trim the ends with a knife.

devil's food cake

Preparation time: 30 minutes
Cooking time: 45 minutes
Serves 8–10

280 g (10 oz/1½ cups) soft brown sugar
40 g (1½ oz/⅓ cup) unsweetened cocoa powder, plus extra, to dust
250 ml (9 fl oz/1 cup) milk
90 g (3¼ oz) dark chocolate, chopped
125 g (4½ oz) unsalted butter, softened
1 teaspoon natural vanilla extract
2 eggs, separated
185 g (6½ oz/1½ cups) plain (all-purpose) flour
1 teaspoon bicarbonate of soda (baking soda)

CHOCOLATE ICING
50 g (1¾ oz) dark chocolate, chopped
30 g (1 oz) unsalted butter
1 tablespoon icing (confectioners') sugar

FILLING
250 ml (9 fl oz/1 cup) pouring (whipping) cream
1 tablespoon icing (confectioners') sugar
1 teaspoon natural vanilla extract

1 Preheat the oven to 160°C (315°F/ Gas 2–3). Lightly grease two deep 20 cm (8 inch) round cake tins and line the bases with baking paper. Combine a third of the brown sugar with the cocoa and milk in a small saucepan. Stir over low heat until the sugar and cocoa have dissolved. Remove from the heat and stir in the chocolate until melted. Cool.

2 Cream the remaining brown sugar with the butter in a small bowl using electric beaters until light and fluffy. Beat in the vanilla and egg yolks and the cooled chocolate mixture. Transfer to a large bowl and stir in the sifted flour and bicarbonate of soda. Whisk the egg whites in a clean, dry small bowl until soft peaks form. Fold into the chocolate mixture.

3 Divide the mixture evenly between the tins and bake for 35 minutes, or until a skewer inserted into the centres of the cakes comes out clean. Leave in the tins for 5 minutes before turning out onto wire racks to cool.

4 To make the chocolate icing (frosting), place the chocolate and butter in a heatproof bowl over a saucepan of simmering water, making sure the base of the bowl doesn't touch the water. Stir

until the mixture is melted and smooth. Gradually add the sifted icing sugar and stir until smooth. Set aside.

5 To make the filling, whip the cream, icing sugar and vanilla using electric beaters until stiff peaks form. Spread over one cooled cake, top with the second cake and then spread the chocolate icing over the top. Dust with extra cocoa.

angel food cake

Preparation time: **30 minutes**
Cooking time: **40 minutes**
Serves **10-12**

125 g (4½ oz/1 cup) self-raising flour
345 g (12 oz/1½ cups) caster (superfine) sugar
12 egg whites
1½ teaspoons cream of tartar
½ teaspoon natural vanilla extract
¼ teaspoon natural almond extract
1–2 tablespoons icing (confectioners') sugar, to dust
whole or sliced fresh fruit (such as strawberries), to decorate

1 Preheat the oven to 180°C (350°F/ Gas 4). Have an ungreased angel food tin ready. Sift the flour and 170 g (6 oz/ ¾ cup) of the caster sugar together four times onto a sheet of paper. Using electric beaters, whisk the egg whites with the cream of tartar and ¼ teaspoon salt until stiff peaks form. Whisk in the remaining sugar, 1 tablespoon at a time. Fold in the vanilla and almond extract.

2 Sift one-quarter of the flour and sugar mixture onto the egg white and, using a spatula, gradually fold in. Repeat with the remaining flour and sugar.

3 Spoon the mixture into the tin and bake for 35–40 minutes, or until puffed and golden and a skewer inserted into the centre of the cake comes out clean. Turn upside-down on a wire rack and leave in the tin until cool. Gently shake the tin to remove the cake. Lightly dust with the icing sugar and decorate with fruit.

sacher torte

sacher torte

✵ ✵

Preparation time: 40 minutes
Cooking time: 50 minutes
Serves 10-12

125 g (4½ oz/1 cup) plain (all-purpose)
   flour
30 g (1 oz/¼ cup) unsweetened cocoa
   powder
230 g (8 oz/1 cup) caster (superfine) sugar
100 g (3½ oz) unsalted butter, cubed
80 g (2¾ oz/¼ cup) strawberry jam
4 eggs, separated

GANACHE TOPPING
170 ml (5½ fl oz/⅔ cup) pouring
   (whipping) cream
80 g (2¾ oz/⅓ cup) caster (superfine)
   sugar
200 g (7 oz) dark chocolate, chopped

1   Preheat the oven to 180°C (350°F/
Gas 4). Lightly grease a 20 cm (8 inch)
round cake tin and line with baking paper.
2   Sift the flour and cocoa into a large
bowl and make a well in the centre.
Combine the sugar, butter and half the
jam in a small saucepan. Stir over low
heat until the sugar has dissolved, then
add to the flour with the lightly beaten
egg yolks and stir until just combined.
3   Whisk the egg whites in a clean, dry,
small bowl using electric beaters until
soft peaks form. Stir one-third of the egg
white into the cake mixture, then fold in
the rest in two batches.
4   Pour the mixture into the tin and
smooth the surface. Bake for 40–45
minutes, or until a skewer inserted into
the centre of the cake comes out clean.
Leave in the tin for 15 minutes before
turning out onto a wire rack to cool.
5   To make the topping, stir the cream,
sugar and chocolate in a small saucepan
over low heat until melted and smooth.
Trim the top of the cake so that it is flat,
then turn it upside down on a wire rack
over a tray. Melt the remaining jam and
brush it over the cake. Pour most of the
topping over the cake and tap the tray to
flatten the surface. Place the remaining
mixture in a piping (icing) bag and pipe
'Sacher' on the top of the cake.

whole orange and almond cake

✵

Preparation time: 30 minutes
Cooking time: 2 hours
Serves 8–10

2 oranges, skins scrubbed with warm
   water to remove wax coating
5 eggs
250 g (9 oz) ground almonds
220 g (7¾ oz/1 cup) sugar
1 teaspoon baking powder
icing (confectioners') sugar, to dust
thin strips of orange zest, to serve

1   Lightly grease a 22 cm (8½ inch)
spring-form cake tin and line the base
with baking paper. Put the whole oranges
in a saucepan, cover with water and boil
for 1 hour. Drain and leave to cool.
2   Preheat the oven to 180°C (350°F/
Gas 4). Using a plate to catch any juice,
cut the cooled oranges into quarters and
remove any seeds. Blend the orange
quarters, including the skin, in a food
processor until they turn to a pulp.
3   Whisk the eggs in a large bowl using
electric beaters until light and fluffy. Add
the orange pulp and any reserved juice,
the almonds, sugar and baking powder,
mix thoroughly, then pour into the tin.
4   Bake for 1–1¼ hours, or until the cake
is firm to the touch and lightly golden.
Cool the cake in the tin before removing
the side and transferring to a wire rack to
cool completely. Dust with icing sugar and
top with the orange zest.

pineapple upside-down cake

☀

Preparation time: **30 minutes**
Cooking time: **1 hour**
Serves **8**

90 g (3¼ oz) unsalted butter, melted
95 g (3¼ oz/½ cup) soft brown sugar
440 g (15½ oz) tin pineapple rings in
  natural juice
6 red glacé cherries
125 g (4½ oz) unsalted butter, extra,
  softened
170 g (5¾ oz/¾ cup) caster (superfine) sugar
2 eggs, lightly beaten
1 teaspoon natural vanilla extract
185 g (6½ oz/1½ cups) self-raising flour
60 g (2¼ oz/½ cup) plain (all-purpose)
  flour
30 g (1 oz/⅓ cup) desiccated coconut

1 Preheat the oven to 180°C (350°F/
Gas 4). Pour the melted butter into a
20 cm (8 inch) round cake tin, brushing
some of it up the side to grease. Sprinkle
the brown sugar over the base. Drain
the pineapple, reserving 125 ml (4 fl oz/
½ cup) of juice. Arrange the pineapple
rings over the base of the tin (five on the
outside and one in the centre) and put a
cherry in the centre of each ring.
2 Cream the extra butter and caster
sugar in a small bowl using electric
beaters until light and fluffy. Add the
egg gradually, beating thoroughly after
each addition. Add the vanilla and beat
until combined. Transfer to a large bowl.
Using a metal spoon, fold in the sifted
flours, then add the coconut and reserved
pineapple juice. Stir until the mixture is
just combined and almost smooth.
3 Spoon the mixture into the tin over the
pineapple and smooth the surface. Indent
the centre slightly with the back of a
spoon to ensure the cake has a reasonably
flat base. Bake for 50–60 minutes, or until
a skewer inserted into the centre of the
cake comes out clean. Leave in the tin for
10 minutes, then turn onto a wire rack.

Arrange the pineapple rings over
the butter and sugar in the base
of the tin.

Fold in the sifted flours using a
large metal spoon.

Spoon the cake mixture into the tin
and indent the centre slightly with
the back of a spoon.

Cook the sugar syrup until it turns a pale caramel colour.

Pour the caramel into the cake tin and press the chopped rhubarb and apple into the caramel.

rhubarb and apple upside-down cake

Preparation time: 40 minutes
Cooking time: 55 minutes
Serves 10–12

250 g (9 oz/1 cup) sugar
250 g (9 oz) trimmed rhubarb, chopped into 2 cm (¾ inch) pieces
1 small granny smith apple, peeled, cored and chopped
2 eggs
40 g (1½ oz/⅓ cup) icing (confectioners') sugar
½ teaspoon natural vanilla extract

100 g (3½ oz) unsalted butter, melted and cooled
125 g (4½ oz/1 cup) self-raising flour

1   Preheat the oven to 180°C (350°F/ Gas 4). Lightly grease a deep 20 cm (8 inch) round cake tin and line the base with baking paper.
2   Put the sugar in a small saucepan with 80 ml (2½ fl oz/⅓ cup) water and heat gently, shaking occasionally, until the sugar has dissolved. Increase the heat and cook until a pale caramel colour — it will turn a deeper colour in the oven. Pour into the tin and then press the rhubarb and apple into the caramel.
3   Whisk the eggs, icing sugar and vanilla in a small bowl using electric beaters until frothy. Fold in the melted butter. Sift the flour over the top and stir until just combined (the mixture will be quite thin). Spoon the mixture gently over the fruit in the tin, being careful not to dislodge it.
4   Bake for about 45 minutes, or until set on top. Run a knife around the side and turn out very carefully onto a plate. Do this straight away or the caramel will cool and stick to the tin. Serve warm.

NOTE: You can serve this cake as a teacake, or with cream as a dessert. Fresh plums, halved, cored and sliced, can be substituted for the apple and rhubarb. Press them into the caramel in a spiral pattern or randomly. Serve either warm or cold.

1 Preheat the oven to 180°C (350°F/ Gas 4). Lightly grease a deep 20 cm (8 inch) round cake tin. Line the base and side with baking paper. Using electric beaters, beat the butter and sugar until light and creamy. Add the egg gradually, beating thoroughly after each addition. Add the vanilla and beat until well combined. Transfer to a large bowl. Using a metal spoon, fold in the sifted flours, bicarbonate of soda and cocoa alternately with the buttermilk. Mix until well combined and smooth.

2 Pour the mixture into the tin and smooth the surface. Bake the cake for 50–60 minutes, or until a skewer inserted into the centre of the cake comes out clean. Leave in the tin for 30 minutes before turning out onto a wire rack to cool. When cooled, cut horizontally into three layers, using a long serrated knife. The easiest way to do this is to rest the palm of one hand lightly on top of the cake while cutting into it. Turn the cake every few strokes so the knife cuts in evenly all the way around the edge. When you have gone the whole way round, cut through the middle. Remove the first layer so it will be easier to see what you are doing while cutting the next one.

3 To make the topping, leave the chocolate in a warm place for 10–15 minutes, or until soft but still firm. With a vegetable peeler, and using long strokes, shave curls of chocolate from the side of the block. If the block is too soft, chill it to firm it up.

4 To assemble, place one cake layer on a serving plate and brush liberally with Kirsch. Spread evenly with one-fifth of the whipped cream. Top with half the pitted cherries. Continue layering with the remaining cake, liqueur, cream and cherries, finishing with the cream on top. Spread the remaining cream evenly over the outside of the cake. Coat the side with chocolate shavings by laying the shavings on a small piece of baking paper and then gently pressing them into the cream. If you use your hands, they will melt, so the paper acts as a barrier. Decorate the top of the cake with more chocolate shavings and fresh or maraschino cherries.

black forest cake (gâteau)

✳ ✳ ✳

Preparation time: 1 hour + 30 minutes standing time
Cooking time: 1 hour
Serves 8-10

125 g (4½ oz) unsalted butter
230 g (8½ oz/1 cup) caster (superfine) sugar
2 eggs, lightly beaten
1 teaspoon natural vanilla extract
40 g (1½ oz/⅓ cup) self-raising flour
125 g (4½ oz/1 cup) plain (all-purpose) flour
1 teaspoon bicarbonate of soda (baking soda)
60 g (2¼ oz/½ cup) unsweetened cocoa powder
185 ml (6 fl oz/¾ cup) buttermilk

TOPPING
100 g (3½ oz) dark chocolate
100 g (3½ oz) milk chocolate
fresh or maraschino cherries with stalks, to decorate

FILLING
60 ml (2 fl oz/¼ cup) Kirsch
750 ml (26 fl oz/3 cups) whipped cream
425 g (15 oz) tinned pitted morello or black cherries, drained

NOTE: Black forest gâteau is probably one of the most famous cakes in the world. It originated in Swabia, Germany, in the Black Forest region. In Germany, it is known as 'Black forest torte'.

flourless chocolate cake

☀

Preparation time: 20 minutes
Cooking time: 1 hour 5 minutes
Serves 10-12

250 g (9 oz) dark chocolate, chopped
100 g (3½ oz) caster (superfine) sugar
100 g (3½ oz) unsalted butter, cubed
1 tablespoon coffee-flavoured liqueur
125 g (4½ oz) ground hazelnuts
5 eggs, separated
icing (confectioners') sugar, to dust

1 Preheat the oven to 180°C (350°F/ Gas 4). Lightly grease a 23 cm (9 inch) spring-form cake tin and line the base with baking paper.
2 Place the chocolate, caster sugar, butter and liqueur in a heatproof bowl over a saucepan of simmering water, making sure the base of the bowl does not touch the water, and stir occasionally to ensure even melting. When the ingredients have melted and the mixture is smooth, remove from the heat and mix thoroughly.

3 Transfer the chocolate mixture to a large bowl. Stir in the hazelnuts, then beat in the egg yolks, one at a time, beating well after each addition. In a clean, dry bowl, whisk the egg whites until they just form stiff peaks. Stir a tablespoonful of the whisked egg white into the chocolate mixture, then gently fold in the rest using a large metal spoon or rubber spatula.
4 Pour the mixture into the tin and bake for 50–60 minutes, or until a skewer inserted into the centre of the cake comes out clean. Leave the cake to cool completely in the tin, then turn it out and dust the top with icing sugar.

dark chocolate

The seeds from the beans of the cacao tree, native to Central America, are fermented, dried, roasted and then formed into a solidified paste known as bitter unsweetened chocolate. The more bitter the chocolate, the more intense the flavour. Bitter-sweet and semi-sweet chocolates have some sugar added. Couverture chocolate, although very expensive, is considered to be the best baking chocolate as it is very high-quality due to its high cocoa butter content.

fruit cakes

With a little careful attention to the lining of the tin,
you will be assured of that special feeling of fulfilment
a homemade fruit cake brings.

fundamentals

Fruit cakes are generally made by the creaming method, so read
the detailed description of this technique on page 50.

Before you begin, read through your recipe, checking you
have all the right equipment and ingredients at hand. Leave
plenty of time, as fruit cakes take a little longer to prepare than
simple cakes and also take a few hours to cook. Line the tin and
make sure the oven rack is positioned so the cake will sit in the
middle of the oven, then preheat the oven.

lining the tin

Lightly grease the tin. Fruit cakes need a double layer of baking
paper for the collar and base. Cut two circles of baking paper,
using the base as a guide. A collar gives extra protection during
cooking. For the collar, cut a double strip of baking paper long
enough to fit around the outside of the tin and wide enough
to extend 5 cm (2 inches) above the top. Fold a 2 cm (¾ inch)
deep cuff along the length of the strip, then make diagonal
cuts up to the fold line about 1 cm (½ inch) apart. Place in
the tin, with the cuts on the base, pressing them out at right
angles so they sit flat around the base. Place the paper circles in
the base over the cuts. Because of the long cooking time, fruit
cakes require extra protection, both around the side and under
the base. This is why we wrap layers of newspaper around the
outside of the tin, and sit the tin on layers of newspaper in the
oven. Because the oven temperature is low, this is quite safe.

making the cake

Weigh all the ingredients and complete preparations such as
softening butter, sifting flour and spices, blanching nuts, tossing
fruit in flour or soaking fruit, if required. Dried fruit is sold
ready for use. Dates and prunes may have stones that need to
be removed. Glacé fruit such as cherries, pineapple or ginger are
better if cut into small pieces as they are heavy and may sink.
If peel is large, cut or chop into smaller pieces.

Following the methods for a creamed butter cake, beat the
butter and sugar using electric beaters until light and fluffy.
Gradually add the eggs, beating thoroughly after each addition.
Add essences, zest, juice, jam, syrup or molasses as specified.
Transfer to a large bowl and add the dried or glacé fruit. Mix
with a large metal spoon until combined. Using a large metal
spoon, fold in the sifted dry ingredients. Alcohol, if specified,
can also be added at this time. Stir until just combined and
almost smooth. Spoon evenly into the tin, spread into the
corners and smooth the top. Some fruit cakes are decorated at
this stage with blanched almonds. Check the oven temperature
is correct. Wrap layers of newspaper around the tin, as high as
the collar, and secure with string or metal paper clips. Some
people like to finish with a layer of brown paper. Place a few
layers of newspaper on the oven rack and put the tin on top. If
the cake browns before it is cooked, cover it loosely with foil.

when is it ready?

As ovens vary, check the cake about 20 minutes before the
specified time. If it is cooked, a skewer inserted into the centre
should come out clean, and the cake should shrink from the
side of the tin. Cool the cake completely in the tin, preferably
overnight, before removing. Fruit cakes improve if kept for
a few weeks wrapped in baking paper and foil, or kept in an
airtight container, before decorating or cutting. Un-iced fruit
cakes can be refrigerated for up to 3 months. They can be 'fed',
by poking holes with a skewer and pouring in brandy or whisky.

glacé fruits

These are also known as candied fruit. They are stoned fruits that have been preserved in a very high concentration of sugar syrup, making them dense, very sweet, moist and sticky. The fruit is usually chopped for adding to fruit cakes to give colour and flavour, and is also used whole to decorate cakes. Mostly available from health food stores, glacé fruits should be bought in small amounts, as needed, although any unused fruits can be refrigerated until the use-by date.

golden fruit cake

Preparation time: 25 minutes
Cooking time: 2 hours
Makes one 20 cm (8 inch) square cake

110 g (3¾ oz) chopped glacé pears
240 g (8¾ oz/1 cup) chopped glacé apricots
220 g (7¾ oz) chopped glacé pineapple
60 g (2¼ oz) chopped mixed peel
95 g (3¼ oz) chopped glacé orange slices
80 g (2¾ oz/½ cup) roughly chopped blanched almonds
185 g (6½ oz/1½ cups) plain (all-purpose) flour
60 g (2¼ oz/½ cup) self-raising flour
250 g (9 oz) unsalted butter, softened

1 tablespoon finely grated orange zest
1 tablespoon finely grated lemon zest
230 g (8 oz/1 cup) caster (superfine) sugar
4 eggs
60 ml (2 fl oz/¼ cup) sweet sherry

1 Preheat the oven to 160°C (315°F/Gas 2–3). Lightly grease a deep 20 cm (8 inch) square cake tin and line with baking paper (page 84).
2 Combine the fruits and almonds in a bowl. Toss with 30 g (1 oz/¼ cup) of plain flour to help keep the fruits separate. Sift together the remaining flours.
3 Beat the butter, orange zest and lemon zest in a small bowl using electric beaters, gradually adding the sugar, until light and fluffy. Beat in the eggs, one at a time,

beating thoroughly after each addition. Transfer the mixture to a large bowl, stir in the sifted flours alternately with the sherry and then fold in the fruit, nut and flour mixture.
4 Spread the mixture evenly into the tin and wrap layers of newspaper around the outside of the tin. Sit the cake tin on several layers of newspaper in the oven. Bake for about 1¾–2 hours, or until a skewer inserted into the centre of the cake comes out clean. Leave the cake in the tin for 20 minutes before turning out onto a wire rack to cool. Store in an airtight container for up to a month.

glacé fruit and nut loaf

✳ ✳

Preparation time: 30 minutes
Cooking time: 1 hour 45 minutes
Makes one 20.5 cm (8¼ inch) loaf

50 g (1¾ oz) unsalted butter, softened
60 g (2¼ oz/⅓ cup) soft brown sugar
2 tablespoons breakfast marmalade
2 eggs, lightly beaten
125 g (4½ oz/1 cup) plain (all-purpose) flour
1 teaspoon baking powder
1 teaspoon ground nutmeg
225 g (8 oz/1¼ cups) stoned dates, chopped
240 g (8¾ oz/1½ cups) raisins
155 g (5½ oz/1 cup) brazil nuts
140 g (5 oz/⅔ cup) red, yellow and green
    glacé cherries
110 g (3¾ oz/½ cup) chopped glacé pear
    or pineapple
120 g (4¼ oz/½ cup) chopped glacé
    apricots
120 g (4¼ oz/½ cup) chopped glacé
    peaches
120 g (4¼ oz/⅓ cup) chopped glacé figs
100 g (3½ oz/1 cup) walnut halves
100 g (3½ oz/⅔ cup) blanched almonds

TOPPING
2 tablespoons breakfast marmalade
2 teaspoons powdered gelatin
150 g (5½ oz) glacé pineapple or pear rings
100 g (3½ oz) red, yellow and green
    glacé cherries
40 g (1½ oz/¼ cup) blanched almonds

1 Preheat the oven to 150°C (300°F/
Gas 2). Lightly grease and line a deep
8 x 20.5 cm (3¼ x 8¼ inch) loaf (bar) tin
(page 84).
2 Cream the butter, sugar and marmalade
in a bowl using electric beaters until pale
and fluffy. Add the egg gradually, beating
thoroughly after each addition.
3 Sift the flour, baking powder and
nutmeg into a large bowl. Add the fruit
and nuts and mix until each piece is
coated in the flour mixture. Add to the
egg mixture and mix to combine well.
4 Spoon the mixture into the tin, pushing
well into each corner. Wrap layers of
newspaper around the outside of the tin
and sit the cake tin on several layers of
newspaper in the oven. Bake for 1½–1¾
hours, or until a skewer inserted into the
centre of the cake comes out clean. Cool
in the tin for 30 minutes, then turn out
onto a wire rack to cool.
5 For the topping, mix the marmalade
with 2 tablespoons water in a small
heatproof bowl. Sprinkle with gelatin.
Bring a saucepan of water to the boil,
then remove from the heat. Stand the
bowl in the pan and stir until the gelatin
has dissolved. Brush the top of the cake
with some of the gelatin mixture and
arrange the pineapple, cherries and
almonds on top. Brush or drizzle with
more gelatin mixture and allow to set.

NOTE: You can toast the blanched
almonds for the topping. To do this,
spread them in a single layer on a baking
tray and bake in a 180°C (350°F/Gas 4)
oven for 8 minutes, or until lightly golden.

rich fruit cakes

Traditionally, rich fruit cakes are baked for celebrations such as Christmas, weddings and anniversaries. For special occasions, they are usually iced with a marzipan or almond paste covering the whole cake, then often decorated with piped and moulded icing. A good fruit cake should be made well in advance to give the flavour time to develop. The addition of sherry, rum or brandy adds to the flavour and helps to keep the cake moist.

boiled fruit cake

✸ ✸

Preparation time: 30 minutes
Cooking time: 1 hour 30 minutes
Makes one 22 cm (8½ inch) round cake

250 g (9 oz) unsalted butter
185 g (6½ oz/1 cup) soft brown sugar
1 kg (2 lb 4 oz) mixed dried fruit
125 ml (4 fl oz/½ cup) sweet sherry
½ teaspoon bicarbonate of soda (baking soda)
185 g (6½ oz/1½ cups) self-raising flour
125 g (4½ oz/1 cup) plain (all-purpose) flour
1 teaspoon mixed (pumpkin pie) spice
4 eggs, lightly beaten

1 Preheat the oven to 180°C (350°F/Gas 4). Lightly grease and line a 22 cm (8½ inch) round cake tin (page 84).
2 Put the butter, sugar, mixed fruit, sherry and 185 ml (6 fl oz/¾ cup) water in a saucepan. Stir over low heat until the butter has melted and the sugar has dissolved. Bring to the boil, reduce the heat and simmer for 10 minutes. Remove from the heat, stir in the bicarbonate of soda and cool.
3 Sift the flours and spice into a large bowl and make a well in the centre. Add the egg to the fruit and mix to combine, then pour into the well and mix thoroughly. Pour into the tin and smooth the surface. Wrap layers of newspaper around the outside of the tin and sit the

cake tin on several layers of newspaper in the oven. Bake for 1–1¼ hours, or until a skewer inserted into the centre of the cake comes out clean. Leave in the tin for at least an hour before turning onto a wire rack. The flavour improves after standing for 3 days. Store the cake in an airtight container for up to 2 months.

rich fruit cake

❋ ❋

Preparation time: 20 minutes
    + overnight soaking time
Cooking time: 3 hours 30 minutes
Makes one 23cm round cake

500 g (1 lb 2 oz) sultanas (golden raisins)
375 g (13 oz) raisins, chopped
250 g (9 oz) currants
250 g (9 oz) glacé cherries, quartered
250 ml (9 fl oz/1 cup) brandy or rum
250 g (9 oz) unsalted butter, softened
230 g (8 oz/1 cup) soft brown sugar
2 teaspoons finely grated orange zest
2 teaspoons finely grated lemon zest
4 eggs
250 g (9 oz/2 cups) plain (all-purpose) flour, sifted
60 g (2¼ oz/½ cup) self-raising flour, sifted
whole blanched almonds, to decorate

1 Put the fruit in a bowl with the brandy. Cover and soak overnight.
2 Preheat the oven to 150°C (300°F/ Gas 2). Grease and line a 23 cm (9 inch) round or square cake tin (page 84).
3 Beat the butter, sugar, orange zest and lemon zest in a bowl using electric beaters until just combined. Add the eggs, one at a time, beating well after each addition. Transfer to a bowl and stir in half of the soaked fruit mix alternately with the plain flour and the self-raising flour. Mix well, then spread evenly into the tin and tap the tin on the bench to remove any air bubbles. Dip your fingers in water and level the surface.
4 Decorate the top of the fruit cake with whole blanched almonds in a pattern of your choice. Wrap layers of newspaper around the outside of the tin and sit the cake tin on several layers of newspaper in the oven.
5 Bake for 3¼–3½ hours, or until a skewer inserted into the centre of the cake comes out clean. Cover the top with baking paper, seal firmly with foil, then wrap the cake and tin in a clean tea towel (dish towel) and leave to cool. Store in an airtight container for up to 2 months.

biscuits

It's one thing to honour a diet and refuse a whole piece of cake, but biscuits are so little and innocent, surely one couldn't do any harm? Especially straight out of the oven. There must be some reward after the tantalising aroma of baking biscuits has been following you around the house. Dear little jam drops with oozy centres, crunchy gingernuts, melt-in-the-mouth Scottish shortbread… You know you can't resist — that's just the way the cookie crumbles.

basic biscuits

Nothing beats the heavenly aroma of freshly baked biscuits. Biscuits are made using several methods, each of which imparts special characteristics.

creaming method: basic butter biscuit

To make about 30 biscuits, line two trays with baking paper or lightly grease with melted butter. Allow 125 g (4½ oz) butter to soften to room temperature, then cut it into cubes. This will make it is easier to work with. Preheat the oven to 210°C (415°F/Gas 6–7) and check the racks are near the centre. Cream the butter with 125 g (4½ oz/½ cup) caster (superfine) sugar in a small bowl using electric beaters, or by hand, until light and creamy. This will take about 3–5 minutes with electric beaters, or 10 minutes by hand. Scrape down the side of the bowl occasionally with a spatula. The mixture should look pale and be quite smooth. The sugar should be almost dissolved.

Add 60 ml (2 fl oz/¼ cup) milk and ¼ teaspoon natural vanilla extract and beat until combined. Add 185 g (6½ oz/1½ cups) self-raising flour and 60 g (2¼ oz/½ cup) custard powder or instant vanilla pudding mix and use a flat-bladed knife to mix to a soft dough with a cutting action, rotating the bowl as you work. Don't overwork the dough or you'll end up with tough biscuits. Roll level teaspoons into balls and place on the trays, leaving 5 cm (2 inches) between each. Flatten the balls lightly with your fingertips, then press with a fork. The biscuits should be about 5 cm (2 inches) in diameter.

Bake for 15–18 minutes, until lightly golden. Avoid opening the oven door until at least two-thirds of the way through baking. Cool on the trays for 3 minutes before transferring to a wire rack to cool completely. Store in an airtight container for up to a week. To freeze, place in freezer bags and seal, label and date. Unfilled and un-iced cooked biscuits can be frozen for up to two months. After thawing, refresh them in a 180°C (350°F/Gas 4) oven for a few minutes, then cool and decorate, as desired, before serving. Uncooked biscuit dough freezes well.

Wrap it in plastic wrap, place in a plastic bag and seal. When ready to use, thaw at room temperature and bake as directed.

Biscuits can be decorated with sifted icing (confectioners') sugar. They can also be iced (frosted) or drizzled with melted chocolate from a plastic bag with the corner snipped off.

citrus butter biscuit

For this variation, omit the vanilla, add 2 teaspoons orange or lemon zest to the creamed butter and sugar and proceed with the recipe. Combine 250 g (9 oz/2 cups) sifted icing (confectioners') sugar, 20 g (¾ oz) softened butter and 1 tablespoon lemon or orange juice and use to ice the biscuits.

nutty butter biscuit

For this variation, mix 55 g (2 oz/½ cup) finely chopped walnuts or pecans into the basic mixture before adding the flour. Press a nut onto each biscuit, instead of pressing with a fork, and bake as above.

melt and mix method

This quick method involves mixing the dry ingredients, then mixing in the melted butter (and any other ingredients) with a wooden spoon until the dry ingredients are well moistened.

rubbing in method

This involves cutting chilled butter into small pieces and rubbing it into the flour with your fingertips until the mixture is crumbly and resembles fine breadcrumbs. Then, almost all the liquid is added and cut into the dry ingredients with a knife, adding more liquid if necessary to bring the mixture together. Don't add the liquid all at once — flours vary, so it may not be needed.

what went wrong: drop biscuits

perfect The biscuit has even golden colouring on both the top and base and has even thickness.

undercooked, sticking These biscuits are pale and the tops soft to touch. This indicates that the cooking time may have been too short, leaving the mixture undercooked and sticky. Alternatively, the oven temperature may have been too low or the oven insufficiently preheated.

overcooked These biscuits are too darkly coloured, indicating the oven may have been too hot or the cooking time may have been too long. The biscuits may have too much sugar, which causes them to darken. Be sure to rest the biscuits for a couple of minutes on the tray after cooking, because they will continue to cook on the tray. Transfer them to a wire rack to cool, unless specified otherwise.

what went wrong: rolled out and cut into shapes

perfect The biscuit has a light golden colouring and even thickness.

too thick The mixture was rolled and cut too thickly. It would need extra baking time as a result.

thin, overcooked The mixture may have been rolled too thinly or the oven may have been too hot, or perhaps the biscuits were cooked for too long.

OTHER PROBLEMS
Biscuit mixture should be put on a baking tray that is at room temperature. When re-using baking trays, don't put the biscuit mixture on a hot tray because the biscuits will spread too much and lose their shape. Don't use trays or tins that have high sides, otherwise the heat distribution during cooking will not be even. Most biscuits are best baked in the middle of the oven, or close to the middle.

what went wrong: shaped by hand or piped

perfect The biscuit has even, golden colouring on both the top and base. It is also the correct thickness.

undercooked The biscuit is a pale colour. The oven temperature may have been too low, the oven not preheated, or the biscuits not cooked for long enough.

overcooked and spread too much The oven may have been too hot or the biscuits cooked for too long.

> STORING BISCUITS
> Most biscuits can be kept for up to 4 days if stored correctly. They should be allowed to cool completely after baking, then stored in an airtight container in a cool place. Moisture is absorbed easily by biscuits so they lose their crispness if not in an airtight jar. It is best not to store different types of biscuits in the same jar and biscuits should definitely not be stored in the same container as cakes. Biscuits that are to be filled should be stored without their filling and then filled just before you want to use them. If you store biscuits after filling them, they tend to soften.

what went wrong: meringues

perfect The meringue is firm and dry, and still very pale in colour, both on the top and the base. The inside of the meringue is crisp.

weeping The meringue is wet and weeping and the inside may look sticky. The mixture may have been under or over-beaten before or after the addition of the sugar.

overcooked The meringue should be white. The oven temperature was probably too high, or the cooking time may have been too long.

jam drops

Preparation time: 20 minutes
Cooking time: 15 minutes
Makes 32

80 g (2¾ oz) unsalted butter, softened
90 g (3¼ oz/⅓ cup) caster (superfine)
  sugar
2 tablespoons milk
½ teaspoon natural vanilla extract
125 g (4½ oz/1 cup) self-raising flour
40 g (1½ oz/⅓ cup) custard powder or
  instant vanilla pudding mix
100 g (3½ oz/⅓ cup) raspberry jam

1 Preheat the oven to 180°C (350°F/
Gas 4). Line two baking trays with
baking paper.
2 Cream the butter and sugar in a small
bowl using electric beaters until light and
creamy. Add the milk and vanilla and
beat until combined. Add the sifted flour
and custard powder and mix to form a
soft dough. Roll heaped teaspoons of the
mixture into balls and place on the trays.
3 Make an indentation in each ball using
the end of a wooden spoon and fill with a
little of the jam. Bake for 15 minutes, cool
slightly, then transfer to a wire rack.

chocolate biscuits

Preparation time: 20 minutes
  + 30 minutes chilling time
Cooking time: 12 minutes
Makes 25

125 g (4½ oz) dark chocolate, chopped
125 g (4½ oz) unsalted butter, cubed
1 egg
185 g (6½ oz1 cup) soft brown sugar
185 g (6½ oz/1½ cups) self-raising flour

1 Preheat the oven to 180°C (350°F/
Gas 4). Line two baking trays with
baking paper.
2 Place the chocolate and butter in a
heatproof bowl. Bring a saucepan of water
to the boil, then remove from the heat. Sit
the bowl over the saucepan, making sure
the base of the bowl does not touch the
water. Stir occasionally until the chocolate
and butter have melted.
3 Break the egg into a large bowl, add
the sugar and beat lightly for 2 minutes,
or until combined. Mix in the melted
chocolate, and stir in the sifted flour until
just combined. Cover and refrigerate for
30 minutes, or until firm.
4 Roll tablespoons of dough into balls
and place on the trays, leaving room
for spreading. Press down gently on the
balls with the back of a spoon. Bake for
10–12 minutes, or until firm to touch and
cracked on top. Cool slightly on the trays
before transferring to a wire rack to cool
completely. When completely cooled,
store in an airtight container.

jam drops

chocolate choc-chip fudge cookies

✳

Preparation time: **20 minutes**
Cooking time: **10 minutes**
Makes **35**

185 g (6½ oz/1½ cups) plain (all-purpose) flour
90 g (3¼ oz/¾ cup) unsweetened cocoa powder
280 g (10 oz/1½ cups) soft brown sugar
180 g (6¼ oz) unsalted butter, cubed
150 g (5½ oz) dark chocolate, chopped
3 eggs, lightly beaten
265 g (9¼ oz/1½ cups) milk chocolate chips

1 Preheat the oven to 180°C (350°F/ Gas 4). Line two baking trays with baking paper.
2 Sift the flour and cocoa into a large bowl, add the sugar and make a well in the centre.
3 Combine the butter and chocolate in a small heatproof bowl. Bring a saucepan of water to the boil, then remove from the heat. Sit the bowl over the saucepan, making sure the base of the bowl does not touch the water. Stir occasionally until the chocolate and butter have melted and are smooth. Mix well.
4 Add the chocolate mixture and the eggs to the dry ingredients. Stir with a wooden spoon until well combined, but do not overbeat. Stir in the chocolate chips. Roll tablespoons of the mixture into balls. Place on the trays, allowing room for spreading, and flatten slightly. Bake for 12 minutes, until firm to touch. Cool on the trays for 5 minutes before transferring to a wire rack to cool completely. Store the cooled cookies in an airtight container.

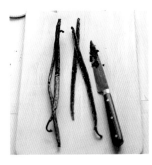

vanilla

Vanilla beans are the seed pod of a climbing orchid plant that is native to South America. The pods are dried and cured and are available at supermarkets and delicatessens. Pure vanilla extract is an aromatic, rich liquid made from the bean. Its flavour is very concentrated so it should be used sparingly. Natural vanilla extract is also taken from the vanilla pod but is a slightly thinner liquid. It has a strong flavour and is often used in cookery for convenience. Imitation vanilla essence is a much cheaper synthetic product.

anzac biscuits

These famous biscuits were developed at the time of the First World War and sent in food parcels to the ANZAC troops (Australia and New Zealand Army Corps). They are an economical, crisp, long-lasting biscuit made without eggs, as these were in short supply at that time. The recipe is still popular, having been handed down through the generations.

gingernuts

syrup and stir until dissolved. Add to the flour mixture and mix to a soft dough using a flat-bladed knife.

3 Roll into balls using 2 heaped teaspoons of mixture at a time. Place on the trays, allowing room for spreading, and flatten out slightly with your fingertips. Bake for 15 minutes, or until well-coloured and firm. Cool on the trays for 10 minutes before transferring to a wire rack to cool completely. Repeat with the remaining mixture. When cooled, store in an airtight container.

NOTE: Make icing (frosting) by combining 2–3 teaspoons lemon juice, 60 g (2¼ oz/ ½ cup) sifted icing (confectioners') sugar and 10 g (¼ oz) melted unsalted butter. Spread over the biscuits and allow to set.

anzac biscuits

Preparation time: **15 minutes**
Cooking time: **25 minutes**
Makes **26**

125 g (4½ oz/1 cup) plain (all-purpose) flour
140 g (5 oz/⅔ cup) sugar
100 g (3½ oz/1 cup) rolled (porridge) oats
90 g (3¼ oz/1 cup) desiccated coconut
125 g (4½ oz) unsalted butter, cubed
90 g (3¼ oz/¼ cup) golden syrup or dark corn syrup
½ teaspoon bicarbonate of soda (baking soda)
1 tablespoon boiling water

1 Preheat the oven to 180°C (350°F/ Gas 4). Line two baking trays with baking paper.
2 Sift the flour into a large bowl. Stir in the sugar, oats and coconut and make a well in the centre.
3 Put the butter and golden syrup in a small saucepan and stir over low heat until melted and smooth. Remove from the heat. Dissolve the bicarbonate of soda in the boiling water and add immediately to the butter mixture. Pour into the well in the dry ingredients and stir with a

gingernuts

Preparation time: **15 minutes**
Cooking time: **15 minutes**
Makes **50**

250 g (9 oz/2 cups) plain (all-purpose) flour
½ teaspoon bicarbonate of soda (baking soda)
1 tablespoon ground ginger
½ teaspoon mixed (pumpkin pie) spice
125 g (4½ oz) unsalted butter, chilled and cubed

185 g (6½ oz/1 cup) soft brown sugar
60 ml (2 fl oz/¼ cup) boiling water
1 tablespoon golden syrup or dark corn syrup

1 Preheat the oven to 180°C (350°F/ Gas 4). Line two baking trays with baking paper.
2 Sift the flour, bicarbonate of soda and spices into a large bowl. Add the butter and sugar and rub into the flour with your fingertips until the mixture resembles fine breadcrumbs. Pour the boiling water into a small heatproof bowl, add the golden

wooden spoon until well combined.

4 Drop level tablespoons of the mixture onto the trays, allowing room for spreading. Gently flatten each biscuit with your fingertips. Bake for 20 minutes, or until just browned. Leave the biscuits on the trays to cool slightly, then transfer to a wire rack to cool completely. Store in an airtight container.

afghans

Preparation time: 25 minutes + cooling time
Cooking time: 20 minutes
Makes 25

150 g (5½ oz) unsalted butter, softened
60 g (2¼ oz/⅓ cup) soft brown sugar
1 egg, lightly beaten
1 teaspoon natural vanilla extract
125 g (4½ oz/1 cup) plain (all-purpose) flour
2 tablespoons unsweetened cocoa powder
30 g (1 oz/⅓ cup) desiccated coconut
75 g (2¾ oz/1½ cups) lightly crushed cornflakes
90 g (3 oz/½ cup) dark chocolate chips

1 Preheat the oven to 180°C (350°F/ Gas 4). Line two baking trays with baking paper.
2 Cream the butter and sugar in a large bowl using electric beaters until light and creamy. Add the egg and vanilla and beat thoroughly.
3 Add the sifted flour and cocoa to the bowl with the coconut and cornflakes. Stir with a metal spoon until the ingredients are just combined. Put level tablespoons of mixture on the trays, allowing room for spreading. Bake for 20 minutes or until lightly browned, then leave on the trays to cool completely.
4 Place the chocolate chips in a small heatproof bowl. Bring a saucepan of water to the boil, then remove from the heat. Sit the bowl over the pan, making sure the base of the bowl does not touch the water. Stir until the chocolate has melted and the mixture is smooth. Spread the biscuits thickly with chocolate and allow to set.

coconut macaroons

Preparation time: 25 minutes
Cooking time: 40 minutes
Makes 60

3 egg whites
310 g (11 oz) caster (superfine) sugar
1 teaspoon finely grated lemon zest
½ teaspoon coconut extract
2 tablespoons sifted cornflour (cornstarch)
270 g (9½ oz/3 cups) desiccated coconut

1 Preheat the oven to 160°C (315°F/ Gas 2–3). Line two baking trays with baking paper.

2 Whisk the egg whites in a clean, dry bowl using electric beaters until soft peaks form. Gradually add the sugar, whisking constantly until thick and glossy and the sugar has dissolved. Add the lemon zest and coconut extract and whisk until just combined. Add the cornflour and coconut and stir gently with a metal spoon.
3 Drop heaped teaspoons onto the trays, about 3 cm (1¼ inches) apart. Bake for 20 minutes, or until golden. Transfer to a wire rack to cool. Repeat with the remaining mixture.

coconut macaroons

storage of biscuits

Biscuits usually have a reasonably high butter, egg and sugar content, making them sweet and moist. Because they are moist, they do not tend to have a long shelf life as exposure to moisture makes them soften and go stale quickly. After cooking and cooling completely on a wire rack, store them in an airtight container. Refrigerate if the weather is hot. If a batch lasts long enough in your household before being consumed, you can freeze half of them in an airtight container for up to a month. Layer them in the container between sheets of baking paper. If biscuits have softened, they can be refreshed by placing, in a single layer on a baking tray, in a 160°C (315°F/Gas 2–3) oven for about 5 minutes. Cool the biscuits on a wire rack.

coffee kisses

Preparation time: 40 minutes
Cooking time: 10 minutes
Makes 30

375 g (13 oz/3 cups) self-raising flour
160 g (5¾ oz) unsalted butter, chopped
115 g (4 oz/½ cup) caster (superfine) sugar
1 egg, lightly beaten
1 tablespoon instant coffee granules,
    dissolved in 1–2 tablespoons water
100 g (3½ oz) white chocolate, melted
chocolate-coated coffee beans, to decorate
    (optional)

COFFEE BUTTERCREAM
80 g (2¾ oz) unsalted butter
125 g (4½ oz/1 cup) icing (confectioners')
    sugar, sifted
2 teaspoons instant coffee granules,
    dissolved in 2 teaspoons water

1 Preheat the oven to 180°C (350°F/ Gas 4). Grease two baking trays and line with baking paper.

2 Sift the flour into a bowl. Using your fingertips, rub in the butter until the mixture resembles fine breadcrumbs.
3 In a separate bowl, whisk together the sugar, egg and coffee. Add to the flour mixture all at once and mix lightly with a flat-bladed knife, using a cutting action, until the mixture forms a soft dough. Gather into a ball and gently knead on a lightly floured surface until smooth.
4 Roll the dough out between two sheets of baking paper to a 5 mm (¼ inch) thickness. Using a 5 cm (2 inch) fluted biscuit (cookie) cutter, cut into 60 rounds. Place on the baking trays and bake for 10 minutes, or until lightly golden. Transfer to a wire rack to cool.
5 To make the coffee buttercream, beat the butter and icing sugar in a bowl using electric beaters until light and creamy. Add the coffee and beat until mixed through.
6 Spoon the coffee buttercream into a piping (icing) bag fitted with a fluted nozzle and pipe onto half the biscuits. Top with the remaining biscuits. Pipe the melted chocolate over and decorate with a coffee bean, if desired.

Cut the dough into shapes with a gingerbread person cutter.

Snip the tip off the end of the piping bag and pipe on clothing.

gingerbread people

❋

Preparation time: 40 minutes + cooling time
Cooking time: 10 minutes
Makes 16

125 g (4½ oz) unsalted butter, softened
60 g (2¼ oz/⅓ cup) soft brown sugar
90 g (3¼ oz/¼ cup) golden syrup or maple syrup
1 egg, lightly beaten
250 g (9 oz/2 cups) plain (all-purpose) flour
30 g (1 oz/¼ cup) self-raising flour
1 tablespoon ground ginger
1 teaspoon bicarbonate of soda (baking soda)
1 tablespoon currants

ICING
1 egg white
½ teaspoon lemon juice
155 g (5½ oz/1¼ cups) icing (confectioners') sugar, sifted
assorted food colourings

1 Preheat the oven to 180°C (350°F/ Gas 4). Line two baking trays with baking paper.
2 Cream the butter, sugar and golden syrup in a small bowl using electric beaters until light and creamy. Add the egg gradually, beating well after each addition. Transfer to a large bowl. Sift the dry ingredients onto the butter mixture and mix with a flat-bladed knife, using a cutting action, until just combined. Turn out onto a well-floured surface and use floured hands to knead for 1–2 minutes, or until smooth. Roll out on a chopping board, between two sheets of baking paper, to 5 mm (¼ inch) thick. Refrigerate on the board for 15 minutes.

3 Cut the dough into shapes with a 13 cm (5 inch) gingerbread person cutter. Press the remaining dough together and re-roll. Cut out more shapes and put the biscuits on the trays. Press on currants as eyes and noses. Bake for 10 minutes, or until lightly browned. Cool completely on the trays.
4 To make the icing (frosting), whisk the egg white using electric beaters in a clean, dry, small bowl until foamy. Gradually add the lemon juice and icing sugar and whisk until thick and creamy. Divide the icing among several bowls. Tint the mixture with food colourings and spoon into small paper or plastic piping (icing) bags. Twist the open ends to seal, snip the tips off the bags and pipe clothing onto the biscuits.

NOTE: When the icing is completely dry, store the biscuits in an airtight container in a cool, dry place for up to 3 days.

peanut biscuits

Preparation time: 30 minutes
Cooking time: 20 minutes
Makes 30

185 g (6½ oz) unsalted butter, softened
370 g (13 oz/2 cups) soft brown sugar
140 g (5 oz) smooth peanut butter
1 teaspoon natural vanilla extract
1 egg
185 g (6½ oz/1½ cups) plain (all-purpose) flour
½ teaspoon baking powder
125 g (4½ oz/1¼ cups) rolled (porridge) oats
120 g (4¼ oz/¾ cup) peanuts

1 Preheat the oven to 180°C (350°F/ Gas 4). Line two baking trays with baking paper. Beat the butter, sugar, peanut butter and vanilla in a small bowl using electric beaters until light and creamy. Add the egg and beat until smooth. Transfer to a large bowl and mix in the combined sifted flour and baking powder. Fold in the oats and peanuts and mix until smooth. Chill until firm.
2 Roll heaped tablespoons of the mixture into balls and place on the trays, leaving room for spreading. Press down gently with a floured fork to make a crisscross pattern. Bake for 15–20 minutes, or until golden. Leave on the trays to cool slightly before transferring to a wire rack to cool completely. Store in an airtight container.

peanut biscuits

toll house cookies

Preparation time: 20 minutes
Cooking time: 10 minutes
Makes 40

180 g (6¼ oz) unsalted butter, softened
140 g (5 oz/¾ cup) soft brown sugar
125 g (4½ oz/½ cup) sugar
2 eggs, lightly beaten
1 teaspoon natural vanilla extract
310 g (11 oz/2¼ cups) plain (all-purpose) flour
1 teaspoon bicarbonate of soda (baking soda)
350 g (12 oz/2 cups) dark chocolate chips
100 g (3½ oz/1 cup) pecans, roughly chopped

1 Preheat the oven to 190°C (375°F/ Gas 5). Line two baking trays with baking paper.
2 Cream the butter and sugars in a large bowl using electric beaters until light and creamy. Gradually add the egg, beating well after each addition. Stir in the vanilla, then the sifted flour and bicarbonate of soda until just combined. Add the chocolate chips and pecans and mix until just combined.
3 Drop tablespoons of mixture onto the trays, leaving room for spreading. Bake the cookies for 8–10 minutes, or until lightly golden. Cool slightly on the trays before transferring to a wire rack to cool completely. When cooled, store in an airtight container.

NOTE: You can use any nuts such as walnuts, almonds or hazelnuts.

digestive biscuits

Preparation time: 35 minutes
+ 1 hour 20 minutes chilling time
Cooking time: 12 minutes
Makes 16

125 g (4½ oz) unsalted butter, softened
60 g (2¼ oz/⅓ cup) soft brown sugar
1 tablespoon malt extract
1 egg, lightly beaten
125 g (4½ oz/1 cup) plain (all-purpose) flour

150 g (5½ oz/1 cup) plain (all-purpose)
   wholemeal (whole-wheat) flour
35 g (1¼ oz/½ cup) unprocessed bran
1 teaspoon baking powder

1 Line two baking trays with baking paper. Cream the butter, sugar and malt in a small bowl using electric beaters until light and creamy. Gradually add the egg, beating well after each addition. Transfer to a large bowl.

2 Sift the flours, bran and baking powder into a small bowl, returning the husks to the bowl. Using a large metal spoon, fold in the dry ingredients in three batches and mix to a firm dough. Cover and refrigerate for at least 1 hour.

3 Preheat the oven to 180°C (350°F/ Gas 4). Roll out half the dough between two sheets of baking paper to 5 mm (¼ inch) thick. Cut out rounds using a 7 cm (2¾ inch) cutter and place the rounds on the trays. Prick the surface of each once with a fork. Repeat with the remaining dough and re-roll any scraps. Refrigerate for 20 minutes to firm.

4 Bake for 12 minutes, or until golden brown and firm. Leave on the trays to cool slightly before transferring to a wire rack to cool completely. Store the biscuits in an airtight container.

NOTE: Digestives can be eaten plain but are delicious served with blue cheese or buttered. They can also be drizzled with melted chocolate.

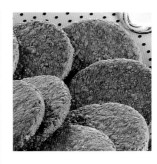

digestive biscuits

These popular biscuits are made from a pastry-like dough, usually using a coarse flour. Although their name implies that your digestion may be improved if you eat them, they actually have no special digestive properties at all. They are also known as 'wheatmeal' biscuits.

shortbread biscuits

Shortbread has a long Scottish history, where it is eaten especially at New Year. However, it has become a traditional snack at Christmas time in many parts of the world. The name comes from the high butter (shortening) content. When mixed thoroughly with the gluten (the protein content of the flour), the butter has the ability to shorten the flour protein strands and results in a tender melt-in-the-mouth biscuit. Rice flour, semolina or cornflour (cornstarch) are often added to help this tenderising process. The first two add texture as well. Shortbread should not be overcooked and dark. It should be pale and lightly golden. If allowed to brown too much, it will taste of slightly bitter and burnt butter.

scottish shortbread

☀

Preparation time: 45 minutes
Cooking time: 35 minutes
Makes 24 pieces

250 g (9 oz) unsalted butter, softened
125 g (4½ oz/½ cup) caster (superfine) sugar
250 g (9 oz/2 cups) plain (all-purpose) flour
115 g (4 oz/⅔ cup) rice flour
1 teaspoon sugar, to decorate

1 Preheat the oven to 160°C (315°F/ Gas 2–3). Line two baking trays with baking paper. Mark a 20 cm (8 inch) circle on the paper on each tray and then turn the paper over.
2 Cream the butter and caster sugar in a small bowl using electric beaters until light and creamy. Add the sifted flours and a pinch of salt and mix with a flat-bladed knife, using a cutting action, to form a soft dough. Gather together and divide into two portions. Refrigerate in plastic wrap for 20 minutes.
3 Place a dough portion on each tray and press into a round, using the drawn circle as a guide. Pinch and flute the edges decoratively and prick the surface with a fork. Use a sharp knife to mark each circle into 12 segments. Sprinkle with sugar and bake for 35 minutes, until firm, pale golden and cooked through. Cool on the trays. Store in an airtight container.

NOTE: Usually, no liquid is used, but if the mixture is very crumbly, moisten with no more than 1 tablespoon of milk or pouring (whipping) cream.

ginger shortbread

Preparation time: **25 minutes**
Cooking time: **45 minutes**
Makes **12 pieces**

250 g (9 oz) unsalted butter, softened
60 g (2¼ oz/½ cup) icing (confectioners')
   sugar
250 g (9 oz/2 cups) plain (all-purpose) flour
1 teaspoon ground ginger
70 g (2½ oz/⅓ cup) chopped crystallised
   ginger

1 Preheat the oven to 150°C (300°F/
Gas 2). Line a 23 cm (9 inch) round
or square tin, or a baking tray, with
baking paper.
2 Cream the butter and sugar in a small
bowl using electric beaters until light
and creamy. Sift the flour into the bowl
with the ground ginger. Add the chopped
ginger and mix with a flat-bladed knife,
using a cutting action, to form a soft
dough. Gently gather together and press
into the tin, or shape into a round about
1 cm (½ inch) thick on the baking tray.
Prick the surface all over with a fork and
score into 12 wedges.
3 Bake for 40–45 minutes, or until lightly
golden. While still warm, cut into wedges.
Cool in the tin or on the tray for about
3 minutes before transferring to a wire
rack to cool completely. When cooled,
store in an airtight container.

ginger shortbread

brown sugar shortbread

Preparation time: **45 minutes**
Cooking time: **20 minutes**
Makes **50**

250 g (9 oz) unsalted butter, softened
140 g (5 oz/¾ cup) soft brown sugar
250 g (9 oz/2 cups) plain (all-purpose) flour
90 g (3¼ oz/½ cup) rice flour
½ teaspoon mixed (pumpkin pie) spice

1 Preheat the oven to 160°C (315°F/
Gas 2–3). Line two baking trays with
baking paper. Cream the butter and sugar
in a small bowl using electric beaters until
light and creamy. Add the sifted flours,
mixed spice and a pinch of salt and mix
with a knife, using a cutting action, to a
soft dough. Gather together and gently
knead for 1 minute. Refrigerate in plastic
wrap for 20 minutes.
2 Divide the mixture into four portions.
Use a lightly floured rolling pin to roll out
one portion on a lightly floured surface

until it is 5 mm (¼ inch) thick. Cut out
shapes using a round 4–5 cm (1½–2 inch)
cutter. Re-roll the trimmings and then
repeat the process with the remaining
portions of dough.
3 Place the shortbread on the trays and
bake for 15–20 minutes, or until lightly
golden and firm to the touch. Remove
from the oven and leave on the trays to
cool for 2 minutes before transferring
to a wire rack to cool completely. When
cooled, store in an airtight container.

melting moments

greek shortbread

☀

Preparation time: **40 minutes**
Cooking time: **15 minutes**
Makes **38**

200 g (7 oz) unsalted butter, softened
125 g (4½ oz/1 cup) icing (confectioners')
    sugar, sifted
1 teaspoon finely grated orange zest
1 egg
1 egg yolk
310 g (11 oz/2½ cups) plain (all-purpose)
    flour
1½ teaspoons baking powder
1 teaspoon ground cinnamon
250 g (9 oz) blanched almonds, toasted,
    finely chopped
125 g (4½ oz/1 cup) icing (confectioners')
    sugar, extra, to dust

1 Preheat the oven to 160°C (315°F/
Gas 2–3). Line two baking trays with
baking paper.
2 Cream the butter, icing sugar and
orange zest in a small bowl using electric
beaters until light and creamy. Add
the egg and egg yolk and beat until
thoroughly combined. Transfer the
mixture to a large bowl.
3 Using a metal spoon, fold in the sifted
flour, baking powder, cinnamon and
almonds, and mix until well combined.
4 Shape level tablespoons of the mixture
into crescent shapes and place on the
trays. Bake for 15 minutes, or until
lightly golden. Cool on the trays for
5 minutes, then transfer to a wire rack.
While still warm, dust heavily with half
of the extra icing sugar. Allow to cool
completely. Just before serving, dust
heavily with the remaining icing sugar.

NOTE: After dusting heavily with icing
sugar the first time, store the cooled
biscuits in an airtight container. They will
keep for a week. Dust again with icing
sugar just before serving.

melting moments

☀

Preparation time: **40 minutes**
    + cooling time
Cooking time: **20 minutes**
Makes **14**

250 g (9 oz) unsalted butter, softened
40 g (1½ oz/⅓ cup) icing (confectioners')
    sugar
1 teaspoon natural vanilla extract
185 g (6½ oz/1½ cups) self-raising
    flour
60 g (2¼ oz/½ cup) custard powder or
    instant vanilla pudding mix

PASSIONFRUIT FILLING
60 g (2¼ oz) unsalted butter
60 g (2¼ oz/½ cup) icing (confectioners')
    sugar
1½ tablespoons passionfruit pulp

1 Preheat the oven to 180°C (350°F/
Gas 4). Line two baking trays with
baking paper.
2 Cream the butter and icing sugar in a
bowl using electric beaters until light and
creamy, then beat in the vanilla. Sift in the
flour and custard powder and mix with a
flat-bladed knife, using a cutting action,
to form a soft dough.
3 Roll level tablespoons of dough into
balls (you should have 28) and place on
the trays, leaving room for spreading.
Flatten slightly with a floured fork. Bake
for 20 minutes, or until lightly golden. Cool
slightly on the trays before transferring to
a wire rack to cool completely.
4 To make the passionfruit filling, beat
the butter and icing sugar in a bowl using
electric beaters until light and creamy,
then beat in the passionfruit pulp. Use to
sandwich the biscuits together. Leave the
filling to firm before serving.

viennese fingers

✺ ✺

Preparation time: 20 minutes + cooling time
Cooking time: 12 minutes
Makes 20

100 g (3½ oz) unsalted butter, softened
40 g (1½ oz/⅓ cup) icing (confectioners')
  sugar
2 egg yolks
1½ teaspoons natural vanilla extract
125 g (4½ oz/1 cup) plain (all-purpose) flour
100 g (3½ oz) dark chocolate, chopped
30 g (1 oz) unsalted butter, extra

1 Preheat the oven to 180°C (350°F/
Gas 4). Line two baking trays with
baking paper.
2 Cream the butter and icing sugar in
a small bowl using electric beaters until
light and creamy. Gradually add the egg
yolks and vanilla and beat thoroughly.
Transfer to a large bowl, then sift in the
flour. Using a flat-bladed knife, mix using
a cutting action until the ingredients are
just combined and the mixture is smooth.
3 Spoon the mixture into a piping (icing)
bag fitted with a 1 cm (½ inch) fluted
nozzle and pipe the mixture into wavy
6 cm (2½ inch) lengths on the trays. Bake
for 12 minutes, or until golden brown. Cool
slightly on the trays before transferring to a
wire rack to cool completely.
4 Place the chocolate and extra butter
in a small heatproof bowl. Half-fill a
saucepan with water and bring to the
boil, then remove from the heat. Sit the
bowl over the pan, making sure the base
of the bowl does not touch the water. Stir
occasionally until the chocolate and butter
have melted and the mixture is smooth.
Dip half of each biscuit in the melted
chocolate mixture and leave to set on
baking paper or foil. Store in an airtight
container for up to 2 days.

NOTE: To make piping easier, fold down
the bag by about 10 cm (4 inches) before
spooning the mixture in, then unfold.
The top will be clean and easy to twist,
stopping the mixture from squirting out.

shortbread shapes

Shortbread-type mixtures
can be made into a variety of
shapes and sizes. Traditional
Scottish shortbreads are
sometimes pressed into a
special-purpose wooden
mould, usually decorated
with a Scottish thistle design.
Petticoat shortbread is pressed
into a circle and fluted on the
edges with your fingers to
represent a petticoat edge.
The mixture can also be piped,
as with the Viennese fingers
shown below, or rolled and
shaped into rounds, triangles,
rectangles or squares. Patterns
can also be pricked onto the top.

langues de chat

✹ ✹

Preparation time: 25 minutes
Cooking time: 7 minutes
Makes 24

75 g (2¾ oz) unsalted butter, softened
90 g (3¼ oz/⅓ cup) caster (superfine) sugar
2 egg whites
75 g (2¾ oz) plain (all-purpose) flour, sifted
icing (confectioners') sugar, to dust

1 Preheat the oven to 220°C (425°F/Gas 7). Line two baking trays with baking paper.

2 Cream the butter and caster sugar in a small bowl using electric beaters until light and creamy. Whisk the egg whites in a small bowl with a fork until frothy, then gradually add to the butter mixture, beating well after each addition. Lightly fold in the sifted flour and a pinch of salt until well combined.

3 Spoon the mixture into a piping bag fitted with a 1 cm (½ inch) plain nozzle and pipe 12 biscuits, 8cm (3¼ inches) long, onto each tray. Cook in batches, if necessary. Bake for 6–7 minutes, or until cooked through and lightly brown around the edges. Cool on the trays for 2 minutes, then transfer to a wire rack to cool completely. Dust with icing sugar just before serving.

NOTE: Langues de chat translates from French as cats' tongues, referring to the biscuit's shape. They are often served with ice creams, sorbets, and other iced or soft desserts such as mousses and sabayons. They are also served as a snack with tea and coffee. They will keep, stored in an airtight container in the refrigerator, for up to a week. They can also be cooked in langues de chat tins (as we have done), available from some kitchenware stores.

Use a knife to mix the butter mixture into the dry ingredients.

Dip one half of each biscuit in the melted chocolate and place on a tray lined with baking paper.

lebkuchen

Preparation time: 25 minutes + cooling time
Cooking time: 30 minutes
Makes 35

290 g (10¼ oz/2⅓ cups) plain
   (all-purpose) flour
60 g (2¼ oz/½ cup) cornflour
   (cornstarch)
2 teaspoons unsweetened cocoa powder
1 teaspoon mixed (pumpkin pie) spice
1 teaspoon ground cinnamon
½ teaspoon freshly grated nutmeg
100 g (3½ oz) unsalted butter, cubed
260 g (9¼ oz/¾ cup) golden syrup or
   dark corn syrup
2 tablespoons milk

150 g (5½ oz/1 cup) white or dark
   chocolate melts
¼ teaspoon mixed (pumpkin pie) spice,
   extra, to sprinkle (optional)

1 Preheat the oven to 180°C (350°F/
Gas 4). Line two baking trays with baking
paper. Sift the flour, cornflour, cocoa and
spices into a large bowl and make a well
in the centre.
2 Place the butter, golden syrup and
milk in a small saucepan, and stir over
low heat until the butter has melted and
the mixture is smooth. Remove from the
heat and add to the dry ingredients. Using
a flat-bladed knife, mix with a cutting
action until the mixture comes together
in small beads. Gather together with your
hands and turn out onto baking paper.

3 Roll the dough out to 8 mm (⅜ inch)
thick. Cut into heart shapes using a
6 cm (2½ inch) cutter. Place on the trays
and bake for 25 minutes, or until lightly
browned. Leave on the trays to cool
slightly before transferring to a wire rack
to cool completely. Place the chocolate in
a small heatproof bowl. Bring a saucepan
of water to the boil, then remove from the
heat. Sit the bowl over the pan, making
sure the base of the bowl does not touch
the water. Stir occasionally until the
chocolate has melted.
4 Dip one half of each biscuit in the
melted chocolate and place on baking
paper until the chocolate has set. Sprinkle
the un-iced side of the biscuits with mixed
spice, if desired. Store in an airtight
container for up to 5 days.

maple and pecan biscuits

maple and pecan biscuits

✳ ✳

Preparation time: 30 minutes
+ 30 minutes chilling time
Cooking time: 15 minutes
Makes about 60

185 g (6½ oz) unsalted butter,
    softened
185 g (6½ oz/1 cup) soft brown
    sugar
60 ml (2 fl oz/¼ cup) maple syrup
1 teaspoon natural vanilla extract
1 egg
280 g (10 oz/2¼ cups) plain (all-purpose)
    flour
1 teaspoon baking powder
120 g (4¼ oz/1 cup) finely chopped
    pecans
whole pecans, to decorate

1 Cream the butter and sugar in a small
bowl using electric beaters until light
and creamy. Add the maple syrup, vanilla
and egg and beat until well combined.
Transfer to a large bowl and add the
sifted flour and baking powder. Using a
flat-bladed knife, mix to a soft dough.
Gather together, then divide the mixture
into two portions.
2 Place a portion of the dough on a sheet
of baking paper and press lightly until the
dough is 30 cm (12 inches) long and 4 cm
(1½ inches) thick. Roll neatly into a log
shape, then roll the log in the chopped
pecans. Repeat with the other portion of
dough. Wrap each log in plastic wrap and
refrigerate for 30 minutes, or until firm.
3 Preheat the oven to 180°C (350°F/
Gas 4). Line two baking trays with baking
paper. Cut the logs into slices about 1 cm
(½ inch) thick. Press a whole pecan
into the top of each biscuit. Place on the
prepared trays, leaving 3 cm (1¼ inches)
between each. Bake for 10–15 minutes, or
until the biscuits are golden. Cool on the
trays for 3 minutes before transferring to
a wire rack to cool completely. Store in an
airtight container.

refrigerator biscuits

✳ ✳

Preparation time: 30 minutes
+ 30 minutes chilling time
Cooking time: 15 minutes
Makes about 60

180 g (6¼ oz) unsalted butter,
    softened
185 g (6½ oz/1 cup) soft brown sugar
1 teaspoon natural vanilla extract
1 egg
280 g (10 oz/2¼ cups) plain (all-purpose)
    flour
1 teaspoon baking powder

1 Cream the butter and sugar in a small
bowl using electric beaters until light and
creamy. Add the vanilla and egg and beat
until well combined. Transfer to a large
bowl and add the sifted flour and baking
powder. Using a flat-bladed knife, mix to
a soft dough. Gather together, then divide
the mixture into two portions.
2 Place a portion of dough on a sheet of
baking paper and press lightly until the
dough is 30 cm (12 inches) long and 4 cm
(1½ inches) thick. Fold the paper around
the dough and roll neatly into a log shape.
Twist the edges of the paper to seal.
Repeat the process with the other portion.
Refrigerate for 30 minutes, or until firm.
3 Preheat the oven to 180°C (350°F/
Gas 4). Line two baking trays with
baking paper.
4 Cut the logs into slices about 1 cm
(½ inch) thick. Place on the prepared
trays, leaving 3 cm (1¼ inches) between
each. Bake for 10–15 minutes, or until
golden. Cool on the trays for 3 minutes
before transferring to a wire rack to
cool completely. Store the biscuits in
an airtight container.

spicy fruit biscuits

✳ ✳

Preparation time: 20 minutes
+ 45 minutes chilling time
Cooking time: 15 minutes
Makes about 60

180 g (6¼ oz) unsalted butter, softened
185 g (6½ oz/1 cup) soft brown sugar
1 teaspoon natural vanilla extract
1 egg
280 g (10 oz/2¼ cups) plain (all-purpose) flour
1 teaspoon baking powder
1 teaspoon mixed (pumpkin pie) spice
½ teaspoon ground ginger
95 g (3¼ oz/½ cup) fruit mince (mincemeat)

1 Cream the butter and sugar in a small bowl using electric beaters until light and creamy. Add the vanilla and egg and beat until well combined. Transfer to a large bowl and add the sifted flour, baking powder, mixed spice and ginger. Using a flat-bladed knife, mix to a soft dough.
2 Divide the mixture into two portions. Roll one portion out on baking paper to a rectangle about 2 mm (¹⁄₁₆ inch) thick and trim the edges. Repeat with other portion. Wrap in plastic wrap and refrigerate until just firm.
3 Spread both portions of dough with the fruit mince. Roll up swiss-roll (jelly-roll) style. Refrigerate for 30 minutes.
4 Preheat the oven to 180°C (350°F/ Gas 4). Line two baking trays with baking paper. Cut the logs into slices about 1 cm (½ inch) thick. Place on the trays, leaving 3 cm (1¼ inches) between each. Bake for 10–15 minutes, or until golden. Cool on the trays for 3 minutes before transferring to a wire rack to cool completely.

marbled biscuits

✳ ✳

Preparation time: 50 minutes + 30 minutes chilling time
Cooking time: 15 minutes
Makes about 60

180 g (6¼ oz) unsalted butter, softened
230 g (8 oz/1 cup) caster (superfine) sugar
1 teaspoon natural vanilla extract
1 egg
a few drops red food colouring
50 g (1¾ oz) dark chocolate, melted
1 tablespoon unsweetened cocoa powder
2 teaspoons milk
270 g (9½ oz) plain (all-purpose) flour
¾ teaspoon baking powder

1 Cream the butter and sugar in a small bowl using electric beaters until light and creamy. Beat in the vanilla and egg until well combined. Divide among three bowls.
2 Add the food colouring to one and the melted chocolate, sifted cocoa powder and milk to another. Leave one plain. Add one-third of the sifted flour and ¼ teaspoon baking powder to each bowl.
3 Using a flat-bladed knife, mix each to a soft dough, then divide in half and roll into thin logs. Twist them all together, then shape into 2 logs. Cover with plastic wrap and refrigerate for 30 minutes.
4 Preheat the oven to 180°C (350°F/ Gas 4). Line two baking trays with baking paper.
5 Cut the logs into slices about 1 cm (½ inch) thick. Place on the trays, leaving 3 cm (1¼ inches) between each. Bake the biscuits for 10–15 minutes, or until golden. Cool on the trays for 3 minutes before transferring to a wire rack to cool completely.

marbled biscuits

amaretti

Amaretti are light, crisp Italian biscuits, similar to the macaroon, with an almond flavour. They are an especially good biscuit to accompany coffee but can also be crushed and used as a flavoursome filling for fruits, particularly cored apples and halved stoned peaches. The crushed biscuits are made into a paste with sugar and butter then stuffed into the apples or spooned onto the peaches. The fruit is then baked in a little wine, which adds to the flavour.

amaretti

amaretti

✹ ✹

Preparation time: **20 minutes**
  + 1 hour standing time
Cooking time: **20 minutes**
Makes **40**

1 tablespoon plain (all-purpose) flour
1 tablespoon cornflour (cornstarch)
1 teaspoon ground cinnamon
160 g (5½ oz/⅔ cup) caster (superfine)
  sugar
1 teaspoon finely grated lemon zest
95 g (3¼ oz/1 cup) ground almonds
2 egg whites
30 g (1 oz/¼ cup) icing (confectioners')
  sugar

1 Line two baking trays with baking
paper. Sift the flour, cornflour, cinnamon
and half the caster sugar into a large
bowl, then add the lemon zest and
ground almonds.
2 Whisk the egg whites in a clean, dry
bowl using electric beaters until firm
peaks form. Gradually add the remaining
caster sugar, whisking constantly until
the mixture is thick and glossy and all the
sugar has dissolved. Using a metal spoon,
fold the egg white mixture into the dry
ingredients and stir until the ingredients
are just combined.
3 Roll 2 level teaspoons of mixture at
a time with oiled or wetted hands into
balls and arrange on the trays, allowing
room for spreading. Set the trays aside,
uncovered, for 1 hour.
4 Preheat the oven to 180°C (350°F/
Gas 4). Sift the icing sugar liberally over
the biscuits, then bake for 15–20 minutes,
or until crisp and lightly browned.
Transfer to a wire rack and leave to cool
completely. These biscuits can be stored in
an airtight container for up to 2 days.

biscotti

✹ ✹

Preparation time: **25 minutes**
Cooking time: **50 minutes**
Makes **45**

250 g (9 oz/2 cups) plain (all-purpose) flour
1 teaspoon baking powder
230 g (8 oz/1 cup) caster (superfine) sugar
3 eggs
1 egg yolk
1 teaspoon natural vanilla extract
1 teaspoon finely grated orange zest
110 g (3¾ oz/¾ cup) pistachio nuts

1 Preheat the oven to 180°C (350°F/
Gas 4). Line two baking trays with baking
paper and lightly dust with flour.

2 Sift the flour and baking powder into a
large bowl. Stir in the sugar. Make a well
in the centre and add 2 of the eggs, the
egg yolk, vanilla and zest. Using a large
metal spoon, stir until just combined. Mix
in the pistachios. Knead for 2–3 minutes
on a lightly floured surface (it will be stiff).
Sprinkle with a little water and divide into
two portions. Roll into logs about 8 x 25
cm (3¼ x 10 inches). Flatten slightly.
3 Place on the trays, a little apart.
Lightly beat the remaining egg and brush
over the logs. Bake for 35 minutes, then
remove from the oven. Reduce the oven
to 150°C (300°F/Gas 2). Cool slightly,
then use a serrated knife to cut into 5 mm
(¼ inch) slices. Bake for 8 minutes, turn
and bake for 8 minutes more, until crisp
and dry. Transfer to a wire rack to cool.

meringues

Just two ingredients are all you require to make a basic mixture for meringues. When egg white and sugar are whisked together, then baked, they miraculously turn into crunchy, delicate delights.

basic meringue recipe

Preheat the oven to 150°C (300°F/Gas 2) and line two baking trays with baking paper. Whisk 2 egg whites to stiff peaks in a clean, dry small bowl using electric beaters. Add 125 g (4½ oz/ ½ cup) caster (superfine) sugar, 1 tablespoon at a time, whisking well after each addition. Whisk until the mixture is thick and glossy and the sugar has dissolved (this will take up to 10 minutes). Spoon into a piping (icing) bag fitted with a plain nozzle and pipe small shapes onto the trays. Bake for 20–25 minutes, or until pale and dry. Turn off the oven, leave the door ajar and cool the meringues in the oven. When cooled, store in an airtight jar. Makes about 30.

custard discs

Prepare the basic mixture until it is thick and glossy. Gently fold in 1 tablespoon sifted custard powder or instant vanilla pudding mix. Spoon into a piping bag with a plain 5 mm (¼ inch) or 1 cm (½ inch) nozzle. Pipe spirals onto trays and bake as above. Dust with icing (confectioners') sugar. Makes about 40.

coffee swirls

Prepare the basic mixture until it is thick and glossy, adding 2–3 teaspoons instant coffee powder with the sugar. Spoon the mixture into a piping bag fitted with a small star nozzle and pipe onto the trays. Bake as for the basic recipe. Coffee swirls are delicious served as is or sandwiched together with 60 g (2¼ oz) melted chocolate. Makes about 30.

chocolate fingers

Prepare the basic mixture until it is thick and glossy, adding 1 tablespoon sifted unsweetened cocoa powder with the sugar. Spoon the mixture into a piping bag fitted with a plain round nozzle and pipe fine 7.5 cm (3 inch) lengths onto lined trays, allowing room for spreading. Bake as for the basic recipe and serve as they are, or drizzled with melted chocolate or lightly dusted with unsweetened cocoa powder combined with a little icing (confectioners') sugar. Makes about 40.

hazelnut snails

Prepare the basic mixture until it is thick and glossy. Gently fold through 2 tablespoons ground hazelnuts. Spoon the mixture into a piping bag fitted with a plain 1 cm (½ inch) nozzle and pipe small spirals onto the trays. Bake as for the basic recipe. These can be served lightly dusted with a mixture of icing (confectioners') sugar and ground cinnamon, or drizzled with melted chocolate. Makes about 30.

meringue nests

Prepare the basic mixture until it is thick and glossy. Spoon into a piping bag fitted with a star nozzle and pipe into small nests on the trays. Bake as for the basic recipe. Meringue nests are delicious if filled with whipped cream flavoured with coffee or chocolate liqueur, topped with a chocolate-coated coffee bean. They can also be filled with a chocolate truffle mixture and topped with a slice of strawberry. Makes about 40.

clockwise from top left: custard discs, chocolate fingers and coffee swirls

brandy snaps

Preparation time: **30 minutes**
Cooking time: **15 minutes**
Makes **15**

60 g (2¼ oz) unsalted butter
2 tablespoons golden syrup or dark corn
   syrup
60 g (2¼ oz/⅓ cup) soft brown sugar
30 g (1 oz/¼ cup) plain (all-purpose) flour
1½ teaspoons ground ginger
60 g (2¼ oz) dark chocolate, chopped

1 Preheat the oven to 180°C (350°F/
Gas 4). Line two baking trays with baking
paper. Place the butter, golden syrup and
sugar in a small saucepan and stir over
low heat until the butter has melted and
the sugar has dissolved. Remove from
the heat and add the sifted flour and
ground ginger to the saucepan. Use a
wooden spoon to stir the mixture until
the ingredients are well combined, taking
care not to overbeat.

2 For each brandy snap, drop 3 level
teaspoons of the mixture onto each tray,
about 12 cm (4½ inches) apart. Bake for
5–6 minutes, or until lightly browned.
Leave on the trays for 30 seconds then,
while still hot, lift one biscuit off the tray
using a large flat knife or spatula, and
wrap around the handle of a thin wooden
spoon. Slide the biscuit off the spoon
and set aside to cool while you curl the
remaining brandy snaps.

3 Put the chocolate in a heatproof bowl.
Bring a saucepan of water to the boil,
then remove from the heat and place the
bowl over the water, making sure the base
of the bowl does not touch the water. Stir
occasionally until melted.

4 Dip both ends of each brandy snap in
the melted chocolate and leave to set on
a foil-lined tray.

NOTE: There is a real art to making these
biscuits: work quickly, as they harden and
crack when cooled. If they cool too much,
return them to the oven for a few minutes
to warm, then try again.

Drop 3 level teaspoons of the
mixture onto the lined trays for
each brandy snap.

While the biscuits are still hot, lift
off the tray and wrap around the
thin handle of a wooden spoon.

Dip both ends of each brandy snap
in melted chocolate and leave to
set on a foil-lined tray.

chocolate peppermint creams

✹ ✹

Preparation time: 40 minutes + cooling time
Cooking time: 15 minutes
Makes 20

65 g (2¼ oz) unsalted butter
55 g (2 oz/¼ cup) caster (superfine) sugar
60 g (2¼ oz/½ cup) plain (all-purpose) flour
40 g (1½ oz/⅓ cup) self-raising flour
2 tablespoons unsweetened cocoa powder
2 tablespoons milk

PEPPERMINT CREAM
1 egg white, at room temperature
215 g (7½ oz/1¾ cups) icing
   (confectioners') sugar, sifted
2–3 drops peppermint extract or oil, to taste

CHOCOLATE TOPPING
150 g (5½ oz/1 cup) chopped dark chocolate
150 g (5½ oz/1 cup) milk chocolate melts

1   Preheat the oven to 180°C (350°F/ Gas 4). Line two baking trays with baking paper. Cream the butter and caster sugar using electric beaters until light and creamy. Add the sifted flours and cocoa alternately with the milk. Mix until the mixture forms a soft dough.
2   Turn out onto a floured surface and gather into a rough ball. Cut the dough in half. Roll each portion between two sheets of baking paper to 2 mm (⅛ inch) thick. Slide onto a tray and refrigerate for 15 minutes, or until firm. Cut the dough into rounds using a 4 cm (1½ inch) cutter, re-rolling the dough scraps and cutting more rounds. Place on the baking trays, allowing room for spreading. Bake for 10 minutes, or until firm. Transfer to a wire rack to cool completely.
3   To make the peppermint cream, put the egg white in a bowl. Whisk in the icing sugar 2 tablespoons at a time, using electric beaters on low. Add more icing sugar, if necessary, to form a soft dough.
4   Turn the dough onto a surface dusted with icing sugar and knead in enough icing sugar so that the dough is not sticky. Knead in the peppermint extract or oil. Roll a teaspoon of peppermint cream into a ball, and flatten slightly. Sandwich between two of the (cooled) chocolate biscuits, pressing together to spread the peppermint to the edges. Repeat with the remaining peppermint cream and chocolate biscuits, keeping the filling covered as you work.
5   To make the topping, put the chopped chocolate and the chocolate melts in a heatproof bowl. Half-fill a saucepan with water and bring to the boil. Remove from the heat and place the bowl over the pan, making sure the base of the bowl doesn't touch the water. Stir until the chocolate has melted. Allow to cool slightly. Use a fork to dip the biscuits in the chocolate and allow any excess to drain away. Place on a tray lined with baking paper to set.

cocoa powder

This is the powder that is ground from the dried solids left when cocoa butter, or fat, is removed from the processed cacao tree seeds. The powder is used extensively in baking. It is usually sifted in with the dry ingredients so it is distributed evenly. Cocoa is sweetened and sold as drinking chocolate. Dutch cocoa is considered the best quality as it has a rich flavour and a dark colour. It is available at delicatessens.

fortune cookies

✹ ✹

Preparation time: 40 minutes
Cooking time: 50 minutes
Makes 30

3 egg whites
60 g (2¼ oz/½ cup) icing (confectioners')
    sugar, sifted
45 g (1¾ oz) unsalted butter, melted
60 g (2¼ oz/½ cup) plain (all-purpose) flour

1 Preheat the oven to 180ºC (350ºF/
Gas 4). Line a baking tray with baking
paper. Draw three circles with 8 cm
(3¼ inch) diameters on the paper.

2 Put the egg whites in a bowl and
whisk until just frothy. Add the icing
sugar and butter and stir until smooth.
Add the flour and mix until smooth.
Allow to stand for 15 minutes.
3 Using a flat-bladed knife, spread
1½ level teaspoons of the mixture over
each circle. Bake for 5 minutes, or until
slightly brown around the edges. Working
quickly, remove the cookies from the tray
by sliding a flat-bladed knife under each.
Place a written fortune message on each
cookie. Fold the cookie in half to form
a semi-circle, then fold it again over a
blunt-edged object like the rim of a glass.
Allow to cool on a wire rack. Repeat with
the remaining mixture.

NOTE: Cook no more than three cookies
at once, or they will cool and harden too
quickly, then break when folded. You can
compose your own messages or look up
traditional ones on the internet.

monte creams

✹

Preparation time: 30 minutes + cooling time
Cooking time: 20 minutes
Makes 25

125 g (4½ oz) unsalted butter, softened
115 g (4 oz/½ cup) caster (superfine) sugar
60 ml (2 fl oz/¼ cup) milk
185 g (6½ oz/1½ cups) self-raising flour
30 g (1 oz/¼ cup) custard powder or
    instant vanilla pudding mix, plus a
    little extra
30 g (1 oz/⅓ cup) desiccated coconut

FILLING
75 g (2¾ oz) unsalted butter, softened
85 g (3 oz/⅔ cup) icing (confectioners')
    sugar
2 teaspoons milk
105 g (3½ oz/⅓ cup) strawberry jam

1 Preheat the oven to 180°C (350°F/
Gas 4). Line two baking trays with baking
paper. Cream the butter and caster sugar
in a small bowl using electric beaters until
light and creamy. Add the milk and beat
until combined. Sift the flour and custard
powder and add to the bowl with the
coconut. Mix to form a soft dough.
2 Roll 2 teaspoons of the mixture into
balls. Place on the trays, allowing room
for spreading and press with a fork. Dip
the fork in the extra custard powder
occasionally to prevent it from sticking.
Bake for 15–20 minutes, or until just
golden. Transfer to a wire rack to cool
completely before filling.
3 To make the filling, beat the butter and
icing sugar in a small bowl using electric
beaters until light and creamy. Beat in the
milk. Spread one biscuit with ½ teaspoon
of the filling and one with ½ teaspoon of
jam, then press them together. Repeat.

Use a flat-bladed knife to spread
mixture over each marked circle.

Fold each cookie in half, then in
half again over a blunt object.

Spread the prepared fig filling lengthways along one side of the pastry, leaving a border.

Place the three rolls on a baking tray lined with baking paper.

fig newtons

❋ ❋

Preparation time: 30 minutes + 2 hours chilling and cooling time
Cooking time: 1 hour 10 minutes
Makes 24

75 g (2¾ oz) unsalted butter, softened
2 tablespoons sour cream
140 g (5 oz/¾ cup) soft brown sugar
1 teaspoon natural vanilla extract
2 eggs, lightly beaten
375 g (13 oz/3 cups) plain (all-purpose) flour
2 teaspoons baking powder
½ teaspoon bicarbonate of soda (baking soda)
½ teaspoon ground cinnamon

FIG FILLING
375 g (13 oz) dried figs, stems removed
80 g (2¾ oz/⅓ cup) caster (superfine) sugar
1 teaspoon finely grated lemon zest

1 Cream the butter, sour cream, sugar and vanilla in a small bowl using electric beaters until light and creamy. Gradually add the egg, beating thoroughly after each addition. The mixture will appear curdled. Transfer to a large bowl and fold in the combined sifted flour, baking powder, bicarbonate of soda and cinnamon. The mixture will be very soft. Wrap in a sheet of floured plastic wrap and refrigerate for at least 2 hours.
2 To make the filling, place the figs and 250 ml (9 fl oz/1 cup) water in a saucepan. Bring to the boil, reduce the heat and simmer, covered, for 30 minutes, or until the figs are soft. Add the sugar and lemon zest, stir well, and simmer for 10 minutes. Cool, drain off any remaining syrup and then chop the figs in a food processor until smooth. Set aside to cool.
3 Preheat the oven to 180°C (350°F/ Gas 4). Line a baking tray with baking paper. Divide the dough into three

portions. Refrigerate two portions and roll the other portion on a floured surface to measure 12 x 28 cm (4½ x 11¼ inches). Spread a third of the filling lengthways along one half of the pastry, leaving a 2 cm (¾ inch) border on that side and on the ends. Brush the border with water. Fold the unfilled half over the filling and press around the edges. Trim 1 cm (½ inch) from the side and ends. Lift onto the tray and refrigerate. Repeat with the remaining portions of dough. Lay all the rolls on the tray, allowing room for spreading. Bake for 25 minutes, or until cooked and golden. Cool for 5 minutes on a wire rack, then trim the ends and cut each roll at 2 cm (¾ inch) intervals. When cooled, store in an airtight container.

graham crackers

Preparation time: 20 minutes
  + 30 minutes chilling time
Cooking time: 10 minutes
Makes 12

350 g (12 oz/2⅓ cups) plain (all-purpose)
  wholemeal (whole-wheat) flour
60 g (2¼ oz/½ cup) cornflour (cornstarch)
55 g (2 oz/¼ cup) caster (superfine) sugar
150 g (5½ oz) butter, chilled and cubed
185 ml (6 fl oz/¾ cup) pouring (whipping)
  cream
strawberry jam, to serve (optional)

1 Sift the flours into a bowl, then stir in
the sugar and ½ teaspoon salt. Rub in
the butter with your fingertips until the
mixture resembles breadcrumbs. Mix in
the cream with a flat-bladed knife, using
a cutting action, to make a pliable dough.
Gather the dough together and shape
into a disc. Wrap in plastic wrap and
refrigerate for 30 minutes.
2 Preheat the oven to 200°C (400°F/
Gas 6). Line two baking trays with
baking paper.
3 Roll out the dough to a rectangle
measuring 24 x 30 cm (9½ x 12 inches).
Cut the dough into 12 rectangles with
a sharp knife or pastry wheel. Place the
rectangles on the baking trays, allowing a
little room for spreading.
4 Bake for 7–10 minutes, or until firm
and golden brown. Leave to cool on the
trays for 2–3 minutes before transferring
to a wire rack to cool completely. Serve
with jam, if desired. Store the cooled
crackers in an airtight container.

graham crackers

In the United States the word 'graham' means
any bread, biscuit or cake made from wholemeal
(whole-wheat) flour, including the bran.
Graham flour was developed and promoted by
Dr Sylvester Graham in the early 19th century.

Dr Graham was an ardent advocate of unrefined
foods and a vegetarian lifestyle. Graham bread,
Graham crackers and Graham rusks all denote
that the baked products have been made with
wholemeal flour.

oat cakes

Preparation time: 15 minutes
Cooking time: 25 minutes
Makes 14

250 g (9 oz/2 cups) oatmeal, plus extra,
    for sprinkling
½ teaspoon baking powder
2 teaspoons soft brown sugar
60 g (2¼ oz) butter, melted

1 Preheat the oven to 180°C (350°F/
Gas 4). Line two baking trays with
baking paper.
2 Combine the oatmeal, baking powder,
sugar and a pinch of salt in a large bowl.
Make a well in the centre and add the
melted butter along with 125 ml (4 fl oz/
½ cup) hot water.
3 Using a flat-bladed knife, mix to form
a dough. Gather the dough together and
turn onto a surface lightly sprinkled with
extra oatmeal. Press into a flattish round.
4 Roll the dough out to a thickness of
5 mm (¼ inch), sprinkling with extra
oatmeal. Use a round 6 cm (2½ inch)
cutter to cut out rounds from the dough.
Place on the baking trays, leaving room
for spreading. Bake for 25 minutes, or
until lightly golden. Allow to cool on the
trays for 5 minutes before transferring
to a wire rack to cool completely. When
cooled, store in an airtight container.

cheese biscuits

Preparation time: 10 minutes
    + 30 minutes chilling time
Cooking time: 10 minutes
Makes 45

125 g (4½ oz) butter, chopped
125 g (4½ oz) cheddar cheese, grated
2 tablespoons grated parmesan cheese
125 g (4½ oz/1 cup) plain (all-purpose) flour
2 tablespoons self-raising flour
pinch of cayenne pepper
2 teaspoons lemon juice

1 Place the butter, cheeses, flours,
cayenne pepper, lemon juice and a pinch
of salt in a food processor. Process for
60 seconds, or until the mixture comes
together and forms a ball.
2 Gently knead the mixture for 2 minutes
on a lightly floured surface. Form the
dough into a sausage shape about
3 cm (1¼ inches) in diameter. Wrap in
plastic wrap, then in foil and freeze for
30 minutes. Remove and leave at room
temperature for 5 minutes.

3 Preheat the oven to 180°C (350°F/
Gas 4). Line two baking trays with
baking paper.
4 Slice the dough into thin slices, about
3 mm (⅛ inch) thick, and place on the
trays, allowing a little room for spreading.
Bake the biscuits for 9–10 minutes, or
until golden. Allow to cool on the trays.
Store in an airtight container.

NOTE: Cheese biscuits are best eaten on
the day of baking.

cheese biscuits (left) and oat cakes

two-seed crackers

☀

Preparation time: **20 minutes**
Cooking time: **25 minutes**
Makes **30**

250 g (9 oz/2 cups) plain (all-purpose) flour
1 teaspoon baking powder
2 tablespoons poppy seeds
2 tablespoons sesame seeds
60 g (2¼ oz) butter, chilled and cubed
125 ml (4 fl oz/½ cup) chilled water

1 Preheat the oven to 180°C (350°F/ Gas 4). Line two baking trays with baking paper.
2 Sift the flour, baking powder and ½ teaspoon salt into a bowl. Stir in the seeds and some pepper. Rub the butter into the flour using your fingertips until the mixture resembles fine breadcrumbs.
3 Make a well in the centre and add the chilled water. Mix together with a flat-bladed knife, using a cutting action, adding a little extra water if necessary, until the mixture comes together in soft

beads. Gather together into a rough ball. Handle the dough gently and do not knead it at any stage. Divide the dough into two portions. Put a portion between two sheets of baking paper and roll out to 2 mm (1⁄16 inch) thick. Cover the other portion with plastic wrap.
4 Using a 6 cm (2½ inch) round cutter, cut rounds from the dough. Prick all over with a fork and transfer to the trays. Repeat with the remaining dough. Pile any dough trimmings together (do not knead) and gently re-roll. Cut out more rounds. Bake for 20–25 minutes, or until golden. Allow to cool on a wire rack.

water crackers

☀ ☀

Preparation time: **15 minutes**
Cooking time: **10 minutes per batch**
Makes **50**

250 g (9 oz/2 cups) self-raising flour
50 g (1¾ oz) unsalted butter, chilled
    and cubed

1 Preheat the oven to 220°C (425°F/ Gas 7). Line two baking trays with baking paper.
2 Sift the flour and ½ teaspoon salt into a bowl, then rub in the butter with your fingertips. Knead in enough water (you may need about 185 ml/6 fl oz/¾ cup) to make a fairly stiff dough. Lightly knead the dough for 5 minutes.
3 On a large floured board, roll the dough out until it is as thin as a wafer. Use a 6.5–7 cm (2½–2¾ inch) cutter to cut out rounds (you can cut a small hole in the centre of each for decoration) and bake in batches for 8–10 minutes each batch, or until the biscuits bubble and brown. Transfer to a wire rack to cool completely.

two-seed crackers

crispbread

✻ ✻

Preparation time: 25 minutes
  + 30 minutes proving time
Cooking time: 30 minutes
Makes 24

250 ml (9 fl oz/1 cup) lukewarm milk
1 tablespoon dried yeast
¼ teaspoon dried fennel seeds
250 g (9 oz) stoneground flour
200 g (7 oz) coarse rye meal

1 Line two baking trays with baking paper. Put the milk in a bowl, add the yeast and stir until dissolved. Leave in a warm place for 10 minutes, or until bubbles appear on the surface. The mixture should be frothy and slightly increased in volume. If your yeast doesn't foam, it is dead, and you will have to discard it and start again.
2 Mix the fennel, flour, rye meal and 1 teaspoon salt in a bowl. Make a well in the centre and add the yeast mixture. Gather together and knead on a floured surface for 5 minutes, adding a little water if necessary. Divide the dough into four portions.
3 Divide each portion into six pieces and shape each into a ball. Cover and leave in a warm, draught-free place for 30 minutes, or until doubled in size.
4 Preheat the oven to 180°C (350°F/ Gas 4). Roll out eight balls of dough to make circles about 13 cm (5 inches) in diameter. Cut out the centre of each circle with a round 2 cm (¾ inch) cutter. Discard the centres, then prick each crispbread with a fork and put on the baking trays. Bake the crispbread for 10 minutes, or until firm, dry and slightly coloured. Cool on the trays. Repeat with the remaining balls of dough. When cooled, store in an airtight container.

Add the yeast mixture to the dry ingredients, then gather the mixture together.

Shape small portions of the mixture into balls and leave in a warm place until doubled in size.

slices

Crunchy, gooey, sticky, fruity, spongy, fudgy, chewy, creamy, nutty, chocolatey — whatever your culinary craving, a slice can satisfy it simply and completely. Loved by children and adults alike, slices grow up with you, becoming more sophisticated as your tastes develop (or not, as the case may be!). The beauty of slices is that they can be as simple or as richly exotic as you like. Easily transportable, they can accompany you to school, to work, to a picnic, or even as far as the sitting room with a cup of coffee and a good book. Cut a piece as little or as large as you like and indulge yourself.

strawberries

These delicious red vine fruits are related to the rose, which accounts for their beautiful aroma and flavour. The strawberry is unusual in that the seeds or small pips are on the outside of the fruit, rather than in the centre as with other fruits. When at the height of the season, in summer, they are often served just as they are or sweetened and eaten with cream or ice cream. Strawberries make beautiful tart and cake fillings and, of course, jam. Sweetened and puréed, they make a simple sauce called a coulis.

coconut jam slice

Preparation time: 30 minutes
Cooking time: 45 minutes
Makes 20 pieces

125 g (4½ oz/1 cup) plain (all-purpose) flour
60 g (2¼ oz/½ cup) self-raising flour
150 g (5½ oz) unsalted butter, chilled and cubed
60 g (2¼ oz/½ cup) icing (confectioners') sugar
1 egg yolk
160 g (5¾ oz/½ cup) strawberry jam
125 g (4½ oz) caster (superfine) sugar
3 eggs
270 g (9½ oz/3 cups) desiccated coconut

1 Preheat the oven to 180°C (350°F/Gas 4). Lightly grease a shallow 23 cm (9 inch) square tin and line with baking paper, extending over two opposite sides.
2 Put the flours, butter and icing sugar in a food processor and process in short bursts until the mixture is fine and crumbly. Add the egg yolk and process until the mixture just comes together. Alternatively, put the flour and icing sugar in a bowl and rub in the butter with your fingertips until the mixture is fine and crumbly. Mix in the egg yolk and then gather together. Press the dough into the tin and refrigerate for 10 minutes. Bake for 15 minutes, or until golden brown. Allow to cool, then spread the jam evenly over the pastry.
3 Beat the caster sugar and eggs together in a small bowl until creamy, then stir in the coconut. Spread the mixture over the jam, gently pressing down with the back of a spoon. Bake for 25–30 minutes, or until lightly golden. Leave to cool in the tin, then lift the slice out, using the paper as handles. Cut the slice into pieces. Store in an airtight container for up to 4 days.

mixed spice

Also known as pumpkin pie spice, this is a blend of freshly ground spices, usually including cloves, nutmeg, cinnamon and allspice, and sometimes ginger. It adds a lightly spiced flavour to puddings, spice cakes, biscuits and fruit cakes. It is often added when apples are being cooked as they seem to complement each other very well. As with all spices, mixed spice should be bought in small amounts and kept in an airtight container in a dark place. Spices can be frozen for up to six months.

muesli slice

Preparation time: 20 minutes
 + 2 hours chilling time
Cooking time: 50 minutes
Makes 18 pieces

250 g (9 oz) unsalted butter, cubed
230 g (8 oz/1 cup) caster (superfine) sugar
2 tablespoons honey
250 g (9 oz/2½ cups) rolled (porridge) oats
65 g (2½ oz/¾ cup) desiccated coconut
30 g (1 oz/1 cup) cornflakes, lightly crushed
45 g (1¾ oz/½ cup) flaked almonds
1 teaspoon mixed (pumpkin pie) spice
45 g (1¾ oz) finely chopped dried apricots
185 g (6½ oz/1 cup) dried mixed fruit

1 Preheat the oven to 160°C (315°F/ Gas 2–3). Lightly grease a shallow tin measuring 20 x 30 cm (8 x 12 inches) and line with baking paper, extending over the two long sides.
2 Put the butter, sugar and honey in a small saucepan and stir over low heat for 5 minutes, or until the butter has melted and the sugar has dissolved.
3 Mix the remaining ingredients together in a bowl and make a well in the centre. Pour in the butter mixture, stir well, then press into the tin. Bake for 45 minutes, or until golden. Cool completely in the tin, then refrigerate for 2 hours, to firm.
4 Lift the slice from the tin, using the paper as handles, before cutting into pieces. This slice will keep for up to 3 days stored in an airtight container.

vanilla slice

25 cm (10 inch) square about 3 mm (⅛ inch) thick and place each on a tray. Prick all over with a fork and bake for 8 minutes, or until golden. Trim each sheet to a 23 cm (9 inch) square. Place one sheet, top side down, in the cake tin.

2 Combine the sugar, cornflour and custard powder in a saucepan. Gradually add the cream and stir until smooth. Place over medium heat and stir constantly for 2 minutes, or until the mixture boils and thickens. Add the butter and vanilla and stir until smooth. Remove from the heat and whisk in the egg yolks until combined. Spread the custard over the pastry in the tin and cover with the remaining pastry, top side down. Allow to cool.

3 To make the icing (frosting), combine the icing sugar, passionfruit pulp and melted butter in a small bowl and stir together until smooth.

4 Lift the slice out, using the foil as handles, spread the icing over the top and leave it to set before carefully cutting into squares with a serrated knife.

apple custard streusel slice

✹ ✹

Preparation time: **40 minutes**
Cooking time: **1 hour 15 minutes**
Makes **16 pieces**

155 g (5½ oz/1¼ cups) plain (all-purpose) flour
1 tablespoon caster (superfine) sugar
80 g (2¾ oz) unsalted butter, melted and cooled
1 egg yolk

APPLE CUSTARD TOPPING
3 green apples
20 g (¾ oz) unsalted butter
80 g (2¾ oz/⅓ cup) caster (superfine) sugar
2 eggs
185 ml (6 fl oz/¾ cup) pouring (whipping) cream
1 teaspoon natural vanilla extract

vanilla slice

✹ ✹

Preparation time: **40 minutes**
Cooking time: **15 minutes**
Makes **9 pieces**

500 g (1 lb 2 oz) block puff pastry, thawed
230 g (8 oz/1 cup) caster (superfine) sugar
90 g (3¼ oz/¾ cup) cornflour (cornstarch)
60 g (2¼ oz/½ cup) custard powder or instant vanilla pudding mix
1 litre (35 fl oz/4 cups) pouring (whipping) cream

60 g (2¼ oz) unsalted butter, cubed
2 teaspoons natural vanilla extract
3 egg yolks

PASSIONFRUIT ICING
185 g (6½ oz/1½ cups) icing (confectioners') sugar
60 g (2¼ oz) passionfruit pulp
15 g (½ oz) unsalted butter, melted

1 Preheat the oven to 210°C (415°F/Gas 6–7). Grease two baking trays with oil. Line the base and sides of a shallow 23 cm (9 inch) square cake tin with foil, extending over two opposite sides. Divide the pastry in half, roll each piece to a

CRUMBLE TOPPING

60 g (2¼ oz/½ cup) plain (all-purpose) flour
2 tablespoons dark brown sugar
40 g (1½ oz/⅓ cup) finely chopped walnuts
60 g (2¼ oz) unsalted butter, chilled and
    cubed

1 Lightly grease a shallow 18 x 28 cm
(7 x 11¼ inch) tin and line with baking
paper, extending over the two long sides.
2 Sift the flour and caster sugar into a
bowl. Add the butter and egg yolk, along
with 2–3 tablespoons water and mix to
form a ball. Roll out the dough between
two sheets of baking paper and fit in the
base of the tin. Refrigerate for 20 minutes.
Preheat the oven to 190°C (375°F/Gas 5).
3 Line the pastry with baking paper,
fill with baking beads or uncooked rice
and bake for 15 minutes. Remove the
paper and rice, reduce the oven to 180°C
(350°F/Gas 4) and bake the pastry for
5 minutes, or until golden. Allow to cool.
4 To make the topping, peel, core and
chop the apples and put in a saucepan
with the butter, half the caster sugar and
2 tablespoons water. Cover and cook
over low heat for 15 minutes, or until
soft. Uncover and simmer for a further
5 minutes to reduce the liquid. Use a
wooden spoon to break down the apples
until they are smooth. Allow to cool.
5 Whisk together the eggs, cream,
remaining sugar and vanilla. Spread
the cooled apple over the pastry in the
tin, then carefully pour over the cream
mixture. Bake for 20 minutes, or until
the custard has half set.
6 To make the crumble, mix the flour,
brown sugar and walnuts and rub in
the butter until the mixture is crumbly.
Sprinkle over the custard and bake for
15 minutes. Cool in the tin before slicing
evenly into 16 pieces. This slice will keep
in the fridge for up to a week.

apple custard streusel slice

streusel

This is an American term
for a crumble topping that
usually consists of flour or
breadcrumbs with sugar and
spices, which is sprinkled over
baked cakes and desserts.
The butter is rubbed in until it
forms a rough crumble. Often
chopped nuts or rolled oats
are added for extra flavour and
texture. The adaptation came
from a European yeast cake,
called a Streusel cake, which
has a spiced crumble mix
baked onto it.

clockwise from top: jaffa triple-choc brownies, blondies and chocolate brownies

jaffa triple-choc brownies

Preparation time: 20 minutes
Cooking time: 45 minutes
Makes 25 pieces

125 g (4½ oz) unsalted butter, cubed
350 g (12 oz) dark chocolate, roughly
  chopped
185 g (6½ oz/1 cup) soft brown sugar
3 eggs
2 teaspoons finely grated orange zest
125 g (4½ oz/1 cup) plain (all-purpose)
  flour
30 g (1 oz/¼ cup) unsweetened cocoa
  powder
100 g (3½ oz) milk chocolate chips
100 g (3½ oz) white chocolate chips

1 Preheat the oven to 180°C (350°F/
Gas 4). Lightly grease a shallow 23 cm
(9 inch) square tin and line with baking
paper, extending over two opposite sides.
2 Place the butter and 250 g (9 oz) of
the dark chocolate in a heatproof bowl.
Half-fill a saucepan with water, bring to
the boil, then remove from the heat.
Sit the bowl over the saucepan, making
sure the base of the bowl does not touch
the water. Stir occasionally until the
butter and chocolate have melted.
Set aside to cool.
3 Beat the sugar, eggs and orange zest
in a bowl until thick and fluffy. Fold in
the chocolate mixture.
4 Sift the flour and cocoa into a bowl,
then stir into the chocolate mixture. Stir
in the remaining dark chocolate and all
the chocolate chips. Spread into the tin
and bake for 40 minutes, or until just
cooked. Allow to cool in the tin before
lifting out, using the paper as handles,
and cutting into squares. The slice can
be drizzled with melted dark chocolate
before cutting, if desired.

blondies

Preparation time: 20 minutes
Cooking time: 45 minutes
Makes 25 pieces

100 g (3½ oz) unsalted butter, cubed
100 g (3½ oz) white chocolate, chopped
125 g (4½ oz/½ cup) caster (superfine)
  sugar
2 eggs, lightly beaten
1 teaspoon natural vanilla extract
125 g (4½ oz/1 cup) self-raising flour
80 g (2¾ oz/½ cup) macadamia nuts,
  roughly chopped

1 Preheat the oven to 180°C (350°F/
Gas 4). Lightly grease a 20 cm (8 inch)
square tin and line with baking paper,
extending over two opposite sides.
2 Place the butter and chocolate in a
heatproof bowl. Half-fill a saucepan with
water and bring to the boil. Remove
from the heat. Place the bowl over the
saucepan, making sure the base of the
bowl does not touch the water. Stir
occasionally until the butter and chocolate
have melted and are smooth.
3 Add the sugar and gradually stir in the
eggs. Add the vanilla, fold in the flour and
macadamia nuts, then pour into the tin.
Bake for 35–40 minutes. If the top starts
to brown too quickly, cover lightly with
a sheet of foil. When cooked, cool in the
tin before lifting out, using the paper as
handles, and cutting into squares. Can be
drizzled with melted white chocolate.

chocolate brownies

Preparation time: 20 minutes
  + 2 hours chilling time
Cooking time: 50 minutes
Makes 24 pieces

40 g (1½ oz/⅓ cup) plain (all-purpose) flour
60 g (2¼ oz/½ cup) unsweetened cocoa
  powder
440 g (15½ oz/2 cups) sugar
120 g (4¼ oz/1 cup) chopped pecans or
  walnuts
250 g (9 oz) good-quality dark chocolate,
  chopped into small pieces
250 g (9 oz) unsalted butter, melted
2 teaspoons natural vanilla extract
4 eggs, lightly beaten

1 Preheat the oven to 180°C (350°F/
Gas 4). Grease a 20 x 30 cm (8 x 12 inch)
cake tin and line with baking paper,
extending over the two long sides.
2 Sift the flour and cocoa into a bowl and
add the sugar, nuts and chocolate. Mix
together and make a well in the centre.
3 Pour the butter into the dry ingredients
with the vanilla and egg and mix well.
Pour into the tin, smooth the surface and
bake for 50 minutes (the mixture will still
be a bit soft inside). Refrigerate for at
least 2 hours before lifting out, using the
paper as handles, and cutting into pieces.

macadamia nuts

These are also called
Queensland nuts, as they are
native to north-east Australia,
although the Hawaiians
cultivated the seeds and have
become large producers of
the nuts. The creamy nut is
enclosed in an extremely
hard shell, which needs to
be cracked with a hammer or
special-purpose clamp. The nut
can be used raw or roasted and
is usually chopped. It is used in
the baking of brownies, cakes
and biscuits. Buy unsalted
macadamia nuts for cooking.

berries

There are many berries that are wonderful to eat ripe off the vine but have multiple uses in baking. The most common varieties, depending on the region and climate, are sold from spring to early autumn. They include blackberries, raspberries, strawberries, blueberries, mulberries, cranberries, currants and gooseberries. Berries are often used in baking and are made into desserts such as pies, puddings and tarts, as well as being used to flavour slices, cakes, muffins and friands.

berry almond slice

✳ ✳

Preparation time: 25 minutes
Cooking time: 1 hour 15 minutes
Makes 15 pieces

1 sheet frozen puff pastry, thawed
150 g (5½ oz) unsalted butter, softened
170 g (5¾ oz/¾ cup) caster (superfine) sugar
3 eggs, beaten
2 tablespoons finely grated lemon zest
125 g (4½ oz/⅔ cup) ground almonds
2 tablespoons plain (all-purpose) flour
150 g (5½ oz) raspberries
150 g (5½ oz) blackberries
icing (confectioners') sugar, to dust

1 Preheat the oven to 200°C (400°F/ Gas 6). Lightly grease a shallow 23 cm (9 inch) square tin and line with baking paper, extending over two opposite sides.
2 Put the pastry on a baking tray lined with baking paper. Prick the pastry all over with a fork and bake for 15 minutes, or until golden. Ease into the tin, trimming the edges if necessary. Reduce the oven to 180°C (350°F/Gas 4).
3 Cream the butter and sugar in a small bowl using electric beaters until light and creamy. Gradually add the egg, beating thoroughly after each addition, then beat in the lemon zest. Fold in the almonds and flour, then spread the mixture over the pastry in the tin.
4 Scatter the fruit on top and bake for 1 hour, or until lightly golden. Cool in the tin, then lift out, using the paper as handles. Cut into pieces and dust with icing sugar to serve.

crunchy peanut meringue slice

❋

Preparation time: 20 minutes
Cooking time: 40 minutes
Makes 15 pieces

125 g (4½ oz/1 cup) plain (all-purpose) flour
2 teaspoons icing (confectioners') sugar
80 g (2¾ oz) unsalted butter, chilled and cubed
1 tablespoon chilled water
105 g (3½ oz/⅓ cup) apricot jam

NUT MERINGUE
240 g (8¾ oz/1½ cups) peanuts, roughly chopped
170 g (5¾ oz/¾ cup) caster (superfine) sugar
30 g (1 oz/⅓ cup) desiccated coconut
1 egg white

1 Preheat the oven to 180°C (350°F/Gas 4). Lightly grease a shallow 18 x 28 cm (7 x 11¼ inch) tin and line with baking paper, extending over the two long sides.
2 Put the flour, icing sugar and butter in a food processor and process in short bursts until fine and crumbly. Add the chilled water and process until the mixture just comes together. Turn out onto a floured surface, gather into a smooth ball, then press out evenly, using floured hands or the base of a floured glass, to cover the base of the tin. Prick well and bake for 15 minutes, or until golden. Cool for 10 minutes before spreading the jam evenly over the surface.
3 To make the nut meringue, put all the ingredients in a large saucepan and stir with a wooden spoon over low heat until just lukewarm. Spread over the slice and bake for 20 minutes, or until golden and crisp. When cool, lift out, using the paper as handles, and cut into pieces.

peanuts

Peanuts are not nuts at all, but a legume or bean that grows underground. They are highly nutritious and are eaten raw or roasted and are also ground into butter and oil. The peanut can be used in all these forms in baking, except the oil, which is too strong in flavour and is better used for frying savoury foods. For baking, use unsalted peanuts. If they are not available, you can wash the salt off the whole nuts, then dry thoroughly before using.

raspberries

Like the strawberry, the raspberry is a member of the rose family, hence the beautiful aroma and flavour. Originally from Europe, they are now grown worldwide in cooler climates. They have a short season, only lasting from summer to early autumn.

They are highly perishable and will only last a few days, so take care when buying them. Check both the top and bottom of the punnet for signs of mould or juices leaching out. Raspberries should be refrigerated if not being used immediately and should never be washed.

princess fingers

Preparation time: 35 minutes
Cooking time: 35 minutes
Makes 24

125 g (4½ oz) unsalted butter, softened
80 g (2¾ oz/⅓ cup) caster (superfine) sugar
1 teaspoon natural vanilla extract
2 egg yolks
250 g (9 oz/2 cups) plain (all-purpose) flour
1 teaspoon baking powder
1 tablespoon milk
160 g (5¾ oz/½ cup) raspberry jam
40 g (1½ oz/⅓ cup) chopped walnuts
80 g (2¾ oz/⅓ cup) chopped red glacé cherries
2 egg whites
1 tablespoon finely grated orange zest
115 g (4 oz/½ cup) caster (superfine) sugar, extra
45 g (1¾ oz/½ cup) desiccated coconut
30 g (1 oz/1 cup) puffed rice cereal

1 Preheat the oven to 180°C (350°F/ Gas 4). Lightly grease a shallow 20 x 30 cm (8 x 12 inch) tin and line with baking paper, extending over the two long sides. Cream the butter, sugar and vanilla using electric beaters until light and creamy. Add the egg yolks, one at a time, beating thoroughly after each addition.
2 Sift the flour and baking powder into a bowl, then fold into the creamed mixture with a metal spoon. Fold in the milk, then press evenly and firmly into the tin. Spread the jam over the top and sprinkle with the chopped walnuts and cherries.
3 Whisk the egg whites in a clean, dry, small bowl until stiff peaks form. Fold in the orange zest and extra sugar with a metal spoon, then fold in the coconut and puffed rice cereal. Spread over the slice with a metal spatula.
4 Bake for 30–35 minutes, or until firm and golden brown. Cool the slice in the tin. Lift out the slice, using the paper as handles, and cut into fingers. Store in an airtight container for up to 4 days.

pecan coffee slice

❋ ❋

Preparation time: **40 minutes**
Cooking time: **30 minutes**
Makes **20**

125 g (4½ oz/1¼ cups) pecans
175 g (6 oz) blanched almonds
2 tablespoons plain (all-purpose) flour
165 g (5¾ oz/¾ cup) sugar
7 egg whites
20 chocolate-coated coffee beans,
    to decorate

COFFEE CREAM
200 g (7 oz) unsalted butter, cubed and
    softened
150 g (5½ oz) dark chocolate, melted and
    cooled
3–4 teaspoons instant coffee granules

1 Preheat the oven to 180°C (350°F/ Gas 4). Lightly grease a shallow 23 cm (9 inch) square tin and line with baking paper, extending over two opposite sides.
2 Roast the pecans and almonds on a baking tray for 5–10 minutes, or until golden. Cool slightly, then chop in a food processor until finely ground. Transfer to a bowl, add the flour and 110 g (3¾ oz/ ½ cup) of the sugar and mix well. Whisk the egg whites in a clean, dry large bowl until soft peaks form. Gradually add the remaining sugar, whisking until the mixture is thick and glossy and the sugar has dissolved. Fold the nut mixture into the egg mixture, a third at a time, using a metal spoon. Spoon into the tin and smooth the surface. Bake for 20 minutes, or until springy when touched. Leave in the tin for 5 minutes, then lift out, using the paper as handles, and transfer to a wire rack to cool completely.

3 To make the coffee cream, beat the butter in a bowl using electric beaters until light and creamy. Gradually pour in the melted chocolate and beat well. Mix the coffee granules with 2 teaspoons water until dissolved, then add to the chocolate mixture and mix well. Refrigerate for 5–10 minutes to thicken slightly.
4 Cut the slice in half horizontally with a sharp, serrated knife. Carefully remove the top layer and spread half the coffee cream over the base. Replace the top and spread evenly with the remaining cream. Run a palette knife backwards and forwards across the top to create a lined pattern, or use an icing (frosting) comb to create swirls. Place the coffee beans at even intervals on the top. Refrigerate until firm. Trim the edges and cut into squares or fingers. Serve at room temperature or chilled. The slice can be refrigerated in an airtight container for up to 5 days.

prunes

These are the whole dried fruit from certain varieties of plum trees. After being dehydrated, they take on a dark wrinkled appearance and have a very sweet flavour. They are suitable to eat on their own or to be used in cakes, slices and puddings. Sold in sealed packets or tins, they should be refrigerated in hot weather. Although mostly used as a sweet addition, they are also combined with meats such as rabbit, pork and game. They have been used for centuries by Arab countries in both sweet and savoury dishes.

fruit mince slice

1   Preheat the oven to 190°C (375°F/ Gas 5). Lightly grease a shallow 18 x 28 cm (7 x 11¼ inch) tin and line the base with baking paper, extending over the two long sides. Sift the flour and icing sugar into a large bowl. Rub in the butter with your fingertips until the mixture resembles fine breadcrumbs. Make a well in the centre and add the egg. Mix with a flat-bladed knife, using a cutting action, until the mixture comes together. Turn onto a lightly floured surface and press together until smooth.

2   Divide the dough in half and press one portion into the tin. Bake for 10 minutes, then leave to cool. Roll the remaining pastry out on a piece of baking paper and refrigerate for 15 minutes.

3   Spread the fruit mince evenly over the baked pastry, topping with the prunes and ginger. Cut the chilled pastry into thin strips using a sharp knife or fluted pastry wheel. Arrange on top of the fruit in a diagonal lattice pattern. Brush with the beaten egg. Bake for 30 minutes, or until golden. Cool in the tin, then lift out, using the paper as handles, and cut into squares or fingers. Serve dusted with icing sugar. The slice can be kept for up to 4 days in an airtight container in a cool place, or in the refrigerator.

plum and almond slice

☀

Preparation time: 30 minutes
Cooking time: 1 hour 10 minutes
Makes 9 pieces

165 g (5¾ oz) unsalted butter, softened
145 g (5½ oz/⅔ cup) caster (superfine)
   sugar
2 eggs
60 g (2¼ oz/½ cup) plain (all-purpose) flour
40 g (1½ oz/⅓ cup) cornflour (cornstarch)
2 tablespoons rice flour
1½ tablespoons thinly sliced glacé ginger
825 g (1 lb 13 oz) tin plums in syrup,
   drained, seeded and halved
90 g (3¼ oz/1 cup) flaked almonds
1 tablespoon honey, warmed

fruit mince slice

☀

Preparation time: 30 minutes
   + cooling time
Cooking time: 40 minutes
Makes 15 pieces

250 g (9 oz/2 cups) plain (all-purpose)
   flour
60 g (2¼ oz/½ cup) icing (confectioners')
   sugar, plus extra, to dust
185 g (6½ oz) unsalted butter, chilled
   and cubed
1 egg
410 g (14½ oz) fruit mince
   (mincemeat)
150 g (5½ oz) pitted prunes, chopped
100 g (3½ oz) glacé ginger, chopped
1 egg, lightly beaten

honey

Honey has the longest history of an ingredient used to sweeten food, dating back hundreds of years before sugar came on the scene. It has a long tradition in baking. The ancient Greeks and Romans made breads and honey spice cakes. Many ancient recipes are still made today, such as the German lebkuchen and English gingerbread. There are also nougats, baklava and halva, all based on honey and almonds. There are many flavours of honey depending on the type of nectar taken by the bees from the flowers.

1   Preheat the oven to 180°C (350°F/ Gas 4). Lightly grease a 20 cm (8 inch) square tin and line with baking paper, extending over the top edge of the tin on all sides. Cream the butter and sugar in a small bowl using electric beaters until light and creamy. Add the eggs one at a time, beating well after each addition. Sift the flours over the mixture and fold into the mixture along with the ginger. Spread into the tin. Arrange the plum halves on top, lightly pressing them into the slice mixture. Scatter with the flaked almonds, pressing in gently, then drizzle with the honey.

2   Bake for 1 hour 10 minutes, or until firm and golden. Cover with foil if the slice starts to brown too much. Cool in the tin, then lift out, using the paper as handles, before cutting into pieces. The slice can be kept for up to 4 or 5 days in an airtight container in the refrigerator.

sweet pies & pastries

To the uncertain cook, pastry can be a scary thing — so many of us find ourselves automatically reaching for the frozen ready-made stuff or avoiding recipes involving pastry altogether. By doing this we really miss out — the thin, flimsy little pies and pastries sold in supermarket freezers cannot compare to the aroma and flavour of a homemade masterpiece. In the following pages, we take the mystery out of pastry and talk you through the potential pitfalls so you can proceed with confidence. You'll soon find making pastry as easy as … well … pie!

shortcrust pastry

For successful shortcrust pastry, work the dough
quickly and lightly on a cool surface, preferably not
on a hot day (or in a cool room at least).

If you don't have a marble slab, rest a tray of iced water on the
work surface for a while before you start. Use real unsalted
butter for pastry, not margarine or softened butter blends.

Unsweetened pastry works well with sweet fillings, giving
a good contrast of flavours. To make a sweet pastry, simply add
2 tablespoons caster (superfine) sugar to the flour. Some recipes
contain egg yolks to enrich the pastry and give good colour.

shortcrust pastry

To make enough to line a 23 cm (9 inch) tin, use 250 g (9 oz/
2 cups) plain (all-purpose) flour, 150 g (5½ oz) chilled,
chopped unsalted butter and 2–4 tablespoons chilled water.
This makes about 500 g (1 lb 2 oz) shortcrust (pie) pastry.

1 Sift the flour into a large bowl. Use your fingertips to rub in
the butter until the mixture resembles fine breadcrumbs.

2 Make a well in the centre, then add 2 tablespoons chilled
water and mix using a flat-bladed knife in a cutting action,
rotating the bowl with your free hand. The mixture will come
together in small beads. To test if you need more water, pinch
a little bit of dough. If it doesn't hold together, add a little more
water. If the pastry is too dry, it will fall apart when you roll it,
and if too wet it will be sticky and shrink when baked.

3 Gently gather the dough together with your hand and lift it
out onto a sheet of baking paper or a floured work surface.

4 Press, don't knead, the dough together into a ball. Handle
gently, keeping your actions light and to a minimum.

5 Press the dough into a flat disc, wrap in plastic wrap and
refrigerate for 20 minutes. Roll out between two sheets of
baking paper or plastic wrap, or on a lightly floured surface.
Always roll from the centre outwards, rotating the dough, rather
than backwards and forwards.

6 If using baking paper, remove the top sheet, carefully invert
the pastry over the tin (make sure you centre the pastry, as it
can't be moved once in place), and then peel away the paper. If
you rolled out on a lightly floured surface, roll the pastry back
over the rolling pin so it is hanging, and ease it into the tin.

7 Once the pastry is in the tin, quickly lift up the sides so they
don't break over the edges of the tin. Use a small ball of excess
dough to help ease and press the pastry into the side of the tin.
If using a tart tin, roll the rolling pin over the top of the tin to
cut off any excess pastry. If you are using a glass or ceramic pie
dish, use a small sharp knife to cut away the excess pastry.

8 Let the pastry sit a little above the side of the tin, to allow
for shrinkage. If you rolled off the excess with a rolling pin and
it has 'bunched' down the side, gently press the side with your
thumbs to flatten and lift it a little. Refrigerate for 15 minutes to
relax the pastry and minimise shrinkage. Preheat the oven.

blind baking

If the pastry is to have a moist filling, it will probably require
partial blind baking to prevent it becoming soggy. If it is
not cooked again after filling, it will need to be fully blind
baked. This means baking the pastry without the filling, but
with weight on it to prevent it rising. Line it with crumpled
greaseproof or baking paper. Pour in baking beads, dried beans
or uncooked rice (these can be used again). Bake for the given
time, then lift out the filled paper. Return the pastry to the
oven to dry it and colour a little. It should look dry with no
greasy patches. Small pastry shells can be pricked with a fork
to prevent them rising or bubbling, but only do this if specified.
Cool the pastry completely before filling. Cooked filling should
also be cooled before adding, to prevent soggy pastry.

puff pastry

This is made by rolling dough with butter and folding to create layers. When cooked, the butter melts and the dough produces steam, which forces the layers apart.

For perfect pastry that rises evenly, the edges must be cut cleanly with a sharp knife or cutter, not torn. Egg glazes give a shine but must be applied carefully, as any drips may glue the layers together and stop them rising evenly. The pastry should be chilled for at least 30 minutes before baking, to relax it.

Always bake puff pastry at a very high temperature — it should rise evenly so, if your oven has areas of uneven heat, turn the pastry around when it has set. If you have an oven with a bottom element, cook your pastry on the bottom shelf. When it is cooked, the top and base should be browned and crisp, and the layers should be visible. Puff pastry is not always perfect — it may fall over or not rise to quite the heights you'd imagined — but as long as it is well cooked, and you don't burn it, it will be absolutely delicious.

making puff pastry

We've given a range of butter quantity. If you've never made puff pastry before, you'll find it easier to use the lower amount. This recipe makes about 500 g (1 lb 2 oz) pastry. You will need 200–250 g (7–9 oz) unsalted butter, 250 g (9 oz/2 cups) plain (all-purpose) flour, ½ teaspoon salt and 170 ml (5½ fl oz/⅔ cup) chilled water.

1 Melt 30 g (1 oz) of the butter in a saucepan. Sift the flour and salt onto a work surface and make a well in the centre. Add the melted butter and water to the centre and blend with your fingertips, gradually drawing in the flour. You should end up with a crumb mixture — if it seems a little dry, add extra drops of water before bringing it all together to form a dough.

2 Cut the dough with a pastry scraper, using a downward cutting action, then turn the dough and repeat in the opposite direction. The dough should now come together to form a soft ball. Score a cross in the top to prevent shrinkage, wrap in plastic wrap and refrigerate for 15–20 minutes.

3 Soften the remaining butter by pounding it between two sheets of baking paper with a rolling pin. Then, still between the sheets of baking paper, roll it into a 10 cm (4 inch) square. The butter must be the same consistency as the dough or they will not roll out the same amount and the layers will not be even. If the butter is too soft, it will squeeze out of the sides. Too hard and it will break through the dough and disturb the layers.

4 Put the pastry on a well-floured surface. Roll it out to form a cross, leaving the centre slightly thicker than the arms. Place the butter in the centre and fold over each 'arm' to make a parcel. Turn the dough so it looks like a book with the hinge side to the left. Tap and roll out the dough to 15 x 45 cm (6 x 17¾ inches). Make it neat and square off the corners, or each time you fold the edges will get messier and the layers won't be even.

5 Fold the dough like a letter, the top third down and bottom third up, to form a square, brushing off any excess flour between the layers. Turn the dough 90 degrees to bring the hinge side to your left and press the seam sides down with the rolling pin to seal them. Re-roll and fold as before to complete two turns and mark the dough by gently pressing into the corner with your fingertip for each turn to remind you where you're up to. Wrap the dough in plastic wrap and chill again for at least 30 minutes.

6 Re-roll and fold twice more and then chill, and then again to complete six turns. If it is a very hot day, you may need to chill for 30 minutes between each turn, rather than doing a double turn as described above. The pastry should now be an even yellow and is ready to use — if it looks a little streaky, roll and fold once more. The aim is to ensure that the butter is evenly distributed throughout. Refrigerate until required.

choux pastry

This pastry is most often used to make profiteroles, éclairs, gougères and the towering French wedding cake called 'croquembouche'.

making choux pastry

Choux pastry is easy to make, but the process is different from pastries such as shortcrust, which have the butter rubbed into the flour. Instead, you melt the butter in the water, then beat in the flour and cook until it is no longer sticky. The mixture is cooled slightly and eggs are gradually beaten in. The dough should be stiff enough to shape.

Before you begin, you should read the recipe and assemble all the necessary ingredients, weighing and measuring carefully. Preheat the oven to 210°C (415°F/Gas 6–7). Sift 185 g (6½ oz/ 1½ cups) plain (all-purpose) flour and ¼ teaspoon salt onto a sheet of baking paper. Place 100 g (3½ oz) chopped unsalted butter in a large heavy-based saucepan with 375 ml (13 fl oz/ 1½ cups) water and stir over medium heat. Once the butter has melted, increase the heat to bring the water just to the boil. Remove from the heat immediately: prolonged boiling will evaporate enough water to alter the proportions of the ingredients. Add the flour and salt all at once and quickly beat into the liquid using hand-held beaters or a wooden spoon. Return to the heat and continue beating until the mixture forms a ball and leaves the side of the saucepan. Transfer to a large bowl and cool slightly.

Lightly beat 6 eggs in a bowl, then gradually add to the butter mixture, about 3 teaspoons at a time. Beat well after each addition. When all the egg has been added the mixture should be thick and glossy — a wooden spoon should stand up in it. If the mixture is too runny, the egg has been added too quickly. To correct this, beat for several more minutes, or until thickened. The pastry is now ready to use and may be piped, spooned or shaped according to the recipe you are following. The pastry is cooked when it is golden and sounds hollow when tapped on the base. Turn off the oven and leave inside to dry out.

profiteroles or puffs

Lightly sprinkle three baking trays with water. Spoon heaped teaspoons of mixture onto the trays, leaving plenty of room between each for spreading. Bake for 20–30 minutes or until golden. Remove from the oven and make a small hole in the base of each puff to assist drying. Return them to the oven for 5 minutes to dry out. Cool on a wire rack. Cooked puffs can be frozen for up to 2 months. Refresh thawed puffs in a 180°C (350°F/Gas 4) oven for 5 minutes before using.

making gougères

By adding grated cheese, such as emmenthal or gruyère, to choux pastry dough, you can make gougères. Substitute half the water with the same quantity of milk and follow the procedure for choux pastry. When all the eggs are incorporated, add 65 g (2¼ oz/½ cup) grated cheese. Using a piping (icing) bag fitted with a plain nozzle, pipe 6 cm (2½ inch) rounds (or smaller for parties) onto a baking tray lined with baking paper. Lightly beat an egg yolk and lightly brush over the gougères. Scatter with a little more grated cheese, using about 35 g (1¼ oz/¼ cup). Bake as for regular choux pastry. This quantity will make about 12 large or 24 small gougères.

helpful tips

Sprinkle the baking tray with water before placing the dough on it as this creates steam in the oven, helping the shapes rise. Prepare and cook the puffs in batches, if necessary.

what went wrong: shortcrust (pie) pastry

perfect The pastry is even and lightly golden. The side has shrunk slightly away from the tin. The base is crisp and dry.

overcooked The cooking time was too long, or the oven too hot. The tin may have been too high or too low in the oven.

stuck to base The pastry may have been too wet, or wasn't chilled. The tin may have been ungreased or unclean.

pastry shrunken The pastry was overworked or not chilled. The weights may have been pressed too firmly against the pastry's side or removed too early.

undercooked The oven was too low, or the cooking time wasn't long enough. The pastry may have been rolled out too thickly. The tin should be put on a preheated tray.

what went wrong: puff pastry

perfect The pastry is well and evenly risen with layers visible. The pastry is deep golden brown, light and flaky.

unevenly risen when cooked The edges weren't trimmed. The glaze dripped down the side, gluing the layers together.

overcooked The oven was too hot, the cooking time too long, or the pastry may have been placed too high in the oven.

what went wrong: filo pastry

perfect The filo pastry is dry, crisp, flaky and puffed and golden brown.

undercooked The pastry is pale and soggy. Many things can cause this. The filling may be heavy and too moist or there may be too many layers of filo. The oven may have been too low or the cooking time too short. Excessive amounts of butter or oil may have been brushed on the layers of filo.

overcooked The pastry is unevenly coloured and too dark in some areas. The oven may have been too high or the layers unevenly brushed with butter or oil. The tin may have been too high in the oven.

what went wrong: choux pastry

perfect The choux pastry is crisp and puffy, hollow inside and has a deep golden colour. To assist in drying and to release steam, make a small hole in the base of each puff with a skewer.

poorly risen The pastry is not puffed and dense inside. Too little egg was added (the more eggs you add, the more the dough will puff). Otherwise, the oven was too low or it was opened too soon during baking. Also, the cooking time may have been too short.

OTHER SHORTCRUST PROBLEMS
If there are holes, the pastry was rolled too thinly or it has split during cooking due to being overworked or not being chilled. If the fork marks are too large, they can cause holes. If the pastry is tough, the dough may have been overworked or there was too much liquid added.

OTHER PUFF PASTRY PROBLEMS
If it is soggy and undercooked, the cooking time may have been too short, or the oven too low. If unevenly risen, it may have been unevenly rolled or the butter wasn't incorporated evenly. If shrunken and poorly risen, it may have been overworked, or not rested and chilled.

OTHER FILO PASTRY PROBLEMS
If the filling leaks, there may be too much filling, or not enough filo layers. The oven may have been too hot or the filling too moist. Otherwise, the parcels were not shaped and secured well enough or were rolled too tightly.

148

apple pie

✳ ✳

Preparation time: 45 minutes
Cooking time: 50 minutes
Serves 6

2 tablespoons marmalade
1 egg, lightly beaten
1 tablespoon sugar

FILLING
6 large granny smith apples

2 tablespoons caster (superfine) sugar
1 teaspoon finely grated lemon zest
pinch of ground cloves

PASTRY
250 g (9 oz/2 cups) plain (all-purpose)
    flour
30 g (1 oz/¼ cup) self-raising flour
150 g (5½ oz) unsalted butter, chilled
    and cubed
2 tablespoons caster (superfine)
    sugar
80–100 ml (2½–3½ fl oz) iced water

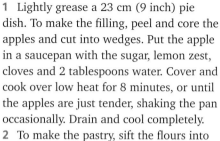

1 Lightly grease a 23 cm (9 inch) pie dish. To make the filling, peel and core the apples and cut into wedges. Put the apple in a saucepan with the sugar, lemon zest, cloves and 2 tablespoons water. Cover and cook over low heat for 8 minutes, or until the apples are just tender, shaking the pan occasionally. Drain and cool completely.
2 To make the pastry, sift the flours into a bowl. Using your fingertips, rub in the butter until the mixture resembles fine breadcrumbs. Stir in the sugar, then make a well in the centre. Add almost all the iced water and mix with a flat-bladed knife, using a cutting action, until the mixture comes together in beads. Add more water if the dough is too dry. Gather together and lift out onto a lightly floured work surface. Press into a ball and divide into two portions, making one a little bigger than the other. Cover with plastic wrap and refrigerate for 20 minutes.
3 Preheat the oven to 200°C (400°F/ Gas 6). Roll out the larger piece of pastry between two sheets of baking paper to line the base and side of the pie dish. Line the pie dish with the pastry. Use a small sharp knife to trim away any excess pastry. Brush the marmalade over the base and spoon the apple mixture into the shell. Roll out the other portion of pastry between the baking paper until large enough to cover the pie. Brush water around the rim then lay the pastry top over the pie. Trim off any excess pastry, pinch the edges and cut a few slits in the top to allow steam to escape.
4 Re-roll the pastry scraps and cut into leaves for decoration. Lightly brush the top with egg, then sprinkle with sugar. Bake for 20 minutes, then reduce the oven to 180°C (350°F/Gas 4) and bake for another 15–20 minutes, or until the pastry is golden.

lemon meringue pie

✳ ✳

Preparation time: 1 hour + cooling time
Cooking time: 40 minutes
Serves 6

185 g (6½ oz/1½ cups) plain (all-purpose)
    flour
2 tablespoons icing (confectioners')
    sugar
125 g (4½ oz) unsalted butter, chilled and
    cubed
60 ml (2 fl oz/¼ cup) chilled water

FILLING AND TOPPING
30 g (1 oz/¼ cup) cornflour (cornstarch)
30 g (1 oz/¼ cup) plain (all-purpose) flour
230 g (8 oz/1 cup) caster (superfine) sugar
185 ml (6 fl oz/¾ cup) lemon juice
3 teaspoons finely grated lemon zest
40 g (1½ oz) unsalted butter, cubed
6 eggs, at room temperature, separated
350 g (12 oz/1½ cups) caster (superfine)
    sugar, extra
½ teaspoon cornflour (cornstarch), extra

1 Sift the flour and icing sugar into a
large bowl. Using your fingertips, rub in
the butter until the mixture resembles
fine breadcrumbs. Add almost all the
water and mix with a flat-bladed knife,
using a cutting action, until the mixture
forms a firm dough. Add more liquid if
the dough is too dry. Turn onto a lightly
floured surface and gather together into
a ball. Roll between two sheets of baking
paper until large enough to fit a 23 cm
(9 inch) pie dish. Line the pie dish with
the pastry, trim the edge and refrigerate
for 20 minutes. Preheat the oven to
180°C (350°F/Gas 4).
2 Line the pastry with a sheet of baking
paper and spread a layer of baking beads
or uncooked rice evenly over the paper.
Bake for 10 minutes, then remove the
paper and beads. Bake for a further
10 minutes, or until the pastry is lightly
golden. Leave to cool.
3 To make the filling, put the flours and
sugar in a saucepan. Whisk in the lemon
juice, zest and 375 ml (13 fl oz/1½ cups)
water. Whisk continually over medium
heat until the mixture boils and thickens.
Reduce the heat and cook for 1 minute,
then whisk in the butter and egg yolks,
one yolk at a time. Transfer to a bowl,
cover the surface with plastic wrap and
allow to cool completely. Preheat the oven
to 220°C (425°F/Gas 7).
4 To make the topping, whisk the egg
whites in a clean, dry, small bowl using
electric beaters until soft peaks form.
Add the extra sugar gradually, whisking
constantly until the meringue is thick and
glossy. Whisk in the extra cornflour. Pour
the cooled filling into the cooled pastry
shell. Spread with meringue to cover,
forming peaks on the top. Bake the pie for
5–10 minutes, or until lightly browned.
Serve hot or cold.

meringues

A soft meringue is a mixture
of stiffly beaten egg white and
sugar, usually in a proportion
of 1 egg white to 60 g (2¼ oz)
sugar. The sugar is gradually
added to the beaten egg white
until the sugar is dissolved
and the mixture is smooth and
glossy. Soft meringues are used
as swirled topping on various
sweet pies such as lemon
meringue pie and fruit pies.
The meringue is piled high onto
the filling, then lightly browned
in the oven. The pie should be
eaten soon after browning as
the meringue topping will start
to 'weep' and lose volume if it
stands too long.

pecan pie

✹ ✹

Preparation time: **30 minutes**
Cooking time: **1 hour 15 minutes**
Serves **6**

vanilla ice-cream, to serve

SHORTCRUST PASTRY
185 g (6½ oz/1½ cups) plain (all-purpose)
    flour
125 g (4½ oz) unsalted butter, chilled and
    cubed
2–3 tablespoons chilled water

FILLING
200 g (7 oz/2 cups) pecans
3 eggs, lightly beaten
50 g (1¾ oz) unsalted butter, melted and
    cooled
140 g (5 oz/¾ cup) soft brown sugar
170 ml (5½ fl oz/⅔ cup) light corn syrup
1 teaspoon natural vanilla extract

1 Preheat the oven to 180°C (350°F/
Gas 4). Sift the flour into a bowl. Using
your fingertips, rub in the butter until the
mixture resembles fine breadcrumbs. Add
almost all the water and mix with a flat-
bladed knife, using a cutting action, until
the mixture comes together in beads. Add
more water if the dough is too dry. Turn
the dough out onto a lightly floured work
surface and gather together into a ball.
2 Roll out to a 35 cm (14 inch) round.
Line a 23 cm (9 inch) round flan (tart) tin
with pastry, trim the edges and refrigerate
for 20 minutes. Roll the pastry trimmings
out on baking paper to a rectangle about
2 mm (¹⁄₁₆ inch) thick, then refrigerate.
3 Line the pastry-lined tin with baking
paper and spread a layer of baking beads
or uncooked rice over the paper. Bake for
15 minutes, remove the paper and beads
and bake for another 15 minutes, or until
lightly golden. Cool completely.
4 To make the filling, spread the pecans
over the pastry base. Whisk together the
eggs, butter, sugar, corn syrup, vanilla and
a pinch of salt until well combined, then
pour over the nuts.

pecans

The pecan is native to America
and is related to the walnut.
It has a mild, creamy and less
bitter flavour than the walnut
but the walnut does make
an adequate substitute. It is
known as a dessert nut as it
is used mostly in desserts and
pies, confectionery and ice

cream. The most famous of the
dessert pies is the American
Pecan pie, popular in the
southern states. The distinctive
flavour is due to corn syrup
which is a by-product of sweet
corn and can be bought in
bottles from health food stores
and delicatessens.

5 Use a fluted pastry wheel or small sharp knife to cut narrow strips from half the pastry trimmings. Cut out small stars with a biscuit (cookie) cutter from the remaining trimmings. Arrange decoratively over the filling. Bake for 45 minutes, or until firm. Cool completely and serve with ice cream.

rhubarb lattice pie

✸ ✸

Preparation time: 35 minutes
  + 40 minutes chilling time
Cooking time: 1 hour
Serves 4–6

150 g (5½ oz/1¼ cups) plain (all-purpose) flour
¼ teaspoon baking powder
90 g (3¼ oz) unsalted butter, chilled and cubed
1 tablespoon caster (superfine) sugar
80–100 ml (2½–3½ fl oz) iced water
milk, to glaze
raw (demerara) sugar, to decorate

RHUBARB FILLING
500 g (1 lb 2 oz) rhubarb, trimmed, leaves discarded
115 g (4 oz/½ cup) caster (superfine) sugar, plus extra, to taste
5 cm (2 inch) piece orange zest, pith removed
1 tablespoon orange juice
410 g (14½ oz) tinned pie apple, drained

1 To make the rhubarb filling, preheat the oven to 180°C (350°F/Gas 4). Cut the rhubarb into 3 cm (1¼ inch) lengths and combine in a large casserole dish with the sugar, orange zest and juice. Cover the dish with a lid or foil and bake for 30 minutes, or until the rhubarb is just tender. Drain away any excess juice and discard the zest. Cool, then stir in the apple. Add more sugar to taste.
2 While the rhubarb is cooking, sift the flour and baking powder into a bowl. Using your fingertips, rub in the butter until the mixture resembles fine breadcrumbs. Stir in the sugar. Make a well in the centre and add almost all the water. Mix with a flat-bladed knife, using a cutting action, until the mixture comes together in beads. Add more water if the dough is too dry. Gather together, wrap in plastic wrap and chill for 20 minutes.
3 Roll the pastry out between two sheets of baking paper to a 28 cm (11¼ inch) circle. Use a sharp knife or a fluted cutter to cut the pastry into 1.5 cm (⅝ inch) strips. Lay half the strips on a sheet of baking paper, leaving a 1 cm (½ inch) gap between each strip. Interweave the remaining strips to form a lattice. Cover with plastic wrap and refrigerate, flat, for 20 minutes.
4 Increase the oven to 210°C (415°F/Gas 6–7). Pour the filling into a 20 cm (8 inch) pie dish and smooth the surface. Invert the pastry lattice on the pie, remove the paper and trim the pastry edge. Bake for 10 minutes. Remove from the oven, brush with milk and sprinkle with sugar. Reduce the oven to 180°C (350°F/Gas 4) and bake the pie for a further 20 minutes, or until the pastry is golden and the filling is bubbling.

Roll the dough out between two sheets of baking paper to a 28 cm (11 inch) circle.

Pour the rhubarb filling into a pie dish and smooth the surface.

custard tarts

✹ ✹

Preparation time: 45 minutes
Cooking time: 45 minutes
Makes 12

PASTRY
250 g (9 oz/2 cups) plain (all-purpose)
   flour
60 g (2¼ oz/⅓ cup) rice flour
30 g (1 oz/¼ cup) icing (confectioners')
   sugar
120 g (4¼ oz) unsalted butter, chilled
   and cubed
1 egg yolk
60 ml (2 fl oz/¼ cup) iced water
1 egg white, lightly beaten

CUSTARD FILLING
3 eggs
375 ml (13 fl oz/1½ cups) milk
55 g (2 oz/¼ cup) caster (superfine)
   sugar
1 teaspoon natural vanilla extract
½ teaspoon freshly grated nutmeg

1   Sift the flours and icing sugar into a
large bowl. Using your fingertips, rub in
the butter until the mixture resembles fine
breadcrumbs. Make a well in the centre
and add the egg yolk and almost all the
water. Mix with a flat-bladed knife, using
a cutting action, until the mixture comes
together in small beads. Add more water
if the dough is too dry. Gather together
and roll out between two sheets of baking
paper. Divide the dough into 12 equal
portions and roll each portion out to fit
the base and side of a 10 cm (4 inch)
loose-based fluted flan (tart) tin. Line the
tins with the pastry and roll the rolling
pin over the tins to trim any excess pastry.
Refrigerate for 20 minutes.
2   Preheat the oven to 180°C (350°F/
Gas 4). Line each pastry-lined tin with
baking paper. Fill with baking beads or
uncooked rice. Place the tins on two large
baking trays and bake for 10 minutes.
Remove the baking paper and beads and
bake for a further 10 minutes, or until
the pastry is lightly golden. Cool. Brush
the base and side of each pastry case with
beaten egg white. Reduce the oven to
150°C (300°F/Gas 2).
3   To make the custard filling, whisk the
eggs and milk in a bowl to combine. Add
the caster sugar gradually, whisking to
dissolve completely. Stir in the vanilla.
Strain, then pour into the cooled pastry
cases. Sprinkle with nutmeg and bake for
25 minutes, or until the filling is just set.
Serve the tarts at room temperature.

apple tarte tatin

✹ ✹

Preparation time: 30 minutes
   + 30 minutes chilling time
Cooking time: 55 minutes
Serves 6

210 g (7½ oz/1⅔ cups) plain (all-purpose)
   flour
125 g (4½ oz) unsalted butter, chilled and
   cubed
2 tablespoons caster (superfine) sugar
1 egg, lightly beaten

tarte tatin

This is traditionally an upside-down apple, or sometimes pear, tart. The fruit is cooked in an ovenproof dish or tin and the rolled pastry cooked on top in the oven. The pie is then inverted to show off the caramelised, juicy cooked fruit. The name commemorates the Tatin sisters who lived in France's Loire Valley in the early 20th century and made their living selling it. The French call it tarte des demoiselles Tatin or 'the tart of two unmarried women named Tatin'.

2 drops natural vanilla extract
8 granny smith apples
110 g (3¾ oz/½ cup) sugar
40 g (1½ oz) unsalted butter, extra, chopped
vanilla ice cream, to serve

1 Sift the flour into a bowl. Using your fingertips, rub in the butter until the mixture resembles fine breadcrumbs. Stir in the caster sugar, then make a well in the centre. Add the egg and vanilla and mix with a flat-bladed knife, using a cutting action, until the mixture comes together in beads. Gather the dough, turn onto a lightly floured surface and shape into a disc. Wrap in plastic wrap and refrigerate for at least 30 minutes, to firm.

2 Peel and core the apples and cut each into eight wedges. Put the sugar and 1 tablespoon water in a heavy-based 25 cm (10 inch) frying pan that has a metal or removable handle, so that it can safely be placed in the oven. Stir over low heat until the sugar dissolves. Increase the heat to medium and cook, without stirring, for 4–5 minutes, or until the mixture becomes golden. Add the extra butter and stir to incorporate. Remove from the heat.

3 Arrange the apple wedges in neat circles to cover the base of the frying pan. Return the pan to low heat and cook for 10–12 minutes, or until the apple is tender and caramelised. Remove the

pan from the heat and leave the apple to cool for 10 minutes.

4 Preheat the oven to 220°C (425°F/ Gas 7). Roll the pastry out on a lightly floured surface to a 27 cm (10¾ inch) circle. Working quickly, place the pastry over the apple to cover it completely, tucking the pastry down firmly at the edge. Bake for 30–35 minutes, or until the pastry is cooked. Leave for 15 minutes before turning out onto a plate. Serve warm or cold with ice cream.

NOTE: High-sided tatin tins are available from speciality kitchenware shops.

summer berry tart

✺ ✺

Preparation time: 40 minutes
Cooking time: 35 minutes
Serves 12

PASTRY
125 g (4½ oz/1 cup) plain (all-purpose)
  flour
90 g (3¼ oz) unsalted butter, chilled and
  cubed
2 tablespoons icing (confectioners') sugar
1–2 tablespoons iced water

FILLING
3 egg yolks
2 tablespoons caster (superfine) sugar
2 tablespoons cornflour (cornstarch)
250 ml (9 fl oz/1 cup) milk
1 teaspoon natural vanilla extract
250 g (9 oz/1⅔ cups) strawberries,
  halved
125 g (4½ oz) blueberries
125 g (4½ oz/1 cup) raspberries
2 tablespoons raspberry jam

1 Preheat the oven to 180°C (350°F/
Gas 4). Lightly grease a round 20 cm
(8 inch) loose-based, fluted flan (tart) tin.
2 To make the pastry, sift the flour into
a bowl. Using your fingertips, rub in the
butter until the mixture resembles fine
breadcrumbs. Mix in the icing sugar. Make
a well in the centre and add almost all the
water. Mix with a flat-bladed knife, using
a cutting action, until the mixture comes
together in beads. Add more water if the
dough is too dry.
3 Roll out the pastry between two sheets
of baking paper to fit the base and side of
the tin. Line the tin with the pastry and
trim away any excess. Refrigerate for
20 minutes. Line the pastry-lined tin with
baking paper and spread a layer of baking
beads or uncooked rice evenly over the
paper. Bake for 15 minutes, remove the
paper and beads and bake for a further
15 minutes, or until golden.
4 To make the filling, put the egg yolks,
sugar and cornflour in a bowl and whisk
until pale. Heat the milk in a saucepan

tarts

A tart has a shallow-sided pastry crust without an
enclosing pastry top. The filling can be sweet or
savoury. Sweet tarts usually have a custard base
and are decorated with fruit or nuts. Savoury
tarts often have a cheesy filling or savoury
custard with meats or vegetables. Small tarts are
called 'tartlets' and are suitable as appetisers or,
if bite-sized, for party food. Special tart tins can
be bought from speciality kitchenware shops.
They come in various sizes with straight or fluted
sides. Most tart tins have a loose base so that the
cooked tart can be easily removed from the tin.

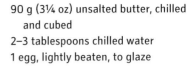

until almost boiling, then remove from the heat and add gradually to the egg mixture, beating constantly. Strain into the pan. Stir constantly over low heat for 3 minutes, or until the mixture boils and thickens. Remove from the heat and add the vanilla. Transfer to a bowl, cover with plastic wrap and set aside to cool.

5 Spread the filling in the pastry shell and top with the berries. Heat the jam in a heatproof bowl over a saucepan of simmering water, or in the microwave, until it liquefies. Strain and then brush over the fruit with a pastry brush.

treacle tart

Preparation time: 20 minutes
  + 40 minutes chilling time
Cooking time: 35 minutes
Serves 4-6

icing (confectioners') sugar and vanilla
  ice cream, to serve

SHORTCRUST PASTRY
150 g (5½ oz/1¼ cups) plain (all-purpose)
  flour

90 g (3¼ oz) unsalted butter, chilled
  and cubed
2–3 tablespoons chilled water
1 egg, lightly beaten, to glaze

FILLING
350 g (12 oz/1 cup) light treacle or golden
  syrup
25 g (1 oz) unsalted butter
½ teaspoon ground ginger
140 g (5 oz/1¾ cups) fresh white
  breadcrumbs

1 To make the pastry, sift the flour into a large bowl. Using your fingertips, rub in the butter until the mixture resembles fine breadcrumbs. Add almost all the water and mix with a flat-bladed knife, using a cutting action, to a firm dough. Add more water if the dough is too dry. Turn onto a lightly floured surface and gather into a ball. Wrap in plastic wrap and refrigerate for 20 minutes.

2 Lightly brush a 20 cm (8 inch) round fluted flan (tart) tin with melted butter or oil. Roll out the pastry large enough to fit the base and side of the tin, allowing a 4 cm (1½ inch) overhang. Ease the pastry into the tin and trim by running a rolling pin firmly across the top of the tin. Re-roll the pastry trimmings to a 10 x 20 cm (4 x 8 inch) rectangle. Using a sharp knife or fluted pastry wheel, cut into long strips 1 cm (½ inch) wide. Cover the pastry case and strips with plastic wrap and refrigerate for 20 minutes. Preheat the oven to 180°C (350°F/Gas 4).

3 To make the filling, combine the treacle or golden syrup, butter and ginger in a small saucepan and stir over low heat until the butter melts. Stir in the breadcrumbs until combined. Pour the mixture into the pastry case. Lay half the pastry strips over the tart, starting at the centre and working outwards. Lay the remaining strips over the tart to form a lattice pattern. Brush the lattice with the beaten egg. Bake the tart for 30 minutes, or until the pastry is lightly golden. Serve warm or at room temperature. Dust the top with icing sugar and serve with vanilla ice cream.

citron tart

citron tart

Preparation time: 30 minutes
  + 30 minutes chilling time
Cooking time: 1 hour
Serves 6–8

3 eggs
2 egg yolks
175 g (6 oz/¾ cup) caster (superfine) sugar
125 ml (4 fl oz/½ cup) pouring (whipping)
  cream
185 ml (6 fl oz/¾ cup) lemon juice
1½ tablespoons finely grated lemon zest
2 small lemons
140 g (5 oz/⅔ cup) sugar
pouring (whipping) cream (optional),
  to serve

PASTRY
125 g (4½ oz/1 cup) plain (all-purpose) flour
80 g (2¾ oz) unsalted butter, softened
1 egg yolk
2 tablespoons icing (confectioners') sugar,
  sifted

1 To make the pastry, sift the flour and a pinch of salt into a large bowl. Make a well in the centre and add the butter, egg yolk and icing sugar. Work together the butter, yolk and sugar with your fingertips, then slowly incorporate the flour. Bring together into a ball — you may need to add a few drops of chilled water. Flatten the ball slightly, then wrap in plastic wrap and refrigerate for 20 minutes.
2 Preheat the oven to 200°C (400°F/ Gas 6). Lightly grease a 21 cm (8¼ inch) round fluted flan (tart) tin.
3 Roll out the pastry between two sheets of baking paper until it is 3 mm (⅛ inch) thick, to fit the base and side of the tin. Gently place in the tin and trim the edge. Refrigerate for 10 minutes. Line the pastry with baking paper, fill with baking beads or uncooked rice and bake for 10 minutes. Remove the paper and beads and bake for another 6–8 minutes, or until the pastry looks dry all over. Allow to cool. Reduce the oven to 150°C (300°F/Gas 2).

4 Whisk the eggs, egg yolks and caster sugar together. Add the cream and lemon juice and mix well. Strain and then add the lemon zest. Place the tin on a baking tray on the middle shelf of the oven and carefully pour in the filling right up to the top. Bake for 40 minutes, or until it is just set — it should wobble in the middle when the tin is firmly tapped. Cool the tart before removing from the tin.
5 Meanwhile, wash and scrub the lemons well to remove the wax from the skin. Slice very thinly (2 mm/1⁄16 inch thick). Combine the sugar and 200 ml (7 fl oz) water in a small frying pan and stir over low heat until the sugar has dissolved. Add the lemon slices and simmer over low heat for 40 minutes, or until the peel is very tender and the pith looks translucent. Lift out of the syrup and drain on baking paper. If serving the tart immediately, cover the surface with the lemon slices. If not, keep the lemon slices covered and decorate the tart when ready to serve. You can serve the tart warm or chilled, with a little cream, if desired.

plum tart

Preparation time: 20 minutes
Cooking time: 35 minutes
Serves 6

500 g (1 lb 2 oz) block puff pastry , thawed

TOPPING
1 tablespoon plum jam
5 large plums, stoned, very thinly sliced
1 tablespoon brandy
1 tablespoon sugar

1 Preheat the oven to 200°C (400°F/ Gas 6). Roll out the pastry on a lightly floured surface to make an irregular rectangular shape, about 20 x 30 cm (8 x 12 inches) and 4 mm (¼ inch) thick.
2 Place the pastry on a greased baking tray. Heat the plum jam with 2 teaspoons of water in a small saucepan over low heat until the jam is softened and

spreadable. Brush the jam over the pastry base, leaving a 2 cm (¾ inch) border. Lay the plum slices along the pastry, leaving a 2 cm (¾ inch) border all around. Lightly brush the fruit with the brandy and sprinkle with the sugar. Bake for 30 minutes, or until the pastry is puffed and golden. Cut into slices and serve warm with cream or ice cream.

NOTE: This tart can also be made using 4 very thinly sliced large nectarines and substituting apricot jam for the plum jam.

plums
There are many varieties of this stone fruit. Most have a shiny skin and they range in colour from deep purple to green, yellow and red. They are available only for a short period during late summer and early autumn. Buy plums that are firm and plump and leave them to fully ripen at room temperature. Refrigerate them once they have ripened. They can be used in pies, tarts and puddings and are also suitable for poaching and serving as an accompaniment to rich cakes. Plums make a beautiful jam as well as sweet and savoury sauces and chutneys. They are also available tinned, which is useful when fresh plums are out of season. When dried, they are sold as prunes.

pumpkin pie

✸ ✸

Preparation time: 40 minutes
Cooking time: 1 hour 10 minutes
Serves 8

FILLING
500 g (1 lb 2 oz) seeded and peeled
   pumpkin (winter squash), chopped into
   small chunks
2 eggs, lightly beaten
140 g (5 oz/¾ cup) soft brown sugar
80 ml (2½ fl oz/⅓ cup) pouring (whipping)
   cream
1 tablespoon sweet sherry
1 teaspoon ground cinnamon
½ teaspoon freshly grated nutmeg
½ teaspoon ground ginger

PASTRY
150 g (5½ oz/1¼ cups) plain (all-purpose)
   flour
100 g (3½ oz) unsalted butter, chilled
   and cubed
2 teaspoons caster (superfine)
   sugar
80 ml (2½ fl oz/⅓ cup) iced water
1 egg yolk, lightly beaten with
   1 tablespoon milk, to glaze

1 Lightly grease a 23 cm (9 inch) pie
dish. Steam or boil the pumpkin for
10 minutes, or until just tender. Drain
thoroughly, mash and set aside to cool.
2 To make the pastry, sift the flour into
a large bowl. Using your fingertips, rub
in the butter until the mixture resembles
fine breadcrumbs. Stir in the caster sugar.
Make a well in the centre, add almost
all the water and mix with a flat-bladed
knife, using a cutting action, until the
mixture comes together in beads. Add the
remaining water if the dough is too dry.
3 Gather the dough together and roll out
between two sheets of baking paper until
large enough to cover the base and side
of the pie dish. Line the dish with pastry,
trim away the excess pastry and crimp
the edges. Roll out the pastry trimmings
to 2 mm (⅟₁₆ inch) thick. Using a sharp
knife, cut out leaf shapes of different sizes
and score vein markings onto the leaves.
Refrigerate the pastry-lined dish and the
leaf shapes for about 20 minutes.
4 Preheat the oven to 180°C (350°F/
Gas 4). Line the pastry-lined dish with
baking paper. Spread baking beads or
uncooked rice over the paper. Bake for
10 minutes, remove the paper and beads
and bake for another 10 minutes, or until
lightly golden. Meanwhile, place the
leaves on a lined baking tray, brush with
the combined egg yolk and milk and bake
for 10–15 minutes, or until lightly golden.
Set aside to cool.

5 To make the filling, whisk the eggs and brown sugar in a large bowl. Add the cooled mashed pumpkin, cream, sherry, cinnamon, nutmeg and ginger and stir to combine thoroughly. Pour the filling into the pastry shell, smooth the surface with the back of a spoon and bake for 40 minutes, or until set. If the pastry edges begin to brown too much during cooking, cover them with foil. Allow the pie to cool to room temperature and then decorate the top with the leaves. Pumpkin pie can be served with ice cream or whipped cream, if desired.

blueberries

These are native to North America but are now grown all over the world. However, America, where blueberries are also called huckleberries, is still the major producer. They are available in the warmer months. The small purplish-blue berries are grown on an evergreen shrub related to heather. Buy firm, dry and unblemished blueberries with their natural whitish 'bloom' still evident. Store them unwashed and in their container. They can be refrigerated for up to two days and can be used for pies, tarts, muffins, jam and fruit salads.

free-form blueberry pie

Preparation time: 30 minutes
Cooking time: 35 minutes
Serves 4

185 g (6½ oz/1½ cups) plain (all-purpose) flour
90 g (3¼ oz/¾ cup) icing (confectioners') sugar, plus extra, for dusting
125 g (4½ oz) unsalted butter, chilled and cubed
60 ml (2 fl oz/¼ cup) lemon juice
500 g (1 lb 2 oz) blueberries
1 teaspoon finely grated lemon zest
½ teaspoon ground cinnamon
1 egg white, lightly beaten
ice cream or whipped cream, to serve

1 Preheat the oven to 180°C (350°F/ Gas 4). Sift together the flour and 60 g (2¼ oz/½ cup) of the icing sugar into a bowl. Using your fingertips, rub in the butter until the mixture resembles fine breadcrumbs. Make a well in the centre and add almost the lemon juice. Mix with a flat-bladed knife, using a cutting action, until the mixture comes together in beads. Add the remaining lemon juice if the dough is too dry.
2 Gently gather the dough together and lift onto a sheet of baking paper. Roll the dough out to a circle about 30 cm (12 inches) in diameter. Wrap in plastic wrap and refrigerate for 10 minutes. Put the blueberries in a bowl and sprinkle with the remaining icing sugar, lemon zest and cinnamon.
3 Place the pastry (still on the baking paper) on a baking tray. Brush the centre lightly with beaten egg white. Pile the blueberry mixture onto the pastry in a 20 cm (8 inch) diameter circle, then fold the edges of the pastry over the filling, leaving the centre uncovered. Bake for 30–35 minutes, until the pastry is golden brown. Dust the pie generously with icing sugar and serve warm with ice cream or whipped cream.

fruit mince pies

✹ ✹

Preparation time: 30 minutes
Cooking time: 25 minutes
Makes 16

icing (confectioners') sugar, to dust

FRUIT MINCE
40 g (1½ oz/⅓ cup) raisins, chopped
60 g (2¼ oz/⅓ cup) soft brown sugar
30 g (1 oz/¼ cup) sultanas (golden raisins)
50 g (1¾ oz/¼ cup) mixed peel (mixed candied citrus peel)
1 tablespoon currants
1 tablespoon chopped almonds
1 small apple, grated
1 teaspoon lemon juice
½ teaspoon finely grated orange zest
½ teaspoon finely grated lemon zest
½ teaspoon mixed (pumpkin pie) spice
pinch of freshly grated nutmeg
25 g (1 oz) unsalted butter, melted
1 tablespoon brandy

PASTRY
250 g (9 oz/2 cups) plain (all-purpose) flour
150 g (5½ oz) unsalted butter, chilled and cubed
85 g (3 oz/⅔ cup) icing (confectioners') sugar
2–3 tablespoons chilled water

1 To make the fruit mince, combine all the ingredients in a bowl, spoon into a sterilised jar and seal. You can use the fruit mince straightaway, but the flavours develop if kept for a while. Store in a cool, dark place for up to 3 months. (Use ready-made fruit mince if short of time.)

2 Preheat the oven to 180°C (350°F/ Gas 4). Lightly grease two 12-hole patty pans.

3 To make the pastry, sift the flour into a bowl. Using your fingertips, rub in the butter until the mixture resembles fine breadcrumbs. Stir in the icing sugar and make a well in the centre. Add almost all the water and mix with a flat-bladed knife, using a cutting action, until the mixture comes together in beads. Add the remaining water if the dough is too dry. Turn out onto a lightly floured work surface and gather into a ball. Roll out two-thirds of the pastry and cut out 24 rounds, slightly larger than the holes in the patty pans, with a round fluted cutter. Fit the rounds into the tins.

4 Divide the fruit mince evenly among the pastry cases. Roll out the remaining pastry, a little thinner than before, and cut 12 rounds with the same cutter. Using a smaller fluted cutter, cut 12 more rounds. Place the large circles on top of half of the pies and press the edges to seal. Place the smaller circles on the remainder. Bake for 25 minutes, or until golden. Leave in the tins for 5 minutes, then lift out with a knife and cool on wire racks. Dust lightly with icing sugar and serve.

pithivier

✵ ✵

Preparation time: **20 minutes**
Cooking time: **20 minutes**
Serves **10**

375 g (13 oz) block puff pastry, thawed
1 egg, lightly beaten

FILLING
90 g (3¼ oz) unsalted butter, softened
85 g (3 oz/⅔ cup) icing (confectioners')
  sugar
2 egg yolks
135 g (4¾ oz/1¼ cups) ground almonds
2 teaspoons almond extract

1 Preheat the oven to 210°C (415°F/
Gas 6–7). Lightly grease a large baking
tray, line with baking paper, then place in
the hot oven to heat.
2 Divide the pastry in half and roll out
each piece between two sheets of baking
paper to 3 mm (⅛ inch) thick. Using
cake tins as a guide, cut a 20 cm (8 inch)
round from one sheet of pastry and an
18 cm (7 inch) round from the other.
Place the smaller round on the baking
tray to form the base.
3 For the filling, beat the butter and icing
sugar in a bowl using electric beaters until
light and creamy. Add the egg yolks and
beat until combined. Add the almonds
and almond extract and stir to combine.
4 Carefully spread the filling over the
pastry base, leaving a 2.5 cm (1 inch)
border. Place the remaining pastry round
over the top and press the edges together
all the way around to seal. Mark into
eight curved wedges, being careful not
to cut all the way through. Make deep
cuts around the border at 2 cm (¾ inch)
intervals and make indentations with the
back of a floured knife. Brush the beaten
egg all over the top of the pastry. Bake the
pithivier for about 20 minutes, or until the
pastry is puffed and golden brown.

Spread the filling evenly over the
pastry base, leaving a border.

Press the pastry edges together all
the way around to seal.

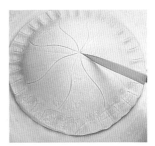

Mark the top into eight curved
wedges, being careful not to cut
all the way through.

bakewell tart

Preparation time: 45 minutes
Cooking time: 55 minutes
Serves 6

125 g (4½ oz/1 cup) plain (all-purpose) flour
90 g (3¼ oz) unsalted butter, chilled and cubed
2 teaspoons caster (superfine) sugar
2 tablespoons iced water
icing (confectioners') sugar, to dust

FILLING
90 g (3¼ oz) unsalted butter, softened
80 g (2¾ oz/⅓ cup) caster (superfine) sugar
2 eggs, lightly beaten
3 drops natural almond extract
70 g (2½ oz/⅔ cup) ground almonds
40 g (1½ oz/⅓ cup) self-raising flour, sifted
160 g (5¾ oz/½ cup) raspberry jam

1 Preheat the oven to 180°C (350°F/ Gas 4). Lightly grease a 20 cm (8 inch) loose-based, fluted flan (tart) tin.
2 Sift the flour into a large bowl and rub in the butter, using your fingertips, until the mixture resembles fine breadcrumbs. Stir in the caster sugar. Make a well in the centre, add almost all the water and mix with a flat-bladed knife, using a cutting action, until the mixture comes together in beads, adding more water if it is too dry. Gently gather the dough together and roll out between two sheets of baking paper to cover the base and side of the tin. Line the tin with the pastry, trim the edges and refrigerate for 20 minutes.
3 Line the pastry with baking paper and spread a layer of baking beads or uncooked rice over the paper. Bake for 10 minutes, then remove the paper and beads and bake the pastry for a further 7 minutes, or until golden. Leave to cool.
4 To make the filling, beat the butter and sugar in a small bowl using electric beaters until light and creamy. Add the egg gradually, beating thoroughly after each addition. Add the almond extract and beat until combined. Transfer to a large bowl and fold in the almonds and

bakewell tart

In the mid-19th century, in Bakewell, a town in Derbyshire, this tart made its first appearance as Bakewell Pudding. The famous recipe writer Eliza Action made reference to it in her *Modern Cookery* book in 1845. The idea of puddings with a jam layer topped with fruit and a sugar,

butter and egg mixture was part of early British cooking. However, the pastry base, a feature of the Bakewell, was not common. Almond flavour was also added, firstly with almond essence and later with ground almonds, which changed the texture.

flour with a metal spoon. Spread the jam over the pastry, then spoon the almond mixture on top and smooth the surface. Bake for 35 minutes, or until risen and golden. Dust with icing sugar.

neenish tarts

✷ ✷ ✷

Preparation time: 45 minutes
  + 30 minutes chilling time
Cooking time: 15 minutes
Makes 12

2 tablespoons plain (all-purpose) flour
70 g (2½ oz/⅔ cup) ground almonds
60 g (2¼ oz/½ cup) icing (confectioners')
  sugar, sifted
1 egg white, lightly beaten

CREAMY FILLING
1 tablespoon plain (all-purpose) flour
125 ml (4 fl oz/½ cup) milk
2 egg yolks
60 g (2¼ oz) unsalted butter, softened
2 tablespoons caster (superfine) sugar
¼ teaspoon natural vanilla extract

ICING
125 g (4½ oz/1 cup) icing (confectioners')
  sugar
2 tablespoons milk
1 tablespoon unsweetened cocoa
  powder

1 Lightly grease a 12-hole shallow patty pan or mini muffin tin. Sift the flour into a bowl and stir in the ground almonds and icing sugar. Make a well in the centre, add the beaten egg white and mix with a flat-bladed knife, using a cutting action, until the mixture comes together in beads and forms a stiff paste. Turn onto a lightly floured surface and gently gather into a ball. Wrap in plastic wrap and refrigerate for 30 minutes, to firm.
2 Preheat the oven to 190°C (375°F/ Gas 5). Roll out the dough between two sheets of baking paper to 3 mm (⅛ inch) thick. Cut the pastry into 12 circles with a 7 cm (2¾ inch) fluted cutter. Press the pastry circles into the greased patty pan and prick evenly with a fork. Bake for 10 minutes, or until lightly golden.
3 To make the filling, stir the flour and milk in a saucepan until smooth, then stir over medium heat for 2 minutes, or until the mixture boils and thickens. Remove from the heat, then quickly stir in the egg yolks until smooth. Cover the surface with plastic wrap and set aside to cool. Using electric beaters, beat the butter, sugar and vanilla in a bowl until light and creamy. Gradually add the cooled egg mixture and beat until smooth. Spoon some of the mixture into each pastry shell and gently smooth the tops with the back of a spoon.

4 To make the icing (frosting), combine the icing sugar and milk in a heatproof bowl, place over a saucepan of simmering water, making sure the base of the bowl does not touch the water, and stir until smooth and glossy. Remove, transfer half the icing to a small bowl, add the cocoa and stir until smooth.
5 Using a small, flat-bladed knife, spread plain icing over half of each tart, starting from the centre and making a straight line with the icing, then pushing the icing out to the edge. Allow to set. Reheat the chocolate icing and ice the other half of each tart. Allow the icing to set completely before serving.

deep-dish apple pie

❋ ❋

Preparation time: 1 hour
  + 40 minutes chilling time
Cooking time: 1 hour
Serves 8

250 g (9 oz/2 cups) plain (all-purpose)
  flour
30 g (1 oz/¼ cup) self-raising flour
150 g (5½ oz) unsalted butter, chilled
  and cubed
2 tablespoons caster (superfine) sugar
4–5 tablespoons iced water
1 egg, lightly beaten, for glazing

FILLING
8 large granny smith apples
2 thick strips lemon zest
6 whole cloves
1 cinnamon stick
125 g (4½ oz/½ cup) sugar

1 Lightly grease a deep 20 cm (8 inch) spring-form tin. Line the base with baking paper and grease the paper, then dust lightly with flour and shake off the excess.
2 Sift the flours into a bowl and rub in the butter with your fingertips until the mixture resembles fine breadcrumbs. Mix in the sugar, then make a well in the centre. Add almost all the water and mix with a flat-bladed knife, using a cutting action, until the mixture comes together in beads. Add more water if necessary. Gather together on a floured surface. Wrap in plastic wrap and refrigerate for 20 minutes.
3 Roll two-thirds of the pastry between two sheets of baking paper until large enough to cover the base and side of the tin. Line the tin with the pastry. Roll out the remaining pastry between the baking paper sheets to fit the top of the tin. Refrigerate the pastry for 20 minutes.
4 To make the filling, peel and core the apples and cut each into 12 wedges. Combine with the lemon zest, cloves, cinnamon, sugar and 500 ml (17 fl oz/ 2 cups) water in a large saucepan. Cover and simmer for 10 minutes, or until tender. Drain well and set aside to cool. Discard the zest, cloves and cinnamon.
5 Preheat the oven to 180°C (350°F/Gas 4). Spoon the apple into the pastry shell. Brush the pastry edges with beaten egg and cover with the pastry top. Trim with a sharp knife, crimping the edges to seal. Prick the top with a fork and brush with beaten egg. Bake for 50 minutes, or until the pastry is cooked. Leave in the tin for 10 minutes before removing to serve.

linzertorte

❋ ❋

Preparation time: 30 minutes
  + 40 minutes chilling time
Cooking time: 30 minutes
Serves 6-8

185 g (6½ oz/1½ cups) plain (all-purpose)
  flour
½ teaspoon ground cinnamon
90 g (3¼ oz) unsalted butter, chilled and
  cubed
55 g (2 oz/¼ cup) caster (superfine)
  sugar
100 g (3½ oz/1 cup) almond meal
2 egg yolks
2–3 tablespoons lemon juice or water
320 g (11¼ oz/1 cup) raspberry jam
80 g (2¾ oz/¼ cup) apricot jam

linzertorte

This beautiful tart originally came from Linz in Austria but is now well known all over the world. Mrs Beeton's famous *Book of Household Management* mentions the tart as far back as 1906. The pastry is rich and contains almond meal and spices. The base is traditionally spread with jam, always raspberry, and the top is decoratively latticed with pastry and glazed with egg yolk to give it a rich, dark crust.

1 Put the flour and cinnamon in a bowl. Using your fingertips, rub in the butter until the mixture resembles fine breadcrumbs. Stir in the sugar and almond meal. Make a well in the centre and add 1 of the egg yolks and the lemon juice. Mix with a flat-bladed knife, using a cutting action, until the mixture comes together in beads. Turn onto a lightly floured work surface and knead briefly until smooth. Wrap in plastic wrap and refrigerate for at least 20 minutes to firm.
2 Roll two-thirds of the pastry out between two sheets of baking paper into a circle to fit a round 20 cm (8 inch) loose-based, fluted flan (tart) tin. Press into the tin and trim away any excess

pastry. Spread the raspberry jam over the base. Roll out the remaining pastry, including scraps, to a thickness of 3 mm (⅛ inch). Cut into long strips, 2 cm (¾ inch) wide, with a fluted cutter. Lay half the strips on a sheet of baking paper, leaving a 1 cm (½ inch) gap between each strip. Interweave the remaining strips to form a lattice. Invert the lattice on top of the tart, then remove the paper and trim the edge with a sharp knife. Cover with plastic wrap and refrigerate for 20 minutes.
3 Preheat the oven to 180°C (350°F/ Gas 4). Place a baking tray in the oven to heat. Combine the remaining egg yolk with 1 teaspoon water and brush over

the tart. Place the tin on the heated tray and bake for 25–30 minutes, or until the pastry is golden brown.
4 Meanwhile, heat the apricot jam with 1 tablespoon of water, then strain the jam and brush over the tart while it is hot. Leave to cool in the tin, then remove and cut into wedges.

NOTE: Fluted cutters or special lattice cutters are available from kitchenware stores. If you cannot obtain these, simply cut the strips with a knife.

pear and almond flan

❉ ❉

Preparation time: 30 minutes
   + 2 hours 30 minutes chilling time
Cooking time: 1 hour 10 minutes
Serves 8

icing (confectioners') sugar, to dust

PASTRY
150 g (5½ oz/1¼ cups) plain (all-purpose) flour
90 g (3¼ oz) unsalted butter, chilled and cubed
55 g (2 oz/¼ cup) caster (superfine) sugar
2 egg yolks, lightly beaten

FILLING
165 g (5¾ oz) unsalted butter, softened
150 g (5½ oz/⅔ cup) caster (superfine) sugar
3 eggs
125 g (4½ oz/1¼ cups) almond meal
1½ tablespoons plain (all-purpose) flour
2 firm, ripe pears

1 Lightly grease a 24 cm (9½ inch) loose-based, fluted flan (tart) tin.
2 To make the pastry, sift the flour into a bowl. Using your fingertips, rub in the butter until the mixture resembles fine breadcrumbs. Stir in the sugar and mix together. Make a well in the centre, add the egg yolks and mix with a flat-bladed knife, using a cutting action, until the mixture comes together in beads. Turn out onto a lightly floured surface and gather into a ball. Wrap in plastic wrap and refrigerate for 30 minutes.
3 Preheat the oven to 180°C (350°F/Gas 4). Roll out the pastry between two sheets of baking paper until large enough to line the base and side of the tin. Line the tin with the pastry and trim the edge. Sparsely prick the base with a fork. Line the base with baking paper, evenly spread a layer of baking beads or uncooked rice over the paper and bake for 10 minutes. Remove the paper and beads and bake for a further 10 minutes. Cool.
4 To make the filling, beat the butter and sugar in a bowl using electric beaters for 30 seconds (don't cream the mixture). Add the eggs one at a time, beating after each addition. Fold in the almond meal and flour and spread the filling smoothly over the cooled pastry base.
5 Peel the pears, halve lengthways and remove the cores. Cut crossways into 3 mm (⅛ inch) slices. Separate the slices slightly, then place the slices on top of the tart to form a cross. Bake for about 50 minutes, or until the filling has set (the middle may still be a little soft). Cool in the tin, then refrigerate for at least 2 hours before serving, dusted with icing sugar.

cherry and cream cheese strudel

✹ ✹

Preparation time: **30 minutes**
Cooking time: **40 minutes**
Serves **8**

250 g (9 oz) cream cheese, at room
    temperature
100 ml (3½ fl oz) whipping (pouring) cream
60 g (2¼ oz/¼ cup) caster (superfine)
    sugar, plus 2 tablespoons, extra
1 tablespoon brandy or cherry brandy
1 teaspoon natural vanilla extract
10 sheets filo pastry
75 g (2¾ oz) unsalted butter, melted
35 g (1¼ oz/⅓ cup) dry breadcrumbs
35 g (1¼ oz/⅓ cup) almond meal
425 g (15 oz) tinned black pitted cherries,
    drained
icing (confectioners') sugar, to dust

1 Preheat the oven to 200°C (400°F/
Gas 6). Lightly grease a large baking
tray. Put the cream cheese, cream, sugar,
brandy and vanilla in a bowl and beat
using electric beaters until smooth.
2 Cover the filo pastry with a damp tea
towel (dish towel) to prevent drying out.
Remove one sheet, brush with melted
butter and sprinkle with some of the
combined crumbs, almond meal and extra
sugar. Repeat with more filo, butter and
crumb mixture until all the filo is used.
3 Spread the cream cheese mixture over
the pastry, leaving a 4 cm (1½ inch)
border all around. Brush butter over the
border. Arrange the cherries over the
cream cheese mixture.
4 Roll the pastry from one long side and
fold in the ends as you roll. Form into a
firm roll and place seam-side-down on
the greased tray. Brush all over with the
remaining butter. Bake for 10 minutes,
then reduce the oven to 180°C (350°F/
Gas 4) and bake for a further 30 minutes,
or until crisp and golden. Place on a wire
rack to cool. Dust liberally with icing
sugar and cut into slices.

Brush the filo pastry with butter,
then sprinkle with the combined
crumbs, almond meal and sugar.

Roll the pastry from a long side
and fold in the ends as you roll.

Roll out the dough between two sheets of baking paper.

Cover the pastry with baking paper, then spread evenly with baking beads or uncooked rice.

Simmer the zest in the sugar syrup until it is translucent.

new york cheesecake

✹ ✹

Preparation time: 1 hour + 6 hours chilling time
Cooking time: 1 hour 50 minutes
Serves 10-12

60 g (2¼ oz/½ cup) self-raising flour
125 g (4½ oz/1 cup) plain (all-purpose)
 flour
55 g (2 oz/¼ cup) caster (superfine) sugar
1 teaspoon finely grated lemon zest
80 g (2¾ oz) unsalted butter, chilled
 and cubed
1 egg
375 ml (13 fl oz/1½ cups) pouring
 (whipping) cream, to serve

FILLING
750 g (1 lb 10 oz/3 cups) cream cheese,
 softened
230 g (8 oz/1 cup) caster (superfine) sugar
30 g (1 oz/¼ cup) plain (all-purpose)
 flour
2 teaspoons finely grated orange zest
2 teaspoons finely grated lemon zest
4 eggs
170 ml (5½ fl oz/⅔ cup) pouring (whipping)
 cream

CANDIED ZEST
finely shredded zest of 3 limes, 3 lemons
 and 3 oranges
230 g (8 oz/1 cup) caster (superfine) sugar

1 Preheat the oven to 210°C (415°F/
Gas 6–7). Lightly grease a 23 cm (9 inch)
spring-form cake tin and line the base
with baking paper.
2 Process the flours, sugar, lemon zest
and butter for about 30 seconds in a food
processor, until crumbly. Add the egg
and process briefly until the mixture just
comes together. Turn out onto a lightly
floured surface and gather together into a
ball. Refrigerate in plastic wrap for about
20 minutes, or until the mixture is firm.
3 Roll the dough between two sheets of
baking paper until large enough to fit the
base and side of the tin. Ease into the tin
and trim the edges. Cover the pastry with

baking paper and spread evenly with a
layer of baking beads or uncooked rice.
Bake for 10 minutes, then remove the
baking paper and rice. Flatten the pastry
lightly with the back of a spoon and bake
for another 5 minutes. Set aside to cool.
4 To make the filling, reduce the oven
to 150°C (300°F/Gas 2). Beat the cream
cheese, sugar, flour and orange and lemon
zest until smooth. Add the eggs, one at
a time, beating well after each addition.
Beat in the cream, pour over the pastry
and bake for 1½ hours, or until almost
set. Turn off the oven and leave to cool
with the door ajar. When cool, refrigerate
for 6 hours or until well chilled.
5 To make the candied zest, place a
little water in a saucepan with the lime,
lemon and orange zest, bring to the boil
and simmer for 1 minute. Drain the zest
and repeat with fresh water (this will
remove any bitterness). Place the sugar
in a saucepan with 60 ml (2 fl oz/
¼ cup) water and stir over low heat
until dissolved. Add the zest, bring to
the boil, reduce the heat and simmer
for 5–6 minutes, or until the zest is
translucent. Allow to cool, then drain the
zest and place on baking paper to dry
(you can save the syrup to serve with
the cheesecake). Whip the cream to soft
peaks, spoon over the cold cheesecake
and top with candied zest.

NOTE: To make the cheesecake easier to
cut, heap the zest in mounds, then cut
between the mounds of zest.

cheesecakes

Cheesecakes vary greatly, from light and fluffy to dense and rich. The uncooked, lighter variety is set with gelatin and has a crushed biscuit base. However, the traditional European cheesecake has a pastry base and is baked. It is smooth, creamy and luscious. A variety of cheeses can be used, often a combination of cream cheese, ricotta, cottage cheese and sour cream. Eggs are added to bind, and flavours such as sugar, grated citrus zest and extracts are beaten in.

1 tablespoon custard powder or instant
   vanilla pudding mix
4 egg yolks
1 teaspoon natural vanilla extract

1 Sift the flour into a large bowl and add about 185 ml (6 fl oz/¾ cup) water, or enough to form a soft dough. Gather the dough into a ball, then roll out on baking paper to form a 24 x 30 cm (9½ x 12 inch) rectangle. Spread the Copha over the surface. Roll up from the short edge to form a log. Roll the dough out into a rectangle again and spread with the butter. Roll up again into a roll and slice into 12 even pieces. Working from the centre outwards, use your fingertips to press each round out to a circle large enough to cover the base and side of twelve 80 ml (2½ fl oz/⅓ cup) muffin holes. Press into the holes and refrigerate while preparing the filling.
2 Put the sugar and 80 ml (2½ fl oz/ ⅓ cup) water in a saucepan and stir over low heat until the sugar dissolves. Stir a little of the milk with the cornflour and custard powder in a small bowl to form a smooth paste. Add to the pan with the remaining milk, egg yolks and vanilla. Stir over low heat until the mixture thickens. Transfer to a bowl, cover and cool.
3 Preheat the oven to 220°C (425°F/ Gas 7). Divide the filling among the pastry bases and bake for 25–30 minutes, or until the custard is set and the tops have browned. Cool in the tins, then transfer to a wire rack.

jalousie

✹ ✹

Preparation time: 40 minutes
Cooking time: 45 minutes
Serves 4-6

30 g (1 oz) unsalted butter
50 g (1¾ oz/¼ cup) soft brown sugar
500 g (1 lb 2 oz) apples, peeled, cored and
   cubed
1 teaspoon finely grated lemon zest
1 tablespoon lemon juice

portuguese custard tarts

✹ ✹ ✹

Preparation time: 40 minutes
Cooking time: 40 minutes
Makes 12

150 g (5½ oz/1¼ cups) plain (all-purpose)
   flour
25 g (1 oz) Copha (white vegetable
   shortening), chopped and softened
30 g (1 oz) unsalted butter, softened
220 g (7¾ oz/1 cup) sugar
500 ml (17 fl oz/2 cups) milk
30 g (1 oz/¼ cup) cornflour (cornstarch)

¼ teaspoon freshly grated nutmeg
¼ teaspoon ground cinnamon
30 g (1 oz/¼ cup) sultanas (golden raisins)
375 g (13 oz) block puff pastry, thawed
1 egg, lightly beaten, to glaze

1 Preheat the oven to 220°C (425°F/ Gas 7). Lightly grease a baking tray and line with baking paper.
2 Melt the butter and sugar in a frying pan. Add the apple, lemon zest and lemon juice and cook over medium heat for 10 minutes, stirring occasionally, until the apples are cooked and the mixture is thick and syrupy. Stir in the nutmeg, cinnamon and sultanas. Cool completely.
3 Cut the block of puff pastry in half. On a lightly floured surface, roll out one half of the pastry to an 18 x 24 cm (7 x 9½ inch) rectangle. Spread the fruit mixture onto the pastry, leaving a 2.5 cm (1 inch) border. Brush the edges lightly with the beaten egg.
4 Roll the second half of the pastry on a lightly floured surface to a 18 x 25 cm (7 x 10 inch) rectangle. Using a sharp knife, carefully cut slashes in the pastry across its width, leaving a 2 cm (¾ inch) border around the edge. The slashes should open slightly and look like a venetian blind ('jalousie' in French). Place over the fruit. then press the edges together. Trim any extra pastry. Knock up the pastry (brush the sides upwards) with a knife to ensure rising during cooking. Glaze the top with egg. Bake for 25–30 minutes, or until puffed and golden.

Stir the apples occasionally until they are cooked and the mixture is golden.

Press the edges of the pastry together to seal.

Knock up the edges of the puff pastry with a knife to ensure it rises during cooking.

chocolate éclairs

✹ ✹

Preparation time: 30 minutes
Cooking time: 40 minutes
Makes 18

125 g (4½ oz) unsalted butter
125 g (4½ oz/1 cup) plain (all-purpose)
   flour, sifted
4 eggs, lightly beaten
300 ml (10½ fl oz) pouring (whipping)
   cream, whipped
150 g (5½ oz) dark chocolate, chopped

1 Preheat the oven to 210°C (415°F/
Gas 6–7). Grease two baking trays.
2 Combine the butter and 250 ml
(9 fl oz/1 cup) water in a large heavy-based saucepan. Stir over medium heat until the butter melts. Increase the heat, bring to the boil, then remove from the heat.
3 Add the flour to the pan and use a wooden spoon to quickly beat into the water. Return to the heat and continue beating until the mixture leaves the side of the pan and forms a ball. Transfer to a large bowl. Cool slightly.
4 Beat the mixture to release any remaining heat. Add the egg gradually, about 3 teaspoons at a time. Beat thoroughly after each addition until all the egg has been added and the mixture is glossy — a wooden spoon should stand upright in the mixture. If it is too runny, the egg has been added too quickly. If this happens, beat for several more minutes, or until the mixture thickens.
5 Spoon the mixture into a piping (icing) bag with a 1.5 cm (⅝ inch) plain nozzle. Sprinkle the baking trays lightly with water. Pipe 15 cm (6 inch) lengths on the trays, leaving room for expansion. Bake for 10–15 minutes.
6 Reduce the oven to 180°C (350°F/ Gas 4). Bake for a further 15 minutes, or until golden and firm. Cool on a wire rack. Split each éclair, removing any uncooked dough. Fill the éclairs with whipped cream.
7 Put the chocolate in a heatproof bowl. Bring a saucepan of water to the boil and remove the pan from the heat. Sit the bowl over the pan, making sure the base of the bowl does not touch the water. Allow to stand, stirring occasionally, until the chocolate has melted. Spread over the tops of the éclairs.

danish pastries

✹ ✹ ✹

Preparation time: 1 hour + 1 hour 30 minutes
   proving and 4 hours chilling time
Cooking time: 25 minutes
Makes about 12

2 teaspoons dried yeast
125 ml (4 fl oz/½ cup) warm milk
1 teaspoon caster (superfine) sugar
250 g (9 oz/2 cups) plain (all-purpose)
   flour
55 g (2 oz/¼ cup) caster (superfine) sugar,
   extra
1 egg, lightly beaten
1 teaspoon natural vanilla extract
250 g (9 oz) unsalted butter, chilled
40 g (1½ oz) flaked almonds
80 g (2¾ oz/¼ cup) apricot jam, to glaze

PASTRY CREAM
2 tablespoons caster (superfine) sugar
2 egg yolks
2 teaspoons plain (all-purpose) flour
2 teaspoons cornflour (cornstarch)
125 ml (4 fl oz/½ cup) hot milk

pastry cream

'Crème patissiere' is the French term for pastry cream. It is a delicious, thick custard based on milk, eggs and sugar and is thickened with flour or cornflour. It becomes firm once cooked and left to stand and is mostly used to fill choux, shortcrust (pie) and puff pastry products. The custard often has a praline of crushed toffee and nuts folded through for added flavour. It is used extensively by French pastry cooks, often to fill elaborate pastry creations.

1 Stir the yeast, milk and sugar in a small bowl until dissolved. Leave in a warm, draught-free place for 10 minutes, or until bubbles appear on the surface. The mixture should be frothy and slightly increased in volume. If your yeast doesn't foam, it is dead, so discard it and start again. Sift the flour and ½ teaspoon salt into a large bowl and stir in the extra sugar. Make a well in the centre and add the yeast, egg and vanilla. Mix to a firm dough. Turn out onto a lightly floured surface and knead for 10 minutes to form a smooth, elastic dough. Place in a lightly greased bowl, cover and set aside in a warm place for 1 hour, or until doubled in size. Cut the butter in half lengthways and place between two sheets of baking paper. Use a rolling pin to pat out to a 15 x 20 cm (6 x 8 inch) rectangle and refrigerate.

2 Knock back the dough (one punch with your fist) and knead for 1 minute. Roll the dough out to a rectangle measuring 25 x 30 cm (10 x 12 inches). Put the butter in the centre of the dough and fold up the bottom and top of the dough over the butter to join in the centre. Seal the edges with a rolling pin. Give the dough a quarter-turn clockwise, then roll out to a 20 x 45 cm (8 x 17¾ inch) rectangle. Fold over the top third of the pastry, then the bottom third and then give another quarter-turn clockwise. Cover and refrigerate for 30 minutes. Repeat the rolling, folding, turning and chilling four more times. Wrap in plastic wrap and chill for at least another 2 hours.

3 To make the pastry cream, put the sugar, egg yolks and flours in a saucepan and whisk to combine. Pour the hot milk over the top and whisk until smooth. Bring to the boil over medium heat, stirring constantly, until the mixture boils and thickens. Cover and set aside.

4 Preheat the oven to 200°C (400°F/ Gas 6) and line two baking trays with baking paper. On a lightly floured surface, roll the dough into a rectangle or square 3 mm (⅛ inch) thick. Cut the dough into 10 cm (4 inch) squares and place on the baking trays. Spoon 1 tablespoon of pastry cream into the centre of each square and top with two apricot halves. Brush one corner with the beaten egg and draw up that corner and the diagonally opposite one to touch in the middle between the apricots. Press firmly in the centre. Repeat with the remaining squares. Leave in a warm place to prove for 30 minutes. Brush each pastry with egg and sprinkle with almonds. Bake for 15–20 minutes, or until golden. Cool on wire racks. Melt the apricot jam with 1 tablespoon water in a saucepan and then strain. Brush the tops of the apricots with the hot glaze and serve.

Take a sheet of filo and place in the greased dish or tin, then brush lightly with melted butter.

Continue layering the filo, brushing each new layer with butter and folding in the edges.

Using a sharp knife, cut the baklava into diamond shapes.

baklava

☀ ☀

Preparation time: 30 minutes
 + 2 hours cooling time
Cooking time: 1 hour 15 minutes
Makes **18** pieces

540 g (1 lb 3 oz/2⅓ cups) caster (superfine) sugar
1½ teaspoons finely grated lemon zest
90 g (3¼ oz/¼ cup) honey
60 ml (2 fl oz/¼ cup) lemon juice
2 tablespoons orange flower water
200 g (7 oz) walnuts, finely chopped
200 g (7 oz) pistachio nuts, finely chopped

200 g (7 oz) almonds, finely chopped
2 tablespoons caster (superfine) sugar, extra
2 teaspoons ground cinnamon
200 g (7 oz) unsalted butter, melted
375 g (13 oz) filo pastry

1 Put the sugar, lemon zest and 375 ml (13 fl oz/1½ cups) water in a saucepan and stir over high heat until the sugar has dissolved, then boil for 5 minutes. Reduce the heat to low and simmer for 5 minutes, or until the syrup has thickened slightly and just coats the back of a spoon. Stir in the honey, lemon juice and orange flower water and cook for 2 minutes. Remove from the heat and cool completely.

2 Preheat the oven to 170°C (325°F/ Gas 3). Combine the nuts, extra sugar and cinnamon in a bowl. Brush the base and sides of a 27 x 30 cm (10¾ x 12 inch) ovenproof dish or tin with the melted butter. Cover the base with a single layer of filo pastry, brush lightly with the butter and fold in any overhanging edges. Continue layering the filo, brushing each new layer with butter and folding in the edges until 10 sheets have been used. Keep the unused filo under a damp tea towel (dish towel).

3 Sprinkle half the nut mixture over the filo pastry in the dish and pat down evenly. Repeat the layering and buttering of five more filo sheets, sprinkle with the remaining nuts, then continue to layer and butter the remaining sheets, including the top layer. Press down with your hands so the pastry and nuts stick to each other. Using a large sharp knife, carefully cut into diamond shapes, making sure you cut right through to the bottom layer of filo. Pour any remaining butter evenly over the top and smooth with your hands. Bake for 30 minutes, then reduce the oven to 150°C (300°F/Gas 2) and cook for a further 30 minutes.

4 Immediately cut through the original diamond markings, then strain the syrup evenly over the top. Cool for 2 hours, then lift the pieces of baklava out onto a serving platter.

NOTE: To achieve the right texture, it is important for the baklava to be piping hot and the syrup cooled when pouring the syrup over at the end.

apple turnovers

✳ ✳

Preparation time: **40 minutes**
Cooking time: **25 minutes**
Makes **12**

500 g (1 lb 2 oz) block puff pastry, thawed
1 egg white, lightly whisked
caster (superfine) sugar, to sprinkle

FILLING
200 g (7 oz/1 cup) tinned pie or stewed apple, drained
1–2 tablespoons caster (superfine) sugar
30 g (1 oz/¼ cup) raisins, chopped
30 g (1 oz/¼ cup) walnut pieces, chopped

1 Preheat the oven to 210°C (415°F/ Gas 6–7). Lightly grease a baking tray. Roll out the pastry on a lightly floured surface to 35 x 45 cm (14 x 17¾ inches). Cut out twelve 10 cm (4 inch) rounds.

2 To make the apple filling, mix the apple, sugar, raisins and walnuts in a small bowl until well combined. Divide the filling among the pastry rounds, then brush the edges with water. Fold in half and pinch firmly together to seal. Use the back of a knife to push up the pastry edge at intervals. Brush the tops with egg white and sprinkle with sugar. Make two small slits in the top of each turnover.

3 Bake the turnovers for 15 minutes, then reduce the oven to 190°C (375°F/ Gas 5) and bake for a further 10 minutes, or until puffed and golden.

profiteroles

❋ ❋ ❋

Preparation time: 30 minutes
Cooking time: 1 hour
Serves 10

110 g (3¾ oz) good-quality dark chocolate
2 teaspoons vegetable oil

CHOUX PASTRY
50 g (1¾ oz) unsalted butter
90 g (3¼ oz/¾ cup) plain (all-purpose)
   flour, sifted twice
3 eggs, lightly beaten

FILLING
375 ml (13 fl oz/1½ cups) milk
4 egg yolks
80 g (2¾ oz/⅓ cup) caster (superfine)
   sugar
30 g (1 oz/¼ cup) plain (all-purpose)
   flour
1 teaspoon natural vanilla extract

1 Preheat the oven to 210°C (415°F/
Gas 6–7). Lightly grease two baking trays.
2 To make the pastry, put the butter
in a large heavy-based saucepan with
185 ml (6 fl oz/¾ cup) water and stir
over medium heat until the mixture
comes to the boil. Remove from the
heat and quickly beat in the flour with a
wooden spoon. Return to the heat and
continue beating until the mixture comes
together, forms a ball and leaves the side
of the pan. Allow to cool slightly.
3 Transfer to a bowl and gradually add
the beaten egg, about 3 teaspoons at a
time, beating well after each addition,
until all the egg has been added and the
mixture is thick and glossy — a wooden
spoon should stand upright in it. If it is
too runny, the egg has been added too
quickly. If this happens, beat for several
more minutes, or until thickened.
4 Sprinkle the baking trays with water
— this creates steam in the oven, helping
the puffs to rise. Spoon heaped teaspoons

of the mixture onto the baking trays,
leaving room for spreading. Bake for
20–30 minutes, or until browned and
hollow sounding, then remove and make
a small hole in the base of each puff with
a skewer. Return to the oven for 5 minutes
to dry out. Cool on a wire rack.
5 To make the filling, put the milk in a
small saucepan and bring to the boil. Set
aside while quickly whisking the yolks
and sugar in a bowl until combined.
Whisk the flour into the egg mixture. Pour
the hot milk slowly onto the egg and flour
mixture, whisking constantly. Wash out
the pan, return the milk mixture to the
pan and bring to the boil, stirring with a
wooden spoon until the mixture comes to
the boil. Boil for 2 minutes, stirring often,
until the mixture thickens. Transfer to a
heatproof bowl and stir in the vanilla. Lay
plastic wrap on the surface to prevent a
skin forming, then refrigerate until cold.
6 Pipe the filling into each profiterole
through the hole in the base, using a
piping (icing) bag with a small nozzle.
7 Chop the chocolate and put it in a
heatproof bowl with the oil. Bring a
saucepan of water to the boil and remove
the pan from the heat. Sit the bowl over
the pan, making sure the base of the bowl
does not touch the water. Allow to stand,
stirring occasionally, until the chocolate
has melted. Stir until smooth, then dip the
top of each profiterole in the chocolate.
Allow the chocolate to set completely
before serving.

croissants

❋ ❋ ❋

Preparation time: 40 minutes
   + 1 hour 40 minutes proving and
   5 hours chilling time
Cooking time: 20 minutes
Serves 12

330 ml (11¼ fl oz/1⅓ cups) warm milk
2 teaspoons dried yeast
55 g (2 oz/¼ cup) caster (superfine) sugar
405 g (14¼ oz/3¼ cups) plain (all-purpose)
   flour

250 g (9 oz) unsalted butter, at room
    temperature
1 egg
butter and strawberry jam, to serve

1 Combine the warm milk, yeast and
1 tablespoon of the sugar in a small bowl
and stir until dissolved. Leave in a warm,
draught-free place for 10 minutes, or
until bubbles appear on the surface. The
mixture should be frothy and slightly
increased in volume. If your yeast doesn't
foam, it is dead, so you will have to
discard it and start again.
2 Put the flour, remaining sugar and
1 teaspoon salt in a large bowl and
make a well in the centre. Pour the yeast
mixture into the well and mix to a rough
dough with a wooden spoon. Turn out
onto a floured surface and knead for
10 minutes, or until smooth and elastic.
Add only a small amount of flour — just
enough to stop the dough sticking. Place
in a large greased bowl, cover and set
aside in a warm place for 1 hour, or until
doubled in bulk.
3 Meanwhile, cut the butter in half
lengthways and place between two sheets
of baking paper. Use a rolling pin to pat
out to a 10 x 20 cm (4 x 8 inch) rectangle.
Cover and refrigerate the butter.
4 Knock back the dough (one punch
with your fist). Knead briefly on a lightly
floured surface, then roll to a rectangle
12 x 45 cm (4½ x 17¾ inches). Place the
butter on the lower half of the dough and
fold down the top half. Seal all around the
edges using your fingertips to completely
seal in the butter. Turn the folded side of
the dough to the right. Roll out the dough
to a rectangle about 22 x 45 cm (8½ x
17¾ inches), then fold up the bottom
third and fold down the top third. Wrap
in plastic wrap and chill for 20 minutes.
Roll again with the fold to the right. Chill
for 20 minutes, then repeat the process
two more times. The butter should be
completely incorporated — roll again
if it's not incorporated.
5 Lightly brush two baking trays with
melted butter. Cut the dough in half.
Roll each half into a large rectangle and

trim each to about 22 x 36 cm (8½ x
14¼ inches). Cut a cardboard triangular
template 18 cm (7 inches) across the
base and 14 cm (5½ inches) along each
side. Cut each rectangle into six triangles.
Stretch each triangle a little to extend its
length. Roll each triangle into a crescent,
starting from the base. Place well apart on
the prepared tray, cover and refrigerate

for a minimum of 4 hours, or overnight.
6 Preheat the oven to 200°C (400°F/
Gas 6). Lightly beat the egg with
2 teaspoons water in a small bowl. Brush
the pastries with the egg glaze and set
aside for 40 minutes, or until doubled in
bulk. Brush again with egg glaze. Bake for
15–20 minutes, or until crisp and golden.
Serve with butter and jam.

Place the rectangle of butter on
the lower half of the dough and
fold down the top half.

Roll each triangle of dough into a
crescent, starting from the base.

Fold the pastry inwards from the short edges so they almost meet.

Fold in again so that the edges almost meet in the middle.

Arrange the palmiers, cut-side up, on the trays. Brush with butter and sprinkle with sugar mixture.

sugar and spice palmiers

☀

Preparation time: 20 minutes
Cooking time: 20 minutes
Makes 32

500 g (1 lb 2 oz) block puff pastry, thawed
2 tablespoons sugar
1 teaspoon mixed (pumpkin pie) spice
1 teaspoon ground cinnamon
40 g (1½ oz) unsalted butter, melted

1 Preheat the oven to 210°C (415°F/ Gas 6–7). Lightly grease two baking trays, then line with baking paper. Roll out the pastry between two sheets of baking paper to make a 30 cm (12 inch) square, 3 mm (⅛ inch) thick. Combine the sugar and spices in a small bowl. Cut the sheet of pastry in half, then brush each pastry sheet with melted butter. Sprinkle with the sugar mixture, reserving 2 teaspoons.
2 Take one half of pastry and fold the short edges of pastry inwards, so that the edges almost meet in the centre. Fold the same way once more, then fold over and

place on baking paper. Do not press down on the folds or the pastry will not puff. Repeat with the other half. Refrigerate both portions for 15 minutes. Using a small, sharp knife, cut each portion into 16 thin slices.
3 Arrange the palmiers cut-side up on the prepared trays. Brush with butter and sprinkle lightly with the reserved sugar mixture. Bake for 20 minutes, until golden. Leave to cool on a wire rack. Serve lightly dusted with sifted icing sugar, if desired.

millefeuille

✻ ✻ ✻

Preparation time: 30 minutes
Cooking time: 1 hour 30 minutes
Makes 6

600 g (1 lb 5 oz) block puff pastry, thawed
625 ml (21½ fl oz/2½ cups) thick (double/
    heavy) cream
500 g (1 lb 2 oz) small strawberries, halved
70 g (2½ oz) blueberries (optional)
icing (confectioners') sugar, to dust

1 Preheat the oven to 220°C (425°F/ Gas 7). Line a baking tray with baking paper. Cut the block of puff pastry into three portions. On a lightly floured surface, roll each portion out to a 25 cm (10 inch) squares. Place one sheet of puff pastry on the tray, prick all over and top with another piece of baking paper and another baking tray and bake for 15 minutes. Flip the trays over together and bake on the other side for 10–15 minutes, or until golden brown. Allow to cool and repeat with the remaining pastry.

2 Trim the edges of each pastry sheet to neaten and cut each into six rectangles. Whisk the cream to firm peaks. Place six pastry pieces on serving plates and spread with half the cream. Arrange half the strawberries and blueberries over the cream, pressing down well. Top each with another pastry piece and repeat with the remaining cream and berries. Top with a final piece of pastry. Dust with icing sugar.

NOTE: You can use 3 ready-rolled sheets of puff pastry instead of the block.

savoury pies & pastries

You'd be hard-pressed to find someone who doesn't love savoury pies: the flaky, melt-in-the-mouth pastry, the scrumptious filling, the rich gravy. Immensely satisfying to eat, they are equally satisfying to make. As well as family pies, we've included recipes for individual pies and pastries because (and let's be honest here) there are times when you simply don't feel like sharing, and want to savour every bite at your own pace. So whether you're at the dinner table or watching a game, these golden pastries will sort out even the most ferocious appetites.

pie & tart decorations

A simple decoration on pastry somehow makes a pie
or tart seem more appealing, so take the opportunity
to make full use of your creative skills.

Traditionally, savoury pies were decorated to differentiate them
from sweet pies when both were served at a meal. These days,
we use trimmings mainly for decorative effect.

Pies are usually double-crusted (a pastry base and top) or
with just a lid on top, whereas tarts are generally open with no
pastry top. As well as giving pies a finished touch, decorating
can be very practical. Not only can you use up pastry trimmings
but it helps seal the edges of a double-crusted pie so the lid
remains securely in place.

decorative edges

Fork-pressed Press a lightly floured fork around the crust's edge.
Fluted Press the pastry between your thumb and forefinger for
a rippled effect.
Crimped Press the pastry between the thumb and forefinger,
while indenting with the other forefinger.
Scalloped Press an upturned teaspoon on the pastry edges to
mark semi-circles.
Checkerboard Make cuts in the pastry edge. Bend every second
square inward.
Leaves Cut out leaf shapes with a cutter or the point of a sharp
knife and mark veins using the back of a knife. Attach to the lip
of the pie using a little water or egg glaze.
Plait Cut three long strips 5 mm (¼ inch) wide. Plait together
and attach to the lip of the pie using a little water or egg glaze,
pressing gently in place.
Rope Twist two long sausages of pastry together and attach to
the edge with a little water or egg glaze.
Feathering Lift the pastry off the lip so that it stands upright and
snip diagonally into the edge of the pie. Push one point inwards
and one point outwards.

decorative tops

There are endless shapes and forms you can use to decorate
pies, from cherries and stars to abstract patterns, or simple
initials. Alternatively, you can buy small biscuit cutters in
various shapes. When rolling out the pastry trimmings, don't
make the shapes too thick or they won't cook through. To attach
them, first brush the pie lid with an egg glaze, then arrange the
decorations and glaze them as well.

You can decorate an open tart with pastry shapes, either
around the edge or on top. However, if the filling is quite liquid,
cook the shapes separately and arrange on the tart after it is
baked and the filling has set.

Another impressive finish for a pie is a lattice top, which is
shown on some of the sweet pies in this book. However, it is
equally suitable for savoury pies and is surprisingly simple to
make. Roll the pastry out on a sheet of baking paper to a square
a little larger than the pie. Using a fluted pastry wheel or a small
sharp knife, cut strips of pastry about 1.5 cm (⅝ inch) wide. On
another sheet of baking paper, lay half the strips vertically, 1 cm
(½ inch) apart. Fold back alternate strips of pastry and lay a
strip of pastry horizontally across the unfolded strips, then fold
the vertical strips back into place. Next, fold the lower strips
back and lay another piece horizontally. Repeat with all the
strips. Refrigerate until firm, then invert the lattice onto the pie
and remove the baking paper. Press the edges to seal and trim
the excess pastry.

You can vary the width of the strips and also the spacing, to
create a tightly woven lattice or one with just a few strips.
Alternatively, you can make life very simple and buy a lattice
cutter. Just roll it over the pastry, then gently open it out, lift it
onto your pie and trim the edges, as before.

chicken and leek pie

✹ ✹

Preparation time: 20 minutes
Cooking time: 40 minutes
Serves 4

50 g (1¾ oz) butter
2 large leeks, thinly sliced
4 spring onions (scallions), sliced
1 garlic clove, crushed
30 g (1 oz/¼ cup) plain (all-purpose) flour
375 ml (13 fl oz/1½ cups) chicken stock
125 ml (4 fl oz/½ cup) whipping (pouring) cream
1 barbecued chicken, flesh chopped
375 g (13 oz) block puff pastry, thawed
60 ml (2 fl oz/¼ cup) milk

1 Preheat the oven to 200°C (400°F/ Gas 6). Grease a 20 cm (8 inch) pie dish.
2 Melt the butter in a saucepan and add the leek, spring onion and garlic. Cook over low heat for 6 minutes, or until the leek is soft but not browned. Sprinkle with the flour and mix well. Gradually pour in the stock and cook, stirring, until thick and smooth. Stir in the cream and add the chicken. Put the mixture in the pie dish and set aside to cool.
3 Divide the pastry into two portions and roll each portion between two sheets of baking paper to a thickness of 3 mm (⅛ inch). Cut a circle out of one of the sheets of pastry to cover the top of the pie. Brush the rim of the pie dish with a little milk. Put the pastry on top and press to seal around the edge. Trim off any excess pastry and press the edge with the back of a fork. Cut the other sheet into 1 cm (½ inch) strips and roll each strip up loosely like a snail. Arrange on top of the pie, starting from the centre and leaving a gap between each one. The spirals may not cover the whole surface of the pie. Make a few small holes between the spirals to let out any steam, and brush the top of the pie lightly with milk.
4 Bake for 25–30 minutes, or until the pastry is brown and crisp. Make sure the spirals look well cooked and are not raw in the middle.

NOTE: You can make small pies by dividing the mixture among four greased 310 ml (10¾ fl oz/1¼ cup) round ovenproof dishes. Cut the pastry into four rounds to fit. Bake for 15 minutes, or until the pastry is crisp.

beef pie

✹ ✹

Preparation time: 35 minutes
  + 30 minutes chilling time
Cooking time: : 2 hours 45 minutes
Serves 6

FILLING
2 tablespoons oil
1 kg (2 lb 4 oz) chuck steak, trimmed, cubed
1 large onion, chopped
1 large carrot, finely chopped
2 garlic cloves, crushed
2 tablespoons plain (all-purpose) flour
250 ml (9 fl oz/1 cup) beef stock
2 teaspoons thyme
1 tablespoon worcestershire sauce

PASTRY
250 g (9 oz/2 cups) plain (all-purpose) flour
150 g (5½ oz) butter, chilled and cubed
1 egg yolk
2–3 tablespoons chilled water
1 egg yolk, extra, to glaze
1 tablespoon milk, to glaze

1 To make the filling, heat half the oil in a large frying pan and brown the beef in batches. Remove from the pan. Heat the remaining oil, add the onion, carrot and garlic and brown over medium heat.
2 Return the beef to the pan and stir in the flour. Cook for 1 minute, then remove from the heat and slowly stir in the stock, mixing it in well. Return to the heat, add the thyme and worcestershire sauce and bring to the boil. Season to taste.
3 Reduce the heat to very low, cover and simmer for 1½–2 hours, or until the beef is tender. Remove the lid for the last 15 minutes of cooking to allow the liquid to reduce so that the sauce is thick and suitable for filling a pie. Cool completely.

4 To make the pastry, sift the flour into a large bowl. Using your fingertips, rub in the butter until it resembles fine breadcrumbs. Add the egg yolk and 2 tablespoons of the water and mix with a flat-bladed knife, using a cutting action, until the mixture comes together in beads. Add more water if the dough is too dry. Turn out onto a lightly floured work surface and gather together to form a smooth dough. Wrap in plastic wrap and refrigerate for 30 minutes.
5 Preheat the oven to 200°C (400°F/ Gas 6). Lightly grease a 23 cm (9 inch) pie dish. Divide the pastry in half and roll out one portion between two sheets of

baking paper until it is large enough to line the pie dish. Line the dish with the pastry, fill with the cooled filling and then roll out the remaining portion of pastry large enough to cover the dish. Brush the pastry edges with water. Lay the pastry over the pie and gently press or pinch to seal. Trim any excess pastry. Re-roll the scraps to make decorative shapes and press on the pie.
6 Cut a few small holes in the top of the pastry to let out any steam. Beat together the extra egg yolk and milk and brush over the top of the pie to glaze. Bake for 20–30 minutes, or until the pastry is golden and the filling is hot.

beef and red wine pies

✳ ✳

Preparation time: **50 minutes**
Cooking time: **2 hours 45 minutes**
Makes **6**

60 ml (2 fl oz/¼ cup) olive oil
1.5 kg (3 lb 5 oz) chuck steak, trimmed and
  cubed
2 onions, chopped
1 garlic clove, crushed
30 g (1 oz/¼ cup) plain (all-purpose)
  flour
310 ml (10¾ fl oz/1¼ cups) good-quality
  dry red wine

500 ml (17 fl oz/2 cups) beef stock
2 bay leaves
2 thyme sprigs
2 carrots, chopped
500 g (1 lb 2 oz) block or 6 sheets
  shortcrust (pie) pastry
500 g (1 lb 2 oz) block puff pastry,
  thawed
1 egg, lightly beaten

1 Lightly grease six metal pie dishes
measuring 9 cm (3½ inches) along the
base and 3 cm (1¼ inches) deep.
2 Heat 2 tablespoons of the oil in a large
frying pan and brown the beef in batches.
Remove from the pan. Heat the remaining

oil in the pan, add the onion and garlic
and stir over medium heat until golden
brown. Add the flour and stir for
2 minutes, until it is well browned.
Remove from the heat and gradually stir
in the combined wine and stock.
3 Return to the heat and stir until the
mixture boils and thickens. Return the
beef to the pan, add the bay leaves
and thyme and simmer for 1 hour. Add
the carrot and simmer for another
45 minutes, or until the meat and carrot
are tender and the sauce has thickened.
Season, then remove the bay leaves and
thyme. Allow to cool.
4 Preheat the oven to 200°C (400°F/
Gas 6). If using a block of shortcrust
pastry, divide it into six portions and roll
out each piece between two sheets of
baking paper to a 25 cm (10 inch) square,
3 mm (⅛ inch) thick. Cut a circle from
each sheet of shortcrust pastry big enough
to line the base and side of each pie dish.
Place in the dishes and trim the edges.
Line each pastry shell with baking paper
and fill with baking beads or uncooked
rice. Place on a baking tray and bake for
8 minutes. Remove the paper and beads
and bake for a further 8 minutes, or until
lightly browned. Allow to cool.
5 Divide the puff pastry into six portions
and roll each portion between two sheets
of baking paper to form a square. Cut
a circle from each square of dough, to
fit the tops of the pie dishes. Divide the
filling evenly among the pastry cases and
brush the edges with some of the beaten
egg. Cover with a circle of puff pastry and
trim any excess pastry, pressing the edges
with a fork to seal. Cut a slit in the top
of each pie. Brush the pie tops with the
remaining beaten egg and bake for
20–25 minutes, or until the pastry is
cooked and golden brown.

NOTE: You can make a family-sized pie
using the same ingredients and one 23 cm
(9 inch) metal pie dish. Bake in a 200°C
(400°F/Gas 6) oven for 30–35 minutes.
Any remaining pastry can be rolled and
used to decorate the pie, or wrapped in
plastic wrap and frozen for later use.

onion tart

✳ ✳

Preparation time: 30 minutes
  + 40 minutes chilling time
Cooking time: 1 hour 30 minutes
Serves 4-6

dressed rocket (arugula) leaves, to serve

SHORTCRUST PASTRY
150 g (5½ oz/1¼ cups) plain (all-purpose)
  flour
90 g (3¼ oz) butter, chilled and cubed
2–3 tablespoons chilled water

FILLING
25 g (1 oz) butter
7 onions, sliced
1 tablespoon dijon mustard

3 eggs, lightly beaten
125 g (4½ oz/½ cup) sour cream
25 g (1 oz/¼ cup) freshly grated
  parmesan cheese

1 Lightly grease a 23 cm (9 inch) round fluted flan (tart) tin. To make the pastry, sift the flour into a bowl. Using your fingertips, rub in the butter until the mixture resembles fine breadcrumbs. Make a well in the centre, add almost all the water and mix with a flat-bladed knife, using a cutting action, until the mixture comes together in beads. Add more water if the dough is too dry.

2 Gather the dough together and lift out onto a lightly floured work surface. Press together until smooth, wrap in plastic wrap and refrigerate for 20 minutes. Roll out between two sheets of baking paper large enough to cover the base and side of the tin. Place the pastry in the tin and trim the edge. Cover with plastic wrap and refrigerate for 20 minutes.

3 Preheat the oven to 180°C (350°F/ Gas 4). Line the pastry case with baking paper and spread with baking beads or uncooked rice. Bake for 10 minutes, remove the paper and beads and bake for another 10 minutes. Cool completely.

4 To make the filling, melt the butter in a large heavy-based frying pan. Add the onion, cover and cook over medium heat for 25 minutes. Uncover and cook for another 10 minutes, stirring often. Cool.

5 Spread the mustard over the pastry, then top with the onion. Whisk together the eggs and sour cream and pour on top. Sprinkle with the parmesan and bake for 35 minutes, or until set. Serve with rocket.

onions

The common dry onion comes in a wide range of varieties, shapes, flavours and sizes. The most readily available are the white, brown and red (also called Spanish), all of which are interchangeable in cooking. The red onion is milder in flavour and can be used raw in salads. High heat will burn onions and give them a bitter flavour so, as a general rule, the longer and slower the chopped or sliced onion is cooked in butter or oil, the sweeter it becomes. Do not buy onions if they have started to sprout. Buy dry-skinned, firm onions and store in a well-ventilated basket so air can circulate to keep them dry. Onions will keep for a month if stored this way.

parmesan cheese

Parmesan is one of the group of cheeses known in Italy as 'formaggi di grana', which are hard, grainy cheeses. They are firm and dry with a strong flavour and are suitable for grating or shredding. In manufacture, the cheese is cooked, then pressed into large wheels and left to mature and dry for up to five years. Parmesan is traditional in Italian recipes, being served with minestrone soup, on pasta dishes and in sauces. It adds flavour to vegetables and is often combined with other cheeses for variation in taste. It keeps well, covered with plastic wrap and refrigerated.

country vegetable pies

Preparation time: 40 minutes
  + 30 minutes chilling time
Cooking time: 45 minutes
Makes 6

PASTRY
250 g (9 oz/2 cups) plain (all-purpose) flour
125 g (4½ oz) butter, chilled and cubed
2 egg yolks
2–3 tablespoons chilled water

FILLING
2 new potatoes, cubed
350 g (12 oz) butternut pumpkin (squash), cubed
100 g (3½ oz) broccoli, cut into small florets
100 g (3½ oz) cauliflower, cut into small florets
1 zucchini (courgette), grated
1 carrot, grated
3 spring onions (scallions), chopped
90 g (3¼ oz/¾ cup) grated cheddar cheese
125 g (4½ oz/½ cup) ricotta cheese
50 g (1¾ oz/½ cup) grated parmesan cheese
3 tablespoons chopped flat-leaf (Italian) parsley
1 egg, lightly beaten

1 To make the pastry, sift the flour into a bowl. Using your fingertips, rub in the butter until the mixture resembles fine breadcrumbs. Make a well in the centre, add the egg yolks and the chilled water and mix with a flat-bladed knife, using a cutting action, until the mixture comes together in beads. Add more water if the dough is too dry. Gently gather the dough together and lift out onto a lightly floured work surface. Press into a ball, wrap in plastic wrap and refrigerate for at least 15 minutes.
2 To make the filling, steam or boil the potato and pumpkin for 10–15 minutes, or until just tender. Drain well and put in a large bowl to cool. Gently fold in the broccoli, cauliflower, zucchini, carrot, spring onion, cheddar, ricotta, parmesan, parsley and egg. Season to taste.

3 Preheat the oven to 190°C (375°F/ Gas 5). Grease six 10 cm (4 inch) pie dishes. Divide the pastry into six portions and roll each portion into a rough 20 cm (8 inch) circle. Place the pastry in the dishes, leaving the excess overhanging.
4 Divide the filling evenly among the pastry cases. Fold over the overhanging pastry, gently folding or pleating as you go. Place on a baking tray, cover and refrigerate for 15 minutes. Bake for 25–30 minutes, or until the pastry is cooked and golden brown. Serve hot.

steak and kidney pie

❋ ❋

Preparation time: **20 minutes**
Cooking time: **1 hour 50 minutes**
Serves **6**

4 lamb kidneys
2 tablespoons plain (all-purpose) flour
750 g (1 lb 10 oz) round steak, trimmed and cut into 2cm (¾ inch) cubes
1 tablespoon oil
1 onion, chopped
30 g (1 oz) butter
1 tablespoon worcestershire sauce
1 tablespoon tomato paste (concentrated purée)
125 ml (4 fl oz/½ cup) red wine
250 ml (9 fl oz/1 cup) beef stock
125 g (4½ oz) button mushrooms, sliced
½ teaspoon dried thyme
4 tablespoons chopped flat-leaf (Italian) parsley
500 g (1 lb 2 oz) block ready-made puff pastry, thawed
1 egg, lightly beaten

1 Peel the skin from the kidneys, quarter them and trim away any fat or sinew. Put the flour in a plastic bag with the beef and kidneys and toss gently. Heat the oil in a frying pan, add the onion and fry for 5 minutes, or until soft. Remove from the pan using a slotted spoon. Add the butter to the pan, brown the beef and kidneys in batches and then return the beef, kidneys and onion to the pan.

2 Add the worcestershire sauce, tomato paste, wine, stock, mushrooms and herbs to the pan. Bring to the boil, reduce the heat and simmer, covered, for 1 hour, or until the meat is tender. Season to taste and allow to cool. Spoon into a 1.5 litre (52 fl oz/6 cup) pie dish.
3 Preheat the oven to 210°C (415°F/ Gas 6–7). Roll the pastry between two sheets of baking paper, to a size 4 cm

(1½ inches) larger than the pie dish. Cut thin strips from the edge of the pastry and press onto the rim of the dish, sealing the joins. Place the pastry on the pie, trim the edges and cut small holes in the top of the pastry to allow any steam to escape. Decorate the pie with leftover pastry and brush the top with egg. Bake for 35–40 minutes, or until the pastry is golden.

steak and kidney pie

This is a traditional British pie. Sometimes oysters, boiled eggs and potatoes are added. The cooled mixture is placed in a casserole dish and topped with a pastry crust. If the pie dish is deep, a decorative funnel, often in the shape of a bird, is placed in the centre of the pie to support the pastry and act as a steam vent during the long cooking. Another traditional dish, known as steak and kidney pudding, uses the same ingredients but they are placed, uncooked, in a pudding basin that is lined with suet pastry. The pudding is then steamed or baked.

bacon

Bacon is meat from the back and side of a pig. It is cured by dry-salting and then smoked to give a distinctive taste. Bacon is usually sold in thin slices called rashers. The middle cut — sometimes called the prime cut — contains the least fat and the most meat. Streaky bacon is cut from the tail end of the loin and is streaked with more fat.

bacon and egg pie

✳ ✳

Preparation time: 40 minutes
Cooking time: 1 hour
Serves 4-6

2 tablespoons oil
4 bacon slices, chopped
250 g (9 oz) block or sheets of shortcrust (pie) pastry
250 g (9 oz) block puff pastry, thawed
5 eggs, beaten
60 ml (2 fl oz/¼ cup) pouring (whipping) cream
1 egg, beaten, extra

1 Lightly grease a 20 cm (8 inch) loose-based pie dish. Heat the oil in a frying pan. Add the bacon and cook over medium heat for a few minutes, or until lightly browned. Drain on paper towels and allow to cool slightly.

2 If using a block of shortcrust pastry, roll out between baking paper until slightly larger than the dish. Line the dish with shortcrust pastry, allowing a slight overlap if using bought sheets. Roll a rolling pin over the dish to trim off any excess pastry. Refrigerate for 20 minutes. Preheat the oven to 210°C (415°F/Gas 6–7).

3 Line the pastry shell with baking paper and spread a layer of baking beads or uncooked rice evenly over the paper. Bake for 10 minutes, then remove the paper and beads and cook for a further 10 minutes, or until the pastry is dry and golden. Allow to cool.

4 Roll out the puff pastry between two sheets of baking paper to a circle large enough to cover the top of the pie. Arrange the bacon over the cooled pastry base and pour the combined egg and cream over the top. Cover the pie with the puff pastry and press on firmly to seal. Trim the pastry edges and decorate the top with shapes cut from the pastry scraps. Brush with the extra egg and bake for 30–35 minutes, or until puffed and golden. Serve at room temperature.

NOTE: This bacon and egg pie can be made a day ahead and refrigerated overnight. Allow to come to room temperature before serving.

cornish pasties

✷ ✷

Preparation time: **40 minutes**
Cooking time: **45 minutes**
Makes **6**

165 g (5¾ oz) round steak, finely chopped
1 small potato, finely chopped
1 small onion, finely chopped
1 small carrot, finely chopped
1–2 teaspoons worcestershire sauce
2 tablespoons beef stock
1 egg, lightly beaten

SHORTCRUST PASTRY
310 g (11 oz/2½ cups) plain (all-purpose)
   flour
125 g (4½ oz) butter, chilled and cubed
80–100 ml (2½–3½ fl oz) chilled water

1 To make the pastry, sift the flour and
a pinch of salt into a large bowl. Using
your fingertips, rub in the butter until
the mixture resembles fine breadcrumbs.
Make a well in the centre and add almost
all the water. Mix with a flat-bladed knife,
using a cutting action, until the mixture
comes together in beads. Add more water
if the dough is too dry. Turn out onto a
lightly floured work surface and form
into a ball. Wrap in plastic wrap and
refrigerate for 20 minutes.
2 Preheat the oven to 210°C (415°F/
Gas 6–7). Lightly grease a baking tray.
Mix together the beef, potato, onion,
carrot, worcestershire sauce and stock in
a bowl and season well.
3 Divide the dough into six portions. Roll
out each portion to 3 mm (⅛ inch) thick.
Using a 16 cm (6¼ inch) diameter plate
as a guide, cut out six circles. Divide the
filling among the circles.
4 Brush the pastry edges with beaten
egg and bring the pastry together to form
a semi-circle. Pinch the edges into a frill
and place on the tray. Brush the pasties
with beaten egg and bake for 15 minutes.
Reduce the oven to 180°C (350°F/Gas 4)
and cook for a further 25–30 minutes, or
until the pastry is golden.

Mix together the beef, potato,
onion, carrot, worcestershire
sauce and stock.

Bring the pastry together to form
a semi-circle and pinch the edges
into a frill.

quiches

These quiches are equally delicious whether served hot or cold. The quantities are suitable to serve up to six people. A green salad is the perfect accompaniment.

pastry for quiches

Sift 215 g (7½ oz/1¾ cups) plain (all-purpose) flour into a bowl and add 100 g (3½ oz) chopped chilled butter. Rub the butter into the flour with your fingertips until it resembles fine breadcrumbs. Make a well in the centre and add 2 tablespoons chilled water. Mix with a flat-bladed knife, using a cutting action, until the mixture comes together in beads. Add a little more water if the dough is too dry. Turn out onto a lightly floured surface and gather into a ball. Wrap in plastic wrap and refrigerate for 20 minutes.

Preheat the oven to 190°C (375°F/Gas 5). Roll out the pastry between two sheets of baking paper to fit a 25 cm (10 inch) fluted flan (tart) tin. Lift the pastry into the tin and press it well into the sides. Trim off any excess by rolling a rolling pin across the top of the tin. Refrigerate the pastry for 20 minutes. Cover the pastry case with baking paper, fill evenly with baking beads or uncooked rice and bake for 15 minutes, or until the pastry is dried out and golden. Cool slightly before filling with one of these fillings. For all these quiches, bake the pastry, then reduce the oven to 180°C (350°F/Gas 4) to cook the filling.

salmon quiche
Drain and flake 415 g (14¾ oz) tinned red salmon and spread over the cooled pastry. Mix 4 lightly beaten eggs, 60 g (2¼ oz/½ cup) grated cheddar cheese, 125 ml (4 fl oz/½ cup) each of milk and pouring (whipping) cream, 4 sliced spring onions (scallions) and 4 tablespoons chopped parsley. Pour over the salmon. Bake for 30 minutes or until set.

quiche lorraine
Melt 30 g (1 oz) butter in a frying pan and cook 1 finely chopped onion and 3 finely chopped bacon slices over medium heat for 10 minutes. Cool, then spread over the cooled pastry. Whisk together 3 eggs, 185 ml (6 fl oz/¾ cup) pouring (whipping) cream and 40 g (1½ oz) grated gruyère cheese. Season. Pour over the onion and sprinkle with 40 g (1½ oz) grated gruyère cheese, extra, and ¼ teaspoon freshly grated nutmeg. Bake for 30 minutes, or until just firm.

crab quiche
Make the pastry as before, then use it to line two greased 12 cm (4½ inch) round, 4 cm (1½ inches) deep flan (tart) tins. Bake as above, then set aside to cool. Heat 20 g (¾ oz) butter in a small frying pan and cook 1 thinly sliced onion until just soft. Remove from the pan and drain on paper towels. Drain a 200 g (7 oz) tin crab meat and squeeze out any excess moisture. Spread the onion and crab over the cooled pastry. Mix 3 eggs, 185 ml (6 fl oz/¾ cup) pouring (whipping) cream and 90 g (3¼ oz/¾ cup) grated cheddar cheese in a bowl. Pour into the pastry case and, if you like, top with some dill sprigs. Bake for 40 minutes, or until lightly golden and set.

asparagus and artichoke quiche
Trim 155 g (5½ oz) asparagus spears, cut into bite-sized pieces and blanch in a saucepan of boiling salted water. Drain, then refresh in iced water. Lightly beat together 3 eggs, 125 ml (4 fl oz/½ cup) pouring (whipping) cream and 40 g (1½ oz/⅓ cup) grated gruyère cheese, then season with salt and pepper. Cut 140 g (5 oz) marinated artichoke hearts into quarters and spread over the cooled pastry with the asparagus. Pour over the egg and cream mixture, then sprinkle with 60 g (2¼ oz/½ cup) grated cheddar cheese. Bake for 25 minutes, or until set and golden. Cover with foil if the pastry browns too quickly.

quiche lorraine (top), asparagus and artichoke quiche (bottom)

raised pork pie

✷ ✷

Preparation time: 50 minutes
  + overnight chilling time
Cooking time: 1 hour 10 minutes
Serves 8

1.2 kg (2 lb 11 oz) minced (ground) pork
100 g (3½ oz/⅔ cup) pistachio nuts,
  chopped
2 green apples, peeled and finely chopped
6 sage leaves, finely chopped
500 g (1 lb 2 oz/4 cups) plain (all-purpose)
  flour
150 g (5½ oz) lard
2 eggs, beaten
1 egg yolk
200 ml (7 fl oz) vegetable stock
200 ml (7 fl oz) unsweetened apple juice
2 teaspoons powdered gelatin

1 Preheat the oven to 200°C (400°F/
Gas 6). Combine the pork, pistachios,
apple and sage in a bowl. Mix well and
season. Cover and refrigerate until ready
to use. Wrap plastic wrap around a 6 cm
(2½ inch) high, round 20 cm (8 inch)
straight-sided tin, then turn the tin over
and grease the plastic wrap.
2 Sift the flour and 1 teaspoon salt into
a bowl and make a well in the centre.
Put the lard in a saucepan with 210 ml
(7½ fl oz) water, bring to the boil and
add to the flour with the egg. Mix with a
wooden spoon until combined, then turn
out onto a work surface and bring the
mixture together to form a smooth dough.
Unlike any other kind of pastry, this
hot-water pastry must be kept warm.
Cover with a tea towel (dish cloth) and
leave in a warm place for 10 minutes until
cool enough to handle.
3 When the pastry is just warm, set
aside one-third — do not refrigerate.
Roll the remainder into a circle large
enough to just cover the outside of the
tin. Lift onto a rolling pin and place over
the tin, working fast before the pastry
sets. Refrigerate until the pastry hardens.
Carefully pull out the tin and remove
the pastry shell and plastic wrap. Attach

Cover the outside of the tin with
the pastry, working quickly so that
the pastry does not set.

The greased paper collar should
fit snugly around the outside of
the pastry.

Gradually pour the gelatin into
the cooked and cooled pie until
it is full.

a paper collar made of two layers of greased baking paper around the outside of the pastry so it fits snugly. Secure with string or a metal paper clip at the top and bottom. Fill the pie with the pork mixture, then roll out the remaining pastry to form a lid. Attach it to the base with some water, pressing or crimping it to make it look neat. Cut a small hole in the top.

4 Put the pie on a baking tray. Bake for 40 minutes and check the pastry top. If it is still pale, bake for a further 10 minutes, then remove the paper. Brush with the egg yolk mixed with 1 tablespoon water and bake for a further 15 minutes, or until the sides are brown. Remove from the oven and allow to cool completely.

5 Bring the stock and half the apple juice to the boil. Place the remaining apple juice in a measuring cup, sprinkle the gelatin over the surface and leave to go spongy, then add to the stock and mix until the gelatin dissolves. Put a small funnel (piping nozzles work well) in the hole of the pie, pour in a little gelatin mixture, leave to settle and then pour in some more until the pie is full. Fill the pie completely so there will be no gaps when the gelatin sets. Refrigerate overnight.

creamy snapper pies

✹ ✹

Preparation time: 25 minutes
Cooking time: 1 hour 20 minutes
Serves 4

2 tablespoons olive oil
4 onions, thinly sliced
375 ml (13 fl oz/1½ cups) fish stock
875 ml (30 fl oz/3½ cups) pouring
    (whipping) cream
1 kg (2 lb 4 oz) skinless, boneless snapper
    fillets, cut into large pieces
2 sheets puff pastry, thawed
1 egg, lightly beaten

1 Preheat the oven to 220°C (425°F/ Gas 7). Heat the oil in a large deep-sided frying pan, add the onion and cook, stirring occasionally, over medium heat

for 20 minutes, or until the onion is golden brown and slightly caramelised.

2 Add the stock, bring to the boil and cook for 10 minutes, or until the liquid has nearly evaporated. Stir in the cream and bring to the boil. Reduce the heat and simmer for about 20 minutes, until the liquid has reduced by half or until it coats the back of a spoon.

3 Divide half the sauce among four deep, 500 ml (17 fl oz/2 cup) ovenproof dishes. Put one-quarter of the fish pieces in each dish, then divide the remaining sauce among the dishes.

4 Cut the pastry sheets into shapes slightly larger than the tops of the dishes. Brush the edges of the pastry with a little of the egg. Press onto the dishes. Brush lightly with the remaining beaten egg. Bake for 30 minutes, or until the pastry is golden and puffed.

NOTE: You can substitute bream, sea perch or garfish for the snapper.

sausage rolls

Preparation time: 30 minutes
Cooking time: 30 minutes
Makes 36

3 sheets puff pastry, thawed
2 eggs, beaten
750 g (1 lb 10 oz) sausage meat
1 onion, finely chopped
1 garlic clove, crushed
80 g (2¾ oz/1 cup) fresh breadcrumbs
3 tablespoons chopped flat-leaf
    (Italian) parsley
3 tablespoons chopped thyme
½ teaspoon ground sage
½ teaspoon freshly grated nutmeg
½ teaspoon ground cloves

1 Preheat the oven to 200°C (400°F/
Gas 6). Lightly grease two baking trays.
Cut the pastry sheets in half and lightly
brush the edges with some beaten egg.
2 Mix half the remaining egg with the
remaining ingredients in a large bowl,
then divide into six portions. Pipe or
spoon the filling down the centre of each
piece of pastry, then brush the edges
with some of the remaining egg. Fold the
pastry over the filling, overlapping the
edges and placing the join underneath.
3 Brush the rolls with more egg, then cut
each into six short pieces. Cut two small
slashes on top of each roll, place on the
baking trays and bake for 15 minutes.
Reduce the temperature to 180°C (350°F/
Gas 4) and bake for a further 15 minutes,
or until puffed and golden.

chicken sausage rolls

Preparation time: 30 minutes
Cooking time: 30 minutes
Makes 36

3 sheets frozen puff pastry, thawed
2 eggs, lightly beaten
750 g (1 lb 10 oz) minced (ground) chicken
4 spring onions (scallions), finely chopped
80 g (2¾ oz/1 cup) fresh breadcrumbs
1 carrot, finely grated
2 tablespoons fruit chutney
1 tablespoon sweet chilli sauce
1 tablespoon grated fresh ginger
sesame seeds, to sprinkle

1 Preheat the oven to 200°C (400°F/
Gas 6). Lightly grease two baking trays.
Cut the pastry sheets in half and lightly
brush the edges with some beaten egg.
2 Mix half of the remaining egg with the
remaining ingredients, except the sesame
seeds, in a large bowl and then divide the
mixture into six portions. Pipe or spoon
the filling along the centre of each piece
of pastry, then brush the edges with some
of the remaining egg. Fold the pastry over
the filling, overlapping the edges and
placing the join underneath.
3 Brush the rolls with more egg, sprinkle
with sesame seeds, then cut each into
six short pieces. Cut two small slashes
on top of each roll, place on the baking
trays and bake for 15 minutes. Reduce
the temperature to 180°C (350°F/Gas 4)
and bake for a further 15 minutes, or until
puffed and golden.

chicken sausage rolls

beef and potato pies

✳ ✳

Preparation time: 25 minutes
Cooking time: 1 hour 5 minutes
Serves 6

1 kg (2 lb 4 oz) all-purpose potatoes,
    chopped
1 tablespoon oil
1 onion, finely chopped
1 garlic clove, crushed
500 g (1 lb 2 oz) minced (ground) beef
2 tablespoons plain (all-purpose) flour
500 ml (17 fl oz/2 cups) beef stock
2 tablespoons tomato paste (concentrated
    purée)
1 tablespoon worcestershire sauce
500 g (1 lb 2 oz) block or 6 sheets
    shortcrust (pie) pastry, thawed
50 g (1¾ oz) butter, softened
60 ml (2 fl oz/¼ cup) milk

1 Steam or boil the potato for 10 minutes,
or until tender. Drain well, then mash.
2 Preheat the oven to 210°C (415°F/
Gas 6–7). Heat the oil in a frying pan, add
the onion and cook for 5 minutes, or until
soft. Add the garlic and cook for 1 minute.
Add the beef and cook for 5 minutes, or
until browned, breaking up any lumps.
3 Sprinkle the flour over the beef and stir
to combine. Add the stock, tomato paste,
worcestershire sauce, salt and pepper and
stir for 2 minutes. Bring to the boil, then
reduce the heat slightly and simmer for
5 minutes, or until reduced and
thickened. Allow to cool completely.
4 Lightly grease six 11 cm (4¼ inch)
pie dishes. If using a block of pastry, roll
between baking paper to 3mm (⅛ inch)
thick. Using a 15 cm (6 inch) plate as a
guide, cut the pastry into circles and line
the dishes. Line the pastry with baking
paper, spread evenly with baking beads
or uncooked rice and bake for 7 minutes.
Remove the paper and beads and cook for
a further 5 minutes. Allow to cool.
5 Divide the filling among the pastry
cases. Stir the butter and milk into the
mashed potato and pipe or spread on top.
Bake for 20 minutes, or until golden.

worcestershire sauce

This condiment was developed in India by an
Englishman. It was first bottled by a company
called Lea and Perrins, in the town of Worcester
in England, hence the name. Today it is still made
by the same company. Widely available the world
over, it is a piquant mixture of onions, garlic,
tamarind, soy sauce, molasses, lime, anchovies
and vinegar. It is used to add flavour to stews,
gravies and soups, and is an essential ingredient
in the cocktail called Bloody Mary.

stir over low heat for 5 minutes. Stir in the garlic and cook for 3 minutes. Remove from the pan.

2 Heat another tablespoon of oil in the pan, add the beef and stir over medium heat until browned, breaking up any lumps with a fork. Return the onion to the pan and stir well. Add the cumin, oregano and a teaspoon each of salt and pepper, and stir for 2 minutes. Transfer to a bowl and allow to cool. Wipe out the pan.

3 Heat the remaining oil in the pan and stir-fry the potato for 1 minute over high heat. Reduce the heat to low and stir for 5 minutes, or until tender. Transfer to a plate to cool, then gently mix into the beef mixture. Preheat the oven to 200°C (400°F/Gas 6). Grease two baking trays.

4 Divide the pastry into two portions and roll each out on a lightly floured surface until 2.5 mm (⅛ inch) thick. Cut out rounds using a 10 cm (4 inch) cutter.

5 Spoon the beef mixture onto one half of each pastry round, leaving a border all around. Place a few olive pieces and some chopped egg on top. Brush the pastry border with egg white. Fold each pastry over to make a half-moon shape, pressing firmly to seal. Press the edges with a floured fork, then transfer to the trays. Combine the egg yolk, paprika and sugar and brush over the empanadas. Bake for 15 minutes, or until golden.

chicken and bacon gougère

✹ ✹

Preparation time: 40 minutes
Cooking time: 50 minutes
Serves 6

60 g (2¼ oz) butter
1–2 garlic cloves, crushed
1 red onion, chopped
3 bacon slices, chopped
30 g (1 oz/¼ cup) plain (all-purpose) flour
375 ml (13 fl oz/1½ cups) milk
125 ml (4 fl oz/½ cup) pouring (whipping) cream

empanadas

✹ ✹

Preparation time: 1 hour 10 minutes
Cooking time: 45 minutes
Serves 8

60 ml (2 fl oz/¼ cup) olive oil
250 g (9 oz) onions, finely diced
4 spring onions (scallions), thinly sliced
3 garlic cloves, crushed
200 g (7 oz) minced (ground) beef
2 teaspoons ground cumin
2 teaspoons dried oregano
250 g (9 oz) potatoes, cut into small cubes
500 g (1 lb 2 oz) block puff pastry
100 g (3½ oz) black olives, pitted and cut into quarters
2 hard-boiled eggs, peeled and finely chopped
1 egg, separated
pinch of paprika
pinch of sugar

1 Heat 1 tablespoon of the oil in a frying pan, add the onion and spring onion and

2 teaspoons wholegrain mustard
250 g (9 oz) cooked chicken, chopped
30 g (1 oz) chopped parsley

CHOUX PASTRY
60 g (2¼ oz/½ cup) plain (all-purpose)
  flour
60 g (2¼ oz) butter, cubed
2 eggs, lightly beaten
35 g (1¼ oz/⅓ cup) freshly grated
  parmesan cheese

1 Melt the butter in a frying pan, add
the garlic, onion and bacon and cook for
5–7 minutes, stirring occasionally, or until
cooked but not brown. Stir in the flour
and cook for 1 minute. Gradually add the
milk, stir until thickened, then simmer for
2 minutes. Add the cream and mustard.
Remove from the heat and fold in the
chicken and parsley. Season with pepper.
2 To make the choux pastry, sift the
flour onto baking paper. Put the butter
in a large saucepan with 125 ml (4 fl oz/
½ cup) water and stir over medium
heat until the mixture comes to the boil.
Remove from the heat, add the flour in
one go and quickly beat it into the liquid
using a wooden spoon. Return to the heat
and continue beating until the mixture
forms a ball and leaves the side of the
pan. Remove from the heat.
3 Transfer to a large clean bowl and
allow to cool slightly. Gradually add the
egg, about 3 teaspoons at a time. Beat
well after each addition until all the egg
has been added and the mixture is thick
and glossy — a wooden spoon should
stand up in it. If it is too runny, the egg
has been added too quickly. If so, beat for
several minutes more, or until thickened.
Stir in the parmesan.
4 Preheat the oven to 210°C (415°F/
Gas 6–7). Grease a deep 23 cm (9 inch)
ovenproof dish, pour in the filling and
spoon heaped tablespoons of choux
pastry around the outside. Bake for
10 minutes, then reduce the oven to
180°C (350°F/Gas 4). Bake for a further
20 minutes, or until the choux is puffed
and golden. Serve sprinkle with a little
grated parmesan, if desired.

mustards

Mustard is produced from three mustard plants
with different-coloured seeds: white or yellow,
brown and black. Its use as a condiment dates
back to Greek and Roman times. The French
have had exclusive rights to make dijon mustard
since 1634. English powdered mustard came into
favour in the 18th century and was later produced
commercially in Norfolk by Mr Colman. This
company still makes the powder today.

tartlets

These savoury tartlet recipes are simplicity itself and will provide you with ideas for quick lunch or first course dishes. Most can be ready in half an hour.

These delicious tartlets can be made with either homemade (page 142) or bought puff pastry. They can be made as four individual serves or two rectangles to serve 4 people.

You will need 500 g (1 lb 2 oz) of puff pastry. The pastry should be divided into two and each portion rolled between two sheets of baking paper. If making four tartlets, cut out two 12 cm (4½ inch) circles of pastry from each portion, or for two long tartlets roll each portion of pastry into a rectangle 12 x 25 cm (4½ x 10 inches). The topping variations are placed on the pastry shapes, leaving a 1.5 cm (⅝ inch) border. The tartlets are then baked in the top half of a preheated 200°C (400°F/Gas 6) oven. These tartlets are best served warm or hot. They are delicious accompanied by a dressed green salad.

tapenade and anchovy tartlets Spread 125 g (4½ oz/ ½ cup) tapenade evenly over the pastry, leaving a 1.5 cm (⅝ inch) border. Drain a 45 g (1¾ oz) tin of anchovies, cut them into thin strips and arrange over the top of the tapenade. Sprinkle 35 g (1¼ oz/⅓ cup) grated parmesan cheese and 75 g (2¾ oz/½ cup) grated mozzarella cheese over the top and bake for 10 minutes, or until risen and golden.

fried green tomato tartlets Thinly slice 2 green tomatoes. Heat 1 tablespoon oil in a large frying pan, add ½ teaspoon ground cumin and 1 crushed garlic clove and cook for 1 minute. Add the tomatoes in two batches and cook for 2–3 minutes each batch, adding more oil and garlic if needed, until slightly softened. Drain on paper towels. Combine 90 g (3¼ oz/⅓ cup) sour cream, 2 tablespoons chopped basil and 2 tablespoons chopped parsley and set aside. Sprinkle 120 g (4¼ oz/1 cup) grated cheddar cheese over the centre of the pastry bases, leaving a 1.5 cm (⅝ inch) border. Arrange the tomato over the cheese and bake for 10 minutes. Place a dollop of the sour cream mixture in the middle and sprinkle the tarts with another tablespoon of shredded basil.

mushroom, asparagus and feta tartlets Heat 2 tablespoons oil in a frying pan, add 400 g (14 oz) sliced button mushrooms and stir until softened. Remove from the heat and add 2 tablespoons chopped parsley. Stir and season. Spoon onto the pastry bases, leaving a 1.5 cm (⅝ inch) border. Bake for 10–15 minutes, until risen and brown. Top with 200 g (7 oz) crumbled feta cheese and steamed asparagus spears.

italian summer tartlets Heat 2 tablespoons olive oil in a saucepan over low heat, add 2 sliced red onions and cook, stirring occasionally, for 10 minutes. Add 1 tablespoon each of balsamic vinegar and soft brown sugar and cook for 10 minutes, or until soft and lightly browned. Remove from the heat, stir in 1 tablespoon chopped thyme, then leave to cool. Spread evenly over the pastry, leaving a 1.5 cm (⅝ inch) border. Bake for 10 minutes. Drain a 170 g (5¾ oz) jar of quartered, marinated artichokes and arrange over the onion. Top with 24 pitted black olives and 6 prosciutto slices, lightly rolled and quartered. Drizzle with extra virgin olive oil and garnish with thyme.

cherry tomato and pesto tartlets Spread 125 g (4½ oz/½ cup) pesto over the pastry, leaving a 1.5 cm (⅝ inch) border. Top with cherry tomatoes (you will need about 375 g/ 13 oz), season with salt and freshly ground black pepper and bake for 10 minutes, or until golden. Drizzle with extra virgin olive oil and garnish with thyme sprigs.

clockwise from top: mushroom, asparagus and feta tartlets; Italian summer tartlets; cherry tomato and pesto tartlets

spinach and feta triangles

✳ ✳

Preparation time: **30 minutes**
Cooking time: **45 minutes**
Makes **8**

1 kg (2 lb 4 oz) English spinach
80 ml (2½ fl oz/⅓ cup) olive oil
1 onion, chopped
10 spring onions (scallions), sliced
4 tablespoons chopped parsley
1 tablespoon chopped dill
large pinch of ground nutmeg
35 g (1¼ oz/⅓ cup) freshly grated
　parmesan cheese
150 g (5½ oz) crumbled feta cheese
90 g (3¼ oz) ricotta cheese
4 eggs, lightly beaten
40 g (1½ oz) butter, melted
12 sheets filo pastry

1　Trim any coarse stems from the spinach, then wash the leaves thoroughly, roughly chop and place in a large saucepan with just a little water clinging to them. Cover and cook over low heat for 5 minutes, or until wilted. Drain well and allow to cool slightly before squeezing tightly to remove the excess water.

2　Heat 60ml (2 fl oz/¼ cup) of the oil in a heavy-based frying pan. Add the onion and cook over low heat for 10 minutes, or until tender and golden. Add the spring onion and cook for another 3 minutes. Remove from the heat. Stir in the spinach, parsley, dill, nutmeg, parmesan, feta, ricotta and egg. Season well.

3　Preheat the oven to 180°C (350°F/ Gas 4). Lightly grease two baking trays.

Combine the butter with the remaining oil. Work with three sheets of filo pastry at a time, keeping the rest covered with a damp tea towel (dish towel). Brush each sheet with butter mixture and layer them, then cut in half lengthways.

4　Place 4 tablespoons of the filling on an angle at the end of each strip. Fold the pastry over to enclose the filling and form a triangle. Continue folding the triangle over until you reach the end of the pastry. Put the triangles on the baking trays and brush with the remaining butter mixture. Repeat with the remaining filo and filling. Bake for 20–25 minutes, or until the pastry is golden brown.

NOTE: Feta is a traditional Greek-style salty cheese that should be stored in lightly salted water and kept refrigerated. Rinse and pat dry before using.

Lift the corner of the filo pastry and fold it over to enclose the spinach and form a triangle.

Continue folding the triangle over until you reach the end of the strip of filo pastry.

filo pastry

This is a pastry commonly used in Middle Eastern, Turkish, Greek, Austrian and Hungarian cuisines. It is a very thin pastry that is layered and used to fill and wrap around both sweet and savoury foods. When baked, the flaky layers are light, crisp and golden. It is readily available in supermarkets. When working with filo, keep the unused sheets covered with a slightly damp tea towel (dish towel). The pastry is so thin that it dries out very quickly and becomes unworkable. Brush the filo lightly with oil or melted butter using a wide pastry brush so that the pastry is covered as quickly as possible and doesn't have time to dry out. Spray oil can also be used if preferred.

lamb and filo pie

Preparation time: 20 minutes
Cooking time: 55 minutes
Serves 6

2 tablespoons oil
2 onions, chopped
1 garlic clove, chopped
1 teaspoon ground cumin
1 teaspoon ground coriander
½ teaspoon ground cinnamon
1 kg (2 lb 4 oz) minced (ground) lamb
3 tablespoons chopped flat-leaf (Italian) parsley
2 tablespoons chopped mint
1 tablespoon tomato paste (concentrated purée)

10 sheets filo pastry
250 g (9 oz) butter, melted

1 Heat the oil in a large frying pan. Add the onion and garlic and cook for 3 minutes, or until just soft. Add the cumin, coriander and cinnamon and cook, stirring continuously, for 1 minute. Add the lamb to the pan and cook over medium heat for 10 minutes, or until the lamb is brown and all the liquid has evaporated. Use a fork to break up any lumps of meat. Add the herbs, tomato paste and ¼ teaspoon salt and mix well. Allow to cool completely.
2 Preheat the oven to 180°C (350°F/ Gas 4). Lightly grease a 23 x 33 cm (9 x 13 inch) ovenproof dish. Remove three sheets of filo. Cover the remainder with a damp tea towel (dish towel) to prevent them drying out. Brush the top sheet of filo with melted butter. Cover with another two sheets of filo and brush the top one with butter. Line the ovenproof dish with these sheets, leaving the excess overhanging the dish.
3 Spread the lamb mixture over the pastry and fold the overhanging pastry over the filling. Butter two sheets of filo, place one on top of the other and fold in half. Place over the top of the filling and tuck in the edges. Butter the remaining sheets of filo, cut roughly into squares and then scrunch these over the top of the pie. Bake the pie for 40 minutes, or until the pastry is crisp and golden.

feta

This Greek cheese is popular in Greek salads and savoury pastries. It is a soft, white cheese with a sharp, salty taste. It is made using the milk from sheep or goats and sometimes cows. The salty taste is intense because the cheese is ripened or pickled in a brine solution. It has a short ripening period of about one month. When buying feta, make sure it looks moist and is sitting in a briny solution. To store feta, place it in a container and cover with a salty solution. Change the solution daily and use the feta within four days. Feta cheese is made in many countries where it is quite popular, including Italy, Bulgaria, Denmark, Germany and Australia.

sweet potato, feta and pine nut strudel

Preparation time: **25 minutes**
Cooking time: **55 minutes**
Serves **6**

450 g (1 lb) sweet potato, cut into 2 cm (¾ inch) cubes
1 tablespoon olive oil
80 g (2¾ oz/½ cup) pine nuts, toasted (see Note)
250 g (9 oz) feta cheese, crumbled
2 tablespoons chopped basil
4 spring onions (scallions), chopped
40 g (1½ oz) butter, melted
2 tablespoons olive oil, extra, for brushing
7 sheets filo pastry
2–3 teaspoons sesame seeds

1 Preheat the oven to 180°C (350°F/ Gas 4). Brush the sweet potato with the oil and bake for 20 minutes, or until softened and slightly coloured. Transfer to a bowl and cool slightly.
2 Add the pine nuts, feta, basil and spring onion to the bowl, mix gently and season to taste.
3 Mix the butter and extra oil. Remove one sheet of filo pastry and cover the rest with a damp tea towel (dish towel) to prevent them from drying out. Brush each sheet of filo with the butter mixture and layer them into a pile.
4 Spread the prepared filling in the centre of the filo, covering an area about 10 x 30 cm (4 x 12 inches). Fold the sides of the pastry into the centre, then tuck in the ends. Carefully turn the strudel over and place, seam-side down, on a baking tray. Lightly brush the top with the butter mixture and sprinkle with the sesame seeds. Bake for 35 minutes, or until the pastry is crisp and golden. Serve warm.

NOTE: You can use 450 g (1 lb) of pumpkin (winter squash) instead of the sweet potato. To toast pine nuts, dry-fry them in a frying pan, stirring and watching constantly so they don't burn.

vol au vents

✳ ✳

Preparation time: **35 minutes**
Cooking time: **30 minutes**
Serves **4**

250 g (9 oz) block puff pastry, thawed
1 egg, lightly beaten

SAUCE AND FILLING
40 g (1½ oz) butter
2 spring onions (scallions), finely chopped
2 tablespoons plain (all-purpose) flour
375 ml (13 fl oz/1½ cups) milk
your choice of filling (see Note)

1 Preheat the oven to 220°C (425°F/Gas 7). Line a baking tray with baking paper. Roll out the pastry to a 20 cm (8 inch) square. Cut out four rounds of pastry with a 10 cm (4 inch) cutter. Place the rounds on the tray and use a 6 cm (2½ inch) cutter to cut a circle into the centre of each, taking care not to cut right through the pastry. Place the baking tray in the refrigerator for 15 minutes.
2 Using a floured knife blade, 'knock up' the side of each pastry round by making even indentations about 1 cm (½ inch) apart around the circumference. This should allow even rising of the pastry as it cooks. The dough can be made ahead of time up to this stage and frozen until needed. Carefully brush the pastry with the egg, avoiding the 'knocked up' edge as any glaze spilt on the sides will stop the pastry from rising. Bake for 15–20 minutes, or until the pastry has risen and is golden brown and crisp. Transfer to a wire rack to cool.
3 Remove the centre from each pastry circle, then pull out and discard any partially cooked pastry from the middle. The pastry cases can be returned to the oven for 2 minutes to dry out if the centre is undercooked. The cases are now ready to be filled with your choice of hot filling before serving.
4 To make the sauce, melt the butter in a saucepan, add the spring onion and stir over low heat for 2 minutes, or until soft.

Add the flour and stir for 2 minutes, or until lightly golden. Gradually add the milk, stirring until smooth. Stir constantly over medium heat for 4 minutes, or until the mixture boils and thickens. Season well. Remove and stir in your choice of filling (see Note).

NOTE: Add 350 g (12 oz) of any of the following to the white sauce: cooked sliced mushrooms; chopped cooked prawns (shrimp); chopped cooked chicken; flaked poached salmon; cooked and dressed crabmeat; oysters; steamed chopped asparagus spears.

Cut out four circles from the puff pastry with a 10 cm (4 inch) cutter.

Cut 6 cm (2½ inch) circles part of the way through the pastry.

Make indentations around the outside of the pastry with a knife.

bread

We've all been there, innocently walking past a bakery, not feeling particularly hungry, but then the smell of freshly baked bread reaches you and suddenly you're hit by a craving that must be satisfied immediately. Well, imagine having a private bakery in your own kitchen, devouring still-warm bread with a slathering of butter or a good drizzle of fruity extra virgin olive oil. Once you've mastered the basics, you'll quickly see how easy it is to add seeds, fruit, nuts, olives or cheese to produce another masterpiece. But remember, as tempting as it may seem, man cannot live by bread alone.

all about bread

When you master the techniques described here, in no time you will be able to rustle up everything from crusty loaves and rolls to pizza bases and panettone.

plain bread

Once you understand some of the important elements of bread making, such as working with yeast, and kneading techniques, you will find that delicious bread is simple to make. As with all cookery, first read the recipe thoroughly, then carefully weigh all the ingredients and assemble the equipment you need.

mysteries of yeast solved

Yeast is available dried or fresh. Dried yeast, available at supermarkets, generally comes in a box containing 7 g (¼ oz) sachets, one of which is enough for a standard loaf. Fresh yeast, sometimes harder to obtain, is available at some health food shops and bakeries. It has quite a short storage life. A 7 g (¼ oz) sachet of dried yeast is equivalent to 15 g (½ oz) of fresh yeast. We have used dried yeast in our recipes as it is readily available, can be stored in the pantry and carries a use-by date. Two teaspoons of dried yeast is equivalent to one 7g sachet.

types of flour

The type and quality of flour you use is vital. The correct flour makes a big difference to the quality of bread. Many recipes call for the use of flour that is labelled as strong, or bread, flour. This is high in protein and will form gluten, which helps the bread rise well and bake into a light, airy loaf with a good crust. Regular wheat flour has less gluten, but for most breads it will still give a good result.

making a plain loaf

This basic recipe is an excellent starting point, as similar techniques are used in all bread making. Put 2 teaspoons dried yeast, 125 ml (4 fl oz/½ cup) warm water and 1 teaspoon caster (superfine) sugar in a small bowl and stir well to combine. Leave in a warm, draught-free place for 10 minutes, or until bubbles appear on the surface. The mixture should be frothy and slightly increased in volume. If it isn't, the yeast is dead, so discard it and start again. Sift 500 g (1 lb 2 oz/4 cups) white strong flour, 1 teaspoon salt, 2 tablespoons dried whole milk powder and 1 tablespoon caster (superfine) sugar into a large bowl. Make a well in the centre, add the yeast mixture, 60 ml (2 fl oz/¼ cup) vegetable oil and 250 ml (9 fl oz/1 cup) lukewarm water. Mix to a soft dough using a large metal spoon. The moisture content of flour can vary between brands and even between batches so add extra water or flour, 1 tablespoon at a time, if the dough is too dry or too sticky. Do not add too much flour because the dough will absorb more flour during kneading.

kneading the dough

Don't be tempted to cut short the kneading time as it affects the texture of the finished bread. Kneading distributes the yeast evenly throughout the dough and allows the flour's protein to develop into gluten. Gluten gives the dough elasticity, strength and the ability to expand, as it traps the carbon dioxide gas created by the yeast and this allows the bread to rise.

The kneading action is simple and it really is quite easy to get into a rhythm. Form the dough into a ball on a lightly floured surface. Hold one end down with one hand, and stretch it away from you with the other hand. Fold the dough back together, make a quarter turn and repeat the action. Continue to knead for 10 minutes, or until the dough is smooth and elastic. When you have finished, gather the dough into a ball, then follow the instructions on the following page to complete the bread-making process.

prepare to bake

Once you've finished kneading the dough, there's little more work to be done. Sit down with a cup of tea while the proving process works its magic.

proving the bread

After kneading, put the dough in a lightly greased bowl to prevent it sticking. Cover loosely with plastic wrap or a clean damp tea towel (dish towel). This helps to retain moisture and stop the formation of a skin. Leave in a warm, draught-free place (around 30°C/86°F is ideal) to allow the dough to rise — this stage is called proving. Do not put the dough in a very hot environment in an attempt to speed up the rising process as it will give an unpleasant flavour and may damage the yeast action. The dough will take longer to rise in a cooler environment, but with no adverse effect. When it is ready it should be doubled in size and not spring back when touched with a fingertip. This will take about 1 hour. Lightly grease a 9 cm (3½ inch) deep, 9 x 22 cm (3½ x 8½ inch) loaf (bar) tin with melted butter or oil.

knocking back

After proving, knock back the dough (give it just one punch to expel the air), and knead briefly for 1 minute, or until smooth. The dough is ready for shaping. Handle it carefully and gently and avoid excessive shaping. Shape it to fit the tin, putting it in with any seam at the base. Cover with plastic wrap or a damp tea towel and place in a warm, draught-free place until well risen and doubled in size. This will take about 45–60 minutes.

baking

Preheat the oven to 210°C (415°F/Gas 6–7). Beat 1 egg with 1 tablespoon milk and brush over the top of the dough. Bake the bread in the middle of the oven for 10 minutes. Don't open the oven during the first 10 minutes, as intense heat is needed during this time. Reduce the oven to 180°C (350°F/Gas 4) and bake for another 30–40 minutes. Turn the loaf out of the tin and tap the base. It will sound hollow when cooked. If not, return it to the tin and bake for 5–10 minutes. Transfer to a wire rack.

other shapes

Bread dough can be made into many shapes. Place on a greased baking tray, sprinkled with polenta or fine cornmeal if desired.

bloomer

At the shaping stage, roll out the dough on a lightly floured surface to a rectangle about 2.5 cm (1 inch) thick. Starting at the short end, roll up the dough quite firmly to make a short, rather thick loaf. Place on the baking tray, seam-side down. Cover with a tea towel and leave in a warm, draught-free place for 1 hour, or until doubled in size. Using a sharp knife, make 6 evenly spaced slashes across the top of the dough. Spray it with a little water and place in a 220°C (425°F/Gas 7) oven for 10 minutes. Reduce the oven to 200°C (400°F/Gas 6) and bake for 30 minutes more, or until golden brown and the loaf sounds hollow when tapped on the base. Cool on a wire rack.

plaited loaf

At the shaping stage, divide the dough into three portions. Gently roll each portion into a 30 cm (12 inch) sausage, then transfer to a greased baking tray. Arrange next to one another on the tray, then join the strands at one end and start plaiting them together. Pinch and tuck under at both ends to seal the plait. Cover with a tea towel (dish towel) and set aside in a warm, draught-free place for 1 hour, or until doubled in size. Brush with milk and bake in a 220°C (425°F/Gas 7) oven for 10 minutes. Reduce the oven to 200°C (400°F/Gas 6) and cook for 30 minutes, or until golden brown and the loaf sounds hollow when tapped on the base. Cool on a wire rack.

storage

Home-baked bread is best eaten on the day of baking, or otherwise used to make toast. It can be tightly wrapped and frozen for up to 3 months. Thaw at room temperature, then refresh in a 180°C (350°F/Gas 4) oven for 10 minutes.

what went wrong: bread

perfect The bread has a good, even crumb and the loaf has risen evenly and well. It has even spring on the sides and sounds hollow when tapped. The bread is coloured to a golden brown.

overcooked The crust is too dark and is cracked on top. The crumb is dry. The oven may have been too hot or the cooking time too long or there may have been too much sugar in the dough. The bread may have been placed too high in the oven.

undercooked The crumb is damp and sticky and the crust soft and pale. If very under-baked, the loaf may not hold its shape and may be wet or have wet holes. If the loaf does not sound hollow when tapped, bake it for another 5–10 minutes. Check that the oven is the correct temperature before putting the dough in.

what went wrong: focaccia

perfect The bread is evenly and well risen and has coloured to a golden brown. The crust is crisp but not hard.

soggy, under-baked The crust is soft and pale and the crumb is dense and wet. The bread may not have been cooked long enough, or the oven temperature may have been too low. The yeast may have been stale or 'killed' by using hot water when dissolving it. Also, the dough may have been too wet because of the addition of too much water.

uneven rising, puffy The dough was not rolled evenly. Also, the dough may not have been sufficiently kneaded during the first stage. The proving time for the dough may have been too long or too much yeast may have been used.

If the focaccia rose poorly, this indicates the yeast may have been old or expired or the dough was overworked during kneading. The yeast may have worked itself out too quickly due to being placed in a spot that was too warm for proving.

what went wrong: pizza

perfect The dough is well risen and lightly browned. It is crisp but not tough. The topping is evenly spread and light golden brown.

risen too much The dough is unevenly risen and may be dry with a yeasty taste. Too much yeast may have been used or the dough may have been allowed to prove too quickly (too warm) or for too long.

uneven rising, puffy The dough was not evenly rolled and the topping not even. The oven temperature may have been uneven or the shelf placed too high or too low.

> If the pizza base is soggy, this may be because the base was rolled too thickly or too much topping was used. The topping may have been too wet or not cooked for long enough. The oven temperature may have been incorrect.

common problems

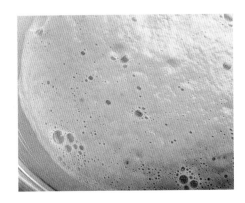

perfect versus dead yeast
The mixture above looks frothy and slightly increased in size — this is perfect. If your yeast mixture has not risen and is not frothy, the yeast is dead. If this happens, you will have to throw it away the mixture and start again. Take care when measuring the yeast. The water should be tepid, not too warm, or you may kill the yeast. If using dried yeast, check the expiry date on the packet.

loaf smells and tastes of yeast
If there is a strong smell and taste of yeast, the bread was undercooked or there was too much yeast used in proportion to the amount of flour.

loaf didn't rise or rose poorly
If the loaf didn't rise or rose poorly, the yeast was old or dead. The liquid may have been too hot and killed the yeast. The yeast may have worked itself out too early by being placed to prove in a spot that was too warm. It may have been left too long to prove.

loaf over-risen and puffy If there are large holes in the loaf and it is risen too much and puffy, the dough may have been insufficiently kneaded during the first kneading stage. The proving time for the dough may have too long, or the dough may not have been correctly knocked back before shaping the loaf.

loaf crust and crumb separate
If the crumb and crust separate from one another, the bread dough was not properly knocked back before shaping the loaf.

loaf rose unevenly If the loaf rises unevenly, or is cracked along one side, the oven tempereature was uneven or the bread was not placed in the centre of the oven or was too close to the oven heating elements. The baking tin used may have been too small.

loaf has uneven colour If the bread is unevenly coloured, the oven temperature was uneven, too high or the bread was too low in the oven.

loaf has a hard crust A hard crust forms if the dough is not covered during the rising stage, allowing the surface to dry out and form a crust.

cottage loaf

☼ ☼

Preparation time: **30 minutes**
 + **1 hour 25 minutes** proving time
Cooking time: **40 minutes**
Makes **1 large loaf**

2 teaspoons dried yeast
1 tablespoon soft brown sugar
250 g (9 oz/2 cups) white strong flour
300 g (10½ oz/2 cups) wholemeal
 (whole-wheat) strong flour
1 tablespoon vegetable oil

1 Put the yeast, 1 teaspoon of the sugar
and 125 ml (4 fl oz/½ cup) warm water
in a small bowl and mix well. Leave in a
warm, draught-free place for 10 minutes,
or until bubbles appear on the surface.
The mixture should be frothy and slightly
increased in volume.
2 Put the flours and 1 teaspoon salt in a
large bowl. Make a well in the centre and
add the yeast mixture, oil, the remaining
sugar and 250 ml (9 fl oz/1 cup) warm
water. Mix with a wooden spoon, then
turn out onto a lightly floured surface.
Knead for 10 minutes, or until smooth
and elastic. Incorporate a little extra flour
as you knead, to stop the dough sticking.
3 Place the dough in an oiled bowl and
lightly brush with oil. Cover with plastic
wrap or a damp tea towel (dish towel)
and leave in a warm, draught-free place
for 45 minutes, or until doubled in size.
4 Knock back the dough, turn out onto
a lightly floured surface and knead for
3–4 minutes. Pull away one-third of the
dough, then knead each portion into a
smooth ball. Place the large ball on a
floured baking tray and brush the top
with water. Sit the smaller ball on top
and, using two fingers, press into the
dough. Cover with plastic wrap or a damp
tea towel and leave in a warm, draught-
free place for 40 minutes, until well risen.
5 Preheat the oven to 190°C (375°F/
Gas 5). Dust the loaf with white flour
and bake for 40 minutes, or until golden
brown and cooked. Leave on the tray for
2–3 minutes, then cool on a wire rack.

cottage loaf

This is a traditional English style of bread with
a distinctive look. It has a large round free-form
base topped with a smaller top-knot. The smaller
loaf is pressed down in the centre with two
fingers to attach it firmly to the base loaf. It can
be made with white or wholemeal (whole-wheat)

flours or a combination of the two. The addition
of oil to bread doughs aids in the keeping quality
of the bread after baking. This basic dough can
be formed into any shape you like, either free-
form or placed in a bread tin. This type of loaf is
also delicious cut into thick slices and toasted.

Soy beans have been cultivated in Asia for centuries and were introduced to Europe in the 17th century. America is now the largest producer of soy beans. They are used mostly to make soy bean oil, but the bean is also used whole and manufactured into a wide range of food products. Soy flour is a high-protein food, but lacks gluten, which is essential for the rising of breads. Soy flour is added to bread to give a different flavour and as it is high in fat, it enriches the bread. A high proportion of wheat flour or added bread improver (gluten flour) is necessary to give a satisfactorily risen loaf based on soy flour.

soy and linseed loaf

✳ ✳

Preparation time: 30 minutes
+ 1 hour 45 minutes proving time
Cooking time: 50 minutes
Makes 1 loaf

110 g (3¾ oz/½ cup) pearl barley
2 teaspoons dried yeast
1 teaspoon caster (superfine) sugar
1 tablespoon linseeds (flax seeds)
2 tablespoons soy flour
2 tablespoons bread improver (gluten flour)
150 g (5½ oz/1 cup) wholemeal (whole-wheat) strong flour
310 g (11 oz/2½ cups) white strong flour
2 tablespoons olive oil

1 Brush a 10 x 26 cm (4 x 10½ inch) loaf (bar) tin with oil. Put the barley in a saucepan with 500 ml (17 fl oz/2 cups) water, bring to the boil and boil for 20 minutes, or until softened. Drain.
2 Combine the yeast, sugar and 150 ml (5 fl oz) warm water in a small bowl. Leave in a warm, draught-free place for 10 minutes, or until bubbles appear on the surface. The mixture should be frothy and slightly increased in volume. If your yeast doesn't foam, it is dead, so you will have to discard it and start again.
3 Place the barley, linseeds, soy flour, bread improver, wholemeal flour, 250 g (9 oz/2 cups) of the white flour and 1 teaspoon salt in a large bowl. Make a well in the centre and add the yeast mixture, oil and 150 ml (5 fl oz) warm water. Mix to a soft dough. Turn out onto a floured surface and knead for

10 minutes, or until smooth and elastic. Incorporate enough of the remaining flour until the dough is no longer sticky.
4 Place the dough in an oiled bowl and brush with oil. Cover with plastic wrap or a damp tea towel (dish towel) and leave in a warm, draught-free place for 45 minutes, until doubled in size. Knock it back, then knead for 2–3 minutes.
5 Pat the dough into a 20 x 24 cm (8 x 9½ inch) rectangle. Roll up firmly from the long side and place, seam-side down, in the bread tin. Cover with plastic wrap or a damp tea towel and set aside in a warm, draught-free place for 1 hour, or until risen to the top of the tin. Preheat the oven to 200°C (400°F/Gas 6).
6 Brush the dough with water and make two slits on top. Bake for 50 minutes, or until golden. Remove from the tin and cool on a wire rack.

mini wholemeal loaves

✹ ✹

Preparation time: 40 minutes
  + 1 hour 45 minutes proving time
Cooking time: 45 minutes
Makes 4 small loaves

2 teaspoons dried yeast
1 tablespoon caster (superfine) sugar
125 ml (4 fl oz/½ cup) warm milk
600 g (1 lb 5 oz/4 cups) wholemeal
  (whole-wheat) strong flour
60 ml (2 fl oz/¼ cup) oil
1 egg, lightly beaten

1   Grease four 13 x 6.5 cm (5 x 2¾ inch) loaf (bar) tins. Place the yeast, sugar and milk in a small bowl and mix well. Leave in a warm, draught-free place for 10 minutes, or until bubbles appear on the surface. The mixture should be frothy and slightly increased in volume. If your yeast doesn't foam, it is dead, so you will have to discard it and start again.
2   Put the flour and 1 teaspoon salt in a large bowl, make a well in the centre and add the yeast mixture, oil and 250 ml (9 fl oz/1 cup) warm water. Mix to a soft dough and gather into a ball. Turn onto a floured surface and knead for 10 minutes. Add a little extra flour if it is too sticky.
3   Place the dough in a large oiled bowl, cover loosely with plastic wrap or a damp tea towel (dish towel) and leave in a warm, draught-free place for 1 hour, or until well risen. Knock back the dough, turn out onto a floured surface and knead for 1 minute, until smooth. Divide into four, knead into shape and put in the tins. Cover loosely with plastic wrap or a damp tea towel and leave in a warm, draught-free place for 45 minutes, or until risen.
4   Preheat the oven to 210°C (415°F/ Gas 6–7). Brush the loaves with beaten egg. Bake for 10 minutes, then reduce the temperature to 180°C (350°F/Gas 4) and bake for 30–35 minutes, or until the bases sound hollow when tapped. Cover with foil if the tops become too brown.

mini baguettes

✹ ✹

Preparation time: 25 minutes
  + 2 hours 20 minutes proving time
Cooking time: 30 minutes
Makes 3 loaves

2 teaspoons dried yeast
1 teaspoon sugar
90 g (3¼ oz/¾ cup) plain (all-purpose)
  flour
375 g (13 oz/3 cups) white strong flour
2 tablespoons polenta, to sprinkle

1   Put the yeast, sugar and 310 ml (10¾ fl oz/1¼ cups) warm water in a small bowl and mix well. Leave in a warm, draught-free place for 10 minutes, or until bubbles appear on the surface. The mixture should be frothy and slightly increased in volume. If your yeast doesn't foam, it is dead, so you will have to discard it and start again.
2   Combine the flours and ½ teaspoon salt and transfer half the dry ingredients to a large bowl. Make a well in the centre and add the yeast mixture. Using a large metal spoon, fold the flour into the yeast mixture. This should form a soft dough. Cover the bowl with a damp tea towel (dish towel) or plastic wrap and set aside in a warm, draught-free place for 30–35 minutes, or until frothy and risen by

baguettes

A baguette, meaning 'little rod', is the famous long, cylindrical and narrow French bread. It has a very crisp, brown crust and a chewy texture. Baguettes always seem to feature in old French movies, sticking out of bicycle baskets. The French say that it is best to buy two baguettes because one always gets half-eaten on the way home! Baguettes can be cooked free-form on a baking tray but special purpose half-cylinder containers can be bought from speciality kitchenware shops.

about a third of its original size.

3 Mix in the remaining dry ingredients and add up to 60 ml (2 fl oz/¼ cup) warm water, enough to form a soft, but slightly sticky dough. Knead the dough on a lightly floured surface for 10 minutes, or until smooth and elastic. If the dough sticks to the work surface while kneading, flour the surface sparingly, but avoid adding too much flour. Shape the dough into a ball and place in a large, lightly greased bowl. Cover with a damp tea towel or plastic wrap and leave in a warm, draught-free place for about 1 hour, or until doubled in size.

4 Lightly grease two large baking trays and sprinkle with polenta. Knock back the dough and knead for 2–3 minutes. Divide the dough into three portions and press or roll each into a rectangle about 20 x 40 cm (8 x 16 inches). Roll each up firmly into a long sausage shape and place, seam-side down, well spaced on the prepared trays. Cover loosely with a damp tea towel or plastic wrap and set aside in a warm, draught-free place for 40 minutes, or until doubled in size.

5 Preheat the oven to 220°C (425°F/ Gas 7). Lightly brush the loaves with water and make diagonal slashes across the top at 6 cm (2½ inch) intervals. Place the trays in the oven and spray the oven with water.

6 Bake the bread for 20 minutes, spraying the oven with water twice during this time. Reduce the oven to 180°C (350°F/Gas 4) and bake for another 5–10 minutes, or until the crust is golden and firm and the bases sound hollow when tapped underneath. Cool on a wire rack. Baguettes are best eaten within a few hours of baking.

sherry

Sherry is a fortified wine made from white grapes that is produced in the Jerez region in southwest Spain. Although "sherry" production takes place the world over, only sherries from the Jerez region are allowed to carry the name. Sherries have a very concentrated flavour and are usually drunk in small glasses as the alcohol content is about 20 per cent (wine is 10–12 per cent). Sherries are sweet, medium or dry in flavour. In baking, sweet sherry is usually used. It is commonly used in sauces, puddings and fruit cakes. A small glass of sherry with a piece of fruit cake is an English tradition.

light fruit bread

Preparation time: **25 minutes**
    + **1 hour 30 minutes proving time**
Cooking time: **35 minutes**
Makes **1 loaf**

125 g (4½ oz/1 cup) raisins
1 tablespoon sherry
1 tablespoon finely grated orange zest
2 teaspoons dried yeast
250 ml (9 fl oz/1 cup) milk, warmed
55 g (2 oz/¼ cup) caster (superfine) sugar
375 g (13 oz/3 cups) white strong flour
30 g (1 oz) butter, cubed

GLAZE
1 egg yolk
2 tablespoons pouring (whipping) cream

1 Combine the raisins, sherry and zest in a small bowl and set aside.
2 Place the yeast, milk and 1 teaspoon of the sugar in a small bowl and mix well. Leave in a warm, draught-free place for 10 minutes, or until bubbles appear on the surface. The mixture should be frothy and slightly increased in volume. If your yeast doesn't foam, it is dead, so you will have to discard it and start again.
3 Place 340 g (11¾ oz/2¾ cups) of the flour and ½ teaspoon salt in a large bowl. Rub in the butter and remaining sugar with your fingertips. Make a well in the centre, add the yeast mixture and mix to a soft dough. Turn out onto a floured surface and knead for 10 minutes, or until smooth and elastic, incorporating the remaining flour as necessary.
4 Place the dough in an oiled bowl and brush with oil. Cover with plastic wrap or

a damp tea towel (dish towel) and leave in a warm, draught-free place for 1 hour, or until well risen. Knock back the dough, knead for 2 minutes, then roll out to a rectangle, 20 x 40 cm (8 x 16 inches). Scatter with the raisins and roll up firmly from the long end.

5 Grease an 8 x 21 cm (3¼ x 8¼ inch) loaf (bar) tin and line the base with baking paper. Place the dough in the tin, cover with plastic wrap or a damp tea towel and leave in a warm, draught-free place for 30 minutes, or until well risen. Preheat the oven to 180°C (350°F/Gas 4).

6 To make the glaze, combine the egg yolk and cream and brush a little over the loaf. Bake for 30 minutes, or until cooked and golden. Glaze, bake for 5 minutes, then glaze again. Cool on a wire rack.

dense fruit bread

✹ ✹

Preparation time: 25 minutes
  + 1 hour 40 minutes proving time
Cooking time: 50 minutes
Makes 1 large loaf

2 teaspoons dried yeast
¼ teaspoon sugar
450 g (1 lb) white strong flour
25 g (1 oz) butter
½ teaspoon ground ginger
¼ teaspoon freshly grated nutmeg
80 g (2¾ oz/⅓ cup) caster (superfine) sugar
250 g (9 oz/2 cups) sultanas (golden raisins)
185 g (6½ oz/1¼ cups) currants
50 g (1¾ oz/¼ cup) mixed peel (mixed candied citrus peel)

1 Put the yeast, sugar and 310 ml (10¾ fl oz/1¼ cups) warm water in a small bowl and mix well. Leave in a warm, draught-free place for 10 minutes, or until bubbles appear on the surface. The mixture should be frothy and slightly increased in volume. If your yeast doesn't foam, it is dead, so you will have to discard it and start again.

2 Put the flour and ¼ teaspoon salt in a large bowl. Using your fingertips, rub in the butter until the mixture resembles coarse breadcrumbs. Stir in the spices and three-quarters of the caster sugar. Make a well in the centre and stir in the yeast mixture. Mix well until the dough comes together and leaves the side of the bowl clean. Turn onto a lightly floured surface and knead for 10 minutes, or until elastic and smooth. Place in a clean bowl, cover with plastic wrap or a damp tea towel (dish towel) and leave in a warm, draught-free place for 1 hour, or until the dough has doubled in size.

3 Turn the dough onto a lightly floured surface, add the fruit and knead for a couple of minutes, or until the fruit is incorporated. Shape the dough into a large round and place on a greased baking tray. Cover with plastic wrap or a damp tea towel and leave in a warm, draught-free place for 30–40 minutes, or until doubled in size.

4 Preheat the oven to 200°C (400°F/Gas 6). Bake on the middle shelf for 40–45 minutes, or until the loaf is nicely coloured and sounds hollow when tapped on the base. Transfer to a wire rack to cool slightly.

5 Place the remaining caster sugar in a small bowl, add 1 tablespoon hot water and stir until the sugar has dissolved. Brush over the loaf, bake for a further 2–3 minutes, then cool on a wire rack.

cheese and herb pull apart

✳ ✳

Preparation time: 30 minutes
+ 1 hour 30 minutes proving time
Cooking time: 30 minutes
Makes 1 loaf

2 teaspoons dried yeast
1 teaspoon sugar

500 g (1 lb 2 oz/4 cups) plain
(all-purpose) flour
2 tablespoons chopped parsley
2 tablespoons snipped chives
1 tablespoon chopped thyme
60 g (2¼ oz) cheddar cheese, grated
milk, to glaze

1 Combine the yeast, sugar and 125 ml (4 fl oz/½ cup) warm water in a small bowl. Leave in a warm, draught-free place for 10 minutes, or until bubbles appear on the surface. The mixture should be frothy and slightly increased in volume.

2 Sift the flour and 1½ teaspoons salt into a large bowl. Make a well in the centre and add the yeast mixture and 250 ml (9 fl oz/1 cup) warm water. Mix to a soft dough. Turn onto a lightly floured surface and knead for 10 minutes, or until smooth. Place the dough in an oiled bowl, cover with plastic wrap or a damp tea towel (dish towel) and leave for 1 hour, or until doubled in size.

3 Knock back the dough and knead for 1 minute. Divide the dough in half and shape each half into 10 flat discs, 6 cm (2½ inches) in diameter. Mix the herbs with the cheddar and put 2 teaspoons of the mixture on one of the discs. Press another disc on top, then repeat with the remaining discs and herb mixture.

4 Grease a deep, 10.5 x 21 cm (4¼ x 8¼ inch) loaf (bar) tin. Stand the filled discs upright in the prepared tin, squashing them together. Cover the tin with plastic wrap or a damp tea towel and leave in a warm place for 30 minutes, or until the dough is well risen.

5 Preheat the oven to 210°C (415°F/ Gas 6–7). Lightly brush the loaf with a little milk and bake for 30 minutes, or until the bread is brown and crusty and sounds hollow when tapped on the base.

cheese and herb pull apart

rosetta rolls

✳ ✳ ✳

Preparation time: 40 minutes
+ 2 hours proving time
Cooking time: 25 minutes
Makes 10 rolls

1 teaspoon dried yeast
1 teaspoon sugar
560 g (1 lb 4 oz/4½ cups) unbleached
plain (all-purpose) flour, sifted
50 g (1¾ oz) butter, softened
60 ml (2 fl oz/¼ cup) olive oil
55 g (2 oz/¼ cup) caster (superfine)
sugar
milk, to glaze
plain (all-purpose) flour, extra, to dust

Press a deep, round indent into the centre of each ball of dough.

Sift a fine layer of plain flour over the tops of the rolls before baking.

1   Lightly grease two baking trays. Put the yeast, sugar and 125 ml (4 fl oz/½ cup) warm water in a small bowl and stir well. Leave in a warm, draught-free place for 10 minutes, or until bubbles appear on the surface. The mixture should be frothy and slightly increased in volume. If your yeast doesn't foam, it is dead, so you will have to discard it and start again.

2   Set aside 30 g (1 oz/¼ cup) of the flour and put the rest in a large bowl with 1 teaspoon salt. Make a well in the centre. Add the yeast mixture, butter, oil, sugar and 310 ml (10¾ fl oz/1¼ cups) warm water. Stir with a wooden spoon until the dough leaves the side of the bowl and forms a rough, sticky ball. Turn out onto a floured surface. Knead for 10 minutes, or until the dough is smooth and elastic. Add enough of the reserved flour, if necessary, to make a smooth dough. Put in a large, lightly oiled bowl and brush the surface with melted butter or oil. Cover with plastic wrap and leave in a warm, draught-free place for 1 hour, or until well risen.

3   Knock back the dough, then knead for 1 minute. Divide into 10 portions and shape each into a smooth ball. Place the balls 5 cm (2 inches) apart on the trays. Using a round 3 cm (1¼ inch) cutter, press a 1 cm (½ inch) deep indent into the centre of each ball. With a sharp knife, score five evenly spaced, 1 cm (½ inch) deep cuts down the side of each roll. Cover with plastic wrap or a damp tea towel (dish towel) and leave in a warm, draught-free place for 1 hour, or until well risen.

4   Preheat the oven to 180°C (350°F/ Gas 4). Brush the rolls with milk and sift a fine layer of the extra flour over them. Bake for 25 minutes, or until golden. Rotate the trays in the oven if one tray is browning faster than the other. Allow to cool on a wire rack.

NOTE: These are best eaten on the day they are cooked, or they can be frozen for up to 1 month.

bread rolls

Create your own selection of delicious rolls using plain (page 208) or wholemeal (page 216) bread dough and the following toppings and glazes.

different types of rolls

spiral rolls Divide the dough into 16–24 even pieces. Roll each into a 30 cm (12 inch) long rope. Shape into tight spirals, tuck under the ends, then seal. Place 5 cm (2 inches) apart on lightly oiled baking trays. Cover with plastic wrap and leave in a warm place for 20 minutes, or until well risen. Brush with a glaze or topping. Bake in a 180°C (350°F/Gas 4) oven for 15–20 minutes, or until risen and golden.

knot rolls Divide the dough into 16–24 even pieces. Roll each into a 30 cm (12 inch) long rope. Tie each rope into a loose knot. Place 5 cm (2 inches) apart on lightly oiled baking trays. Proceed as for spiral rolls.

clover leaf rolls Divide the dough into 16–24 even pieces. Divide each piece into 3 even-sized balls. Place the trio of balls from each piece close together on lightly oiled baking trays and 5 cm (2 inches) apart. Proceed as for spiral rolls.

oval rolls Divide the dough into 16–24 even pieces, and then shape into ovals. Leave plain or slash the tops once lengthways, or twice diagonally. Place 5 cm (2 inches) apart on lightly oiled baking trays. Proceed as for spiral rolls.

toppings and glazes

Glazing dough and adding toppings will change the appearance as well as the taste of the bread. Glazing affects the result of the crust and is done before or after baking, depending on the result you are after. Toppings are sprinkled over the dough before baking. The high oven temperature used for baking bread may cause some toppings to brown too quickly — if this is happening, lower the oven temperature slightly or cover the rolls with foil or a double thickness of baking paper.

toppings Lightly sprinkle the dough with flour, rolled oats, crushed rock salt, cracked wheat or grated cheese. You can also try poppy, sesame, caraway, pumpkin, dill, fennel or sunflower seeds. Cornmeal (polenta), barley flakes, cracked wheat and rye flakes also make interesting toppings and add a little flavour.

glazes Use a wide pastry brush to brush one of these glazes over the uncooked dough or cooked bread (as specified), choosing the appropriate glaze for your desired result.
Deep colour in the crust: Beat 1 whole egg with 1 teaspoon water and brush over the rolls before baking. For a very deep colour, use 1 egg yolk beaten with 1 teaspoon water.
Rich, dark gleam on savoury breads: Beat 1 egg together with 1 teaspoon oil, salt and freshly ground black pepper, then brush over the rolls before baking.
Crisp crust: Whisk together 1 egg white with 1 teaspoon water and brush over the rolls before baking.
Light sheen: Brush the rolls with milk, cream or melted butter before baking.
Soft crust: Brush the cooked, hot bread with melted butter and return to the oven for 2 minutes. Remove, brush again with melted butter and leave to cool.
Glossy crust: Whisk 1 egg white with 1 tablespoon water. Brush the cooked, hot bread with the glaze, then return to the oven for 5 minutes. Cool.
Sweet glossy crust: Mix 1 tablespoon sugar with 2 tablespoons milk and brush over the cooked, hot bread. Return to the oven for 5 minutes. Cool.
Sugar glaze: Mix 60 g (2¼ oz/¼ cup) sugar and 2 tablespoons water over low heat until the sugar dissolves. Boil for 2 minutes, or until the mixture is syrupy. Brush on the hot, cooked bread.

Gradually draw the flour into the yeast mixture and stir to form a thick paste.

Stir the flour into the starter mixture and whisk in warm water to form a smooth mixture.

Knead the dough until it is smooth and elastic, incorporating more flour if necessary.

Use a sharp knife to make diagonal cuts along the loaves.

sourdough bread

✳ ✳ ✳

Preparation time: 30 minutes + 2 days, 1 hour and 45 minutes proving time
Cooking time: 40 minutes
Makes 2 loaves

STARTER
125 g (4½ oz/1 cup) white strong flour
2 teaspoons fresh yeast

SPONGE
125 g (4½ oz/1 cup) white strong flour

DOUGH
375 g (13 oz/3 cups) white strong flour
2 teaspoons fresh yeast

1 To make the starter, sift the flour into a bowl and make a well in the centre.

Cream the yeast and 250 ml (9 fl oz/ 1 cup) warm water together, pour into the flour and gradually draw the flour into the centre to form a thick, smooth paste. Cover with plastic wrap or a damp tea towel (dish towel) and leave at room temperature for 24 hours. The starter will begin to ferment and bubble.

2 To make the sponge, stir the flour into the starter mixture and gradually whisk in 125 ml (4 fl oz/½ cup) warm water to form a smooth mixture. Cover with plastic wrap and leave for 24 hours.

3 To make the dough, sift the flour and 1 teaspoon salt into a large bowl and make a well in the centre. Cream the yeast and 80 ml (2½ fl oz/⅓ cup) warm water together and add to the dry ingredients with the starter and sponge mixture. Gradually incorporate the flour into the well. Turn the dough onto a lightly floured surface and knead for 10 minutes, or until smooth and elastic, incorporating extra flour if needed.

4 Place the dough in a lightly oiled bowl, cover with plastic wrap or a damp tea towel and place in a warm, draught-free place for 1 hour, or until doubled in size. Lightly grease two baking trays and dust lightly with flour. Knock back the dough and turn onto the work surface. Knead for 1 minute, or until smooth. Divide into two equal portions and shape each into a 20 cm (8 inch) round. Using a sharp knife, score diagonal cuts 1 cm (½ inch) deep along the loaves.

5 Place the loaves on the trays and cover with plastic wrap or a damp tea towel. Leave in a warm, draught-free place for 45 minutes, or until doubled in size. Preheat the oven to 190°C (375°F/Gas 5). Bake the loaves for 35–40 minutes, swapping the trays around halfway through cooking, until golden and crusty and they sound hollow when tapped on the base. Cool on a wire rack.

potato bread

✳ ✳

Preparation time: 45 minutes
  + 1 hour 45 minutes proving time
Cooking time: 35 minutes
Makes 1 loaf

2 teaspoons dried yeast
500 g (1 lb 2 oz/4 cups) unbleached plain (all-purpose) flour
2 tablespoons full-cream milk powder
235 g (8½ oz/1 cup) warm cooked mashed potato
25 g (1 oz) snipped chives
1 egg white, to glaze
2 teaspoons cold water
sunflower seeds and pepitas (pumpkin seeds), to sprinkle

1 Lightly grease a round 25 cm (10 inch) cake tin and line the base with baking paper. Put the yeast and 60 ml (2 fl oz/ ¼ cup) warm water in a small bowl and stir well. Leave in a warm, draught-free place for 10 minutes, or until bubbles appear on the surface. The mixture should be frothy and slightly increased in volume. If your yeast doesn't foam, it is dead, so you will have to discard it and start again.

2 Sift 440 g (15½ oz/3½ cups) of the flour, the milk powder and 1 teaspoon salt into a large bowl. Using a fork, mix the potato and chives through the dry ingredients. Add the yeast mixture and 250 ml (9 fl oz/1 cup) warm water and mix until combined. Add enough of the remaining flour to make a soft dough.

3 Turn onto a lightly floured surface and knead for 10 minutes, or until smooth and elastic. Place in an oiled bowl and brush the top with oil. Cover with plastic wrap and leave in a warm, draught-free place for 1 hour, until well risen.

4 Knock back the dough, then knead for 1 minute. Divide into 12 equal pieces and form each piece into a smooth ball. Place evenly spaced balls in a daisy pattern in the tin, piling two balls in the centre. Cover with plastic wrap and leave in a warm, draught-free place for 45 minutes, or until the dough has risen to the top of the tin. Preheat the oven to 210°C (415°F/Gas 6–7).

5 Brush the top with the combined egg white and water and sprinkle with the seeds and pepitas. Bake for 15 minutes. Reduce the oven to 180°C (350°F/ Gas 4) and bake for a further 20 minutes, or until a skewer inserted into the centre of the loaf comes out clean. Leave for 10 minutes, then turn onto a wire rack.

NOTE: Depending on the moisture content of the potato, extra flour may need to be added to make a soft, slightly sticky dough. The bread will keep for 3 days in an airtight container.

1 Grease a round 20 cm (8 inch) cake tin and a 12 x 28 cm (4½ x 11¼ inch) loaf (bar) or bread tin, or use any baking tin with a 1.75 litre (60½ fl oz/7 cup) capacity. Line the base of each tin with baking paper. Put the yeast, sugar and 125 ml (4 fl oz/½ cup) warm water in a small bowl and stir well. Leave in a warm, draught-free place for 10 minutes, or until bubbles appear on the surface. The mixture should be frothy and slightly increased in volume. If your yeast doesn't foam, it is dead, so you will have to discard it and start again.

2 Put the molasses, vinegar, butter, chocolate, coffee powder and 500 ml (17 fl oz/2 cups) cold water in a saucepan and stir over low heat until the butter and chocolate have melted and the mixture is just warmed and smooth.

3 Put the rye flour, bran, caraway and fennel seeds, 440 g (15½ oz/3½ cups) of the plain flour and 1 teaspoon salt in a large bowl. Make a well in the centre and add the yeast and chocolate mixtures. Using a wooden spoon, and then your hands, bring in the flour and combine the mixture until it leaves the side of the bowl and forms a firm, sticky ball of dough.

4 Turn out onto a heavily floured surface and knead for 10 minutes. Incorporate enough of the remaining plain flour to make a dense, but smooth and elastic dough. Divide into two evenly sized portions and place in separate lightly oiled bowls. Brush the surface of the dough with melted butter or oil. Cover with plastic wrap or a damp tea towel (dish towel) and leave in a warm, draught-free place for 1¼ hours, or until well risen. Knock back the dough and knead each portion for 1 minute. Shape each portion to fit one of the prepared tins and place one in each tin. Cover with lightly oiled plastic wrap or a damp tea towel and leave in a warm, draught-free place for 1 hour, or until well risen.

5 Preheat the oven to 180°C (350°F/ Gas 4). Glaze the dough with the combined egg white and 1 tablespoon water, then sprinkle with caraway seeds. Bake for 50 minutes, or until well

pumpernickel

✳✳

Preparation time: 1 hour + 2 hours 15 minutes
    proving time
Cooking time: 50 minutes
Makes 2 loaves

1 tablespoon dried yeast
1 teaspoon caster (superfine) sugar
90 g (3¼ oz/¼ cup) molasses
60 ml (2 fl oz/¼ cup) cider vinegar

90 g (3¼ oz) butter
30 g (1 oz) dark chocolate, chopped
1 tablespoon instant coffee powder
300 g (10½ oz/3 cups) rye flour
75 g (2¾ oz/1 cup) bran
1 tablespoon caraway seeds
2 teaspoons fennel seeds
560 g (1 lb 4 oz/4½ cups) unbleached
    plain (all-purpose) flour
1 egg white
caraway seeds, extra, to sprinkle

browned. During the last 15 minutes, cover the surface with foil to prevent excess browning. Leave in the tins for 15 minutes before turning out onto a wire rack to cool.

NOTE: Pumpernickel is a dense rye bread that originated in Germany.

english muffins

✷ ✷

Preparation time: 20 minutes
+ 1 hour 40 minutes proving time
Cooking time: 15 minutes
Makes 15

2 teaspoons dried yeast
½ teaspoon sugar
530 g (1 lb 3 oz/4¼ cups) plain (all-purpose) flour
350 ml (12 fl oz) lukewarm milk
1 egg, lightly beaten
40 g (1½ oz) butter, melted

1 Lightly dust two 28 x 32 cm (11¼ x 12¾ inch) baking trays with flour. Put the yeast, sugar, 1 teaspoon of the flour and 60 ml (2 fl oz/¼ cup) warm water in a small bowl and mix well. Leave in a warm, draught-free place for 10 minutes, or until bubbles appear on the surface. The mixture should be frothy and slightly increased in volume. If your yeast doesn't foam, it is dead, so you will have to discard it and start again.
2 Sift the remaining flour and 1 teaspoon salt into a large bowl. Make a well in the centre and add the milk, egg, butter and yeast mixture all at once. Using a flat-bladed knife, mix to a soft dough.
3 Turn the dough onto a lightly floured surface and knead lightly for 2 minutes, or until smooth. Shape the dough into a ball and place in a large, lightly oiled bowl. Cover with plastic wrap or a damp tea towel (dish towel) and leave in a warm, draught-free place for 1½ hours, or until the dough is well risen.
4 Preheat the oven to 210°C (415°F/ Gas 6–7). Knock back the dough and knead again for 2 minutes, or until smooth. Roll to 1 cm (½ inch) thick, then cut into rounds with a lightly floured, plain 8 cm (3¼ inch) cutter and place on the trays. Cover with plastic wrap or a damp tea towel and leave in a warm, draught-free place for 10 minutes.
5 Bake for 15 minutes, turning halfway through cooking. Transfer to a wire rack to cool. Serve warm or cold.

focaccia

✳ ✳

Preparation time: 50 minutes
+ 1 hour 50 minutes proving time
Cooking time: 25 minutes
Makes 1 flat loaf

2 teaspoons dried yeast
1 teaspoon caster (superfine) sugar
2 tablespoons olive oil
405 g (14¼ oz/3¼ cups) white strong
    flour
1 tablespoon full-cream milk powder

TOPPING
1 tablespoon olive oil
1–2 garlic cloves, crushed
black olives
rosemary sprigs or leaves
1 teaspoon dried oregano
1–2 teaspoons coarse sea salt

1 Lightly grease a 18 x 28 cm (7 x 11¼
inch) baking tin. Put the yeast, sugar
and 250 ml (9 fl oz/1 cup) warm water
in a small bowl and stir well. Leave in a
warm, draught-free place for 10 minutes,
or until bubbles appear on the surface.
The mixture should be frothy and slightly
increased in volume. If your yeast doesn't
foam, it is dead, so you will have to
discard it and start again. Add the oil.
2 Sift 375 g (13 oz/3 cups) of the flour,
the milk powder and ½ teaspoon salt into
a large bowl. Make a well in the centre
and add the yeast mixture. Beat with a
wooden spoon until the mixture is well
combined. Add enough of the remaining
flour to form a soft dough, and then turn
onto a lightly floured surface.
3 Knead for 10 minutes, or until the
dough is smooth and elastic. Place the
dough in a large, lightly oiled bowl.
Brush the surface of the dough with oil.
Cover with plastic wrap or a damp tea
towel (dish towel) and leave in a warm,
draught-free place for 1 hour, or until well
risen. Knock back the dough and knead
for 1 minute. Roll out to 18 x 28 cm
(7 x 11¼ inches) and place in the tin.
Cover with plastic wrap and leave in a

warm, draught-free place for 20 minutes to rise. Using the handle of a wooden spoon, form indents 1 cm (½ inch) deep all over the dough at regular intervals. Cover with plastic wrap and set aside in a warm, draught-free place for a further 30 minutes, or until well risen. Preheat the oven to 180°C (350°F/Gas 4).

4 To make the topping, brush the combined olive oil and garlic over the surface of the dough. Top with the olives and rosemary sprigs, then sprinkle with the oregano and salt.

5 Bake for 20–25 minutes, or until golden and crisp. Cut into large squares and serve warm.

NOTE: Focaccia is best eaten on the day of baking. It can be reheated if necessary.

malt bread

✷✷

Preparation time: 45 minutes
   + 1 hour 40 minutes proving time
Cooking time: 40 minutes
Makes 1 loaf

2 teaspoons dried yeast
1 teaspoon sugar
300 g (10½ oz/2 cups) wholemeal (whole-wheat) plain (all-purpose) flour
125 g (4½ oz/1 cup) plain (all-purpose) flour
2 teaspoons ground cinnamon
60 g (2¼ oz/½ cup) raisins
30 g (1 oz) butter, melted
1 tablespoon treacle
1 tablespoon liquid malt extract
1 tablespoon hot milk
½ teaspoon liquid malt extract, extra

1 Brush a deep, 14 x 21 cm (5½ x 8¼ inch) loaf (bar) tin with oil and line the base with baking paper. Combine the yeast, sugar and 250 ml (9 fl oz/1 cup) lukewarm water in a small bowl. Cover with plastic wrap and set aside in a warm, draught-free place for 10 minutes, or until bubbles appear on the surface. The mixture should be frothy and slightly

increased in volume. If your yeast doesn't foam, it is dead, so you will have to discard it and start again.

2 Sift the flours and cinnamon into a large bowl, then add the raisins and stir. Make a well in the centre. Add the melted butter, treacle, 1 tablespoon of malt extract and the yeast mixture. Mix to a soft dough using a flat-bladed knife. Turn onto a lightly floured surface and knead for 10 minutes, or until smooth. Shape the dough into a ball and place in a lightly oiled bowl. Set aside, covered with plastic wrap, in a warm, draught-free

place for 1 hour, or until well risen. Knock back the dough, then knead until smooth.

3 Roll the dough into a 20 cm (8 inch) square, then roll up. Place in the tin, seam-side down. Cover with plastic wrap and leave in a warm, draught-free place for 40 minutes, or until well risen.

4 Preheat the oven to 180°C (350°F/Gas 4). Brush the dough with the combined milk and extra malt extract. Bake for 40 minutes or until a skewer inserted into the centre of the bread comes out clean. Set aside for 3 minutes in the tin, then cool on a wire rack.

pitta bread

Preparation time: **20 minutes**
+ 40 minutes proving time
Cooking time: **5 minutes**
Makes **12**

1 teaspoon dried yeast
1 teaspoon caster (superfine) sugar
435 g (15¼ oz/3½ cups) plain (all-purpose)
    flour
2 tablespoons olive oil

1 Place the yeast, sugar and 375 ml (13 fl oz/1½ cups) lukewarm water in a bowl and stir until dissolved. Leave in a warm, draught-free place for 10 minutes, or until bubbles appear on the surface. The mixture should be frothy and slightly increased in volume. If your yeast doesn't foam, it is dead, so you will have to discard it and start again.
2 Process the flour, yeast mixture and oil in a food processor for 30 seconds, or until the mixture forms a ball. If you prefer, place the ingredients in a bowl and mix with a wooden spoon, or your hand, until the mixture forms a smooth dough.
3 Turn the dough onto a well-floured surface and knead until smooth and elastic. Place in a well-oiled bowl, cover with plastic wrap, then a tea towel (dish towel) and leave in a warm, draught-free place for 20 minutes, or until the dough has almost doubled in size.
4 Knock back the dough and divide into 12 equal portions. Roll each portion into a 5 mm (¼ inch) thick round. Place on greased baking trays and brush well with water. Set aside in a warm, draught-free place for another 20 minutes to rise.
5 Preheat the oven to 250°C (500°F/ Gas 9). If the dough has dried, brush again with water. Bake for 4–5 minutes. The pitta breads should be soft and pale, slightly swollen, and hollow inside. Eat warm with kebabs or falafel, or cool on wire racks and serve with salad.

pitta bread

This is the staple bread of the Middle East. It is known as 'khubz' in Arabic but is more commonly known in the west by its Greek name, pitta. It is a flat bread with a chewy crust and a hollow pouch which makes it very versatile. Typically, it is split open and filled with a variety of meats, salads and dips, such as hummus or baba ghanoush. It can also be used as a scoop for dips and even to wrap foods such as kebabs. Keep pitta bread sealed in a plastic bag in the refrigerator. To refresh, sprinkle lightly with water and reheat in a 160°C (315°F/Gas 2–3) oven.

pretzels

✳ ✳

Preparation time: 50 minutes
  + 1 hour 30 minutes proving time
Cooking time: 15 minutes
Makes 12

1 teaspoon dried yeast
¼ teaspoon sugar
150 ml (5 fl oz) warm milk
185 g (6½ oz/1½ cups) white strong flour
30 g (1 oz) butter, melted
1 egg yolk, lightly beaten
coarse sea salt, to sprinkle

1 Put the yeast, sugar and warm milk in a small bowl and stir well. Leave in a warm, draught-free place for 10 minutes, or until bubbles appear on the surface. The mixture should be frothy and slightly increased in volume. If your yeast doesn't foam, it is dead, so you will have to discard it and start again.
2 Put the flour and ¼ teaspoon salt in a large bowl and make a well in the centre. Add the yeast mixture and butter and mix to a rough dough with a wooden spoon. Turn out onto a floured surface and knead for 10 minutes until smooth and elastic.
3 Place in an oiled bowl, oil the surface of the dough, cover with plastic wrap or a clean tea towel (dish towel) and set aside in a warm, draught-free place for 1 hour, until the dough has doubled in size.
4 Preheat the oven to 190°C (375°F/Gas 5). Line a large baking tray with baking paper. Knock back the dough and knead again for 2–3 minutes. Divide into 12 pieces. Cover the dough while working with each piece. Roll each piece into a long rope 40 cm (16 inches) long. Form into a circle and knot into a pretzel shape. Place, well spaced, on the tray. Cover with a tea towel. Leave in a warm, draught-free place for 20–30 minutes to rise.
5 Lightly brush the pretzels with the egg yolk and sprinkle with sea salt. Place in the oven and spray the pretzels twice with water before baking for 12–15 minutes, or until crisp and golden brown. Transfer to a wire rack to cool.

Leave the yeast mixture until bubbles appear on the surface.

Knead the dough until it is smooth and quite stiff.

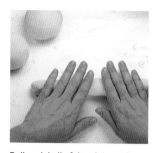

Roll each ball of dough into a long rope, the same thickness all the way along.

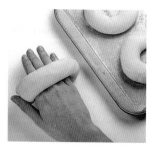

With the circle around the base of your fingers and the overlap under your palm, roll the rope several times. Apply firm pressure to seal the seam.

bagels

❋ ❋

Preparation time: **35 minutes**
+ 12 hours chilling time
Cooking time: **16 minutes**
Makes **8**

2 teaspoons dried yeast
1 teaspoon sugar
1 tablespoon barley malt syrup or honey
500 g (1 lb 2 oz/4 cups) white strong flour
2 teaspoons salt
coarse polenta, to dust

1 Put the yeast, sugar and 375 ml (13 fl oz/1½ cups) warm water in a small bowl and stir until dissolved. Leave in a warm, draught-free place for 10 minutes, or until bubbles appear on the surface.

The mixture should be frothy and slightly increased in volume.

2 Put 250 g (9 oz/2 cups) of the flour in a large bowl, make a well in the centre and add the yeast mixture and salt. Stir with a wooden spoon, adding more flour as necessary to make a firm dough. Turn out onto a floured work surface and knead for 10–12 minutes, or until smooth and stiff. Add more flour, if necessary, to make the dough quite stiff, then divide into eight portions and roll them into smooth balls. Cover with plastic wrap or a clean tea towel (dish towel) and leave in a warm, draught-free place for 5 minutes.

3 Roll each ball under your palms to form a rope 28 cm (11¼ inches) long. Do not taper the ends of the rope. Dampen the ends slightly, overlap by 4 cm (1½ inches) and pinch firmly together. Place one at a time around the base of your fingers and, with the overlap under your palm, roll the rope several times. Apply firm pressure to seal the seam. It should be the same thickness all the way around. Place all the balls on polenta-dusted baking trays, cover with plastic wrap and refrigerate for 12 hours.

4 Preheat the oven to 240°C (475°F/ Gas 8). Line two baking trays with baking paper. Remove the bagels from the fridge 20 minutes before cooking. Bring a large saucepan of water to the boil and drop the bagels, in batches of three or four, into the water for 30 seconds. Remove and drain briefly, base-down, on a wire rack.

5 Transfer the bagels to the baking trays and bake for 15 minutes, or until they are deep golden-brown and crisp. Transfer to a wire rack to cool.

scottish baps

✳ ✳

Preparation time: 40 minutes
+ 1 hour 15 minutes proving time
Cooking time: 30 minutes
Makes 12

2 teaspoons dried yeast
1 teaspoon caster (superfine) sugar
440 g (15½ oz/3½ cups) white strong flour
250 ml (9 fl oz/1 cup) lukewarm milk
50 g (1¾ oz) butter, melted
1 tablespoon plain (all-purpose) flour

1 Lightly dust two baking trays with flour. Place the yeast, sugar and 2 tablespoons of the white strong flour in a small bowl. Gradually add the milk, blending until smooth and dissolved. Leave in a warm, draught-free place for 10 minutes, or until bubbles appear on the surface. The mixture should be frothy and slightly increased in volume.

2 Sift together the remaining flour and 1½ teaspoons salt into a large bowl. Make a well in the centre and add the yeast mixture and butter. Using a flat-bladed knife, mix to form a soft dough. Turn the dough onto a lightly floured surface and knead for 3 minutes, or until smooth. Shape into a ball and place in a large oiled bowl. Cover with plastic wrap or a damp tea towel (dish towel) and leave in a warm, draught-free place for 1 hour, or until the dough is well risen.

3 Preheat the oven to 210°C (415°F/ Gas 6–7). Knock back the dough with your fist. Knead the dough again for 2 minutes, or until smooth. Divide into 12 pieces. Knead one portion at a time on a lightly floured surface for 1 minute, roll into a ball and shape into a flat oval. Repeat with the remaining dough.

4 Place the baps on the trays and dust with plain flour. Cover with plastic wrap and leave in a warm, draught-free place for 15 minutes, or until well risen. Make an indent in the centre of each with your finger. Bake for 30 minutes, until browned and cooked through. Serve warm.

pide (turkish bread)

pide (turkish bread)

✳ ✳

Preparation time: 30 minutes
  + 1 hour 30 minutes proving time
Cooking time: 30 minutes
Makes 3 loaves

1 tablespoon dried yeast
½ teaspoon sugar
60 g (2¼ oz/½ cup) plain (all-purpose) flour
440 g (15½ oz/3½ cups) white strong flour
80 ml (2½ fl oz/⅓ cup) olive oil
1 egg, lightly beaten with 2 teaspoons water
nigella or sesame seeds, to sprinkle

1 Put the yeast, sugar and 125 ml (4 fl oz/½ cup) warm water in a small bowl and stir well. Add a little of the flour and mix to a paste. Leave in a warm, draught-free place for 10 minutes, or until bubbles appear on the surface. The mixture should be frothy and slightly increased in volume.

2 Combine the remaining flours and 1½ teaspoons salt in a large bowl and make a well in the centre. Add the yeast mixture, olive oil and 250 ml (9 fl oz/ 1 cup) warm water. Mix to a rough dough, then turn out onto a floured surface and knead for 5 minutes. Add minimal flour as the dough needs to be damp and springy.

3 Shape the dough into a ball and place in a large oiled bowl. Cover with plastic wrap or a damp tea towel (dish towel) and leave in a warm, draught-free place for 1 hour to triple in size. Knock back the dough and divide into three. Knead each portion for 2 minutes and shape each into a ball. Cover with plastic wrap or a damp tea towel and leave in a warm, draught-free place for 10 minutes.

4 Roll the dough into rectangles, 15 x 35 cm (6 x 14 inches). Cover with damp tea towels and leave in a warm, draught-free place for 20 minutes. Indent all over the surface with your fingers, brush with egg glaze and sprinkle with seeds. Preheat the oven to 220°C (425°F/Gas 7).

5 For the best results, bake each loaf separately. Place a baking tray in the oven for a couple of minutes until hot, remove and sprinkle lightly with flour. Place one portion of dough on the hot tray and bake for 10–12 minutes, until puffed and golden brown. Wrap in a clean tea towel and set aside to cool. Meanwhile, repeat baking the remaining portions of dough.

unleavened lavash

✳ ✳

Preparation time: 40 minutes
  + 1 hour chilling time
Cooking time: 35 minutes
Makes 4

125 g (4½ oz/1 cup) plain (all-purpose) flour
½ teaspoon sugar
20 g (¾ oz) butter, chilled and cubed
80 ml (2½ fl oz/⅓ cup) milk
sesame and poppy seeds, to sprinkle

1 Process the flour, sugar, butter and ½ teaspoon salt in short bursts in a food processor until the butter is incorporated. With the machine running, gradually pour in the milk and process until the dough comes together — you may need to add an extra 1 tablespoon milk. Turn out onto a lightly floured surface and knead briefly until smooth. Wrap in plastic wrap and refrigerate for 1 hour.

2 Preheat the oven to 190°C (375°F/ Gas 5). Lightly grease a large baking tray. Cut the dough into four pieces. Working with one piece at a time, roll until very thin, into a rough square shape measuring about 20 cm (8 inches) along the sides. Place the dough shape on the tray, brush the top lightly with water and sprinkle with the seeds. Roll a rolling pin lightly over the surface of the dough to press in the seeds. Bake for 6–8 minutes, or until golden brown and dry. Transfer to a wire rack until cool and crisp.

3 Repeat the process with the remaining portions of dough. Break the lavash into large pieces to serve.

pizza

The idea of cooking a flat piece of dough with a savoury topping was known to the ancient Greeks and Romans even though the Armenians claim to have invented the pizza. In more modern times, the world was introduced to the pizza via Naples in Italy, although every region in Italy has its own variations. The classic Naples version is basically a very thin dough with a simple tomato and mozzarella cheese sauce, maybe with a few herbs, anchovies and black olives added for extra flavour. It was the Americans, though, who transformed pizza into the ultimate fast food item with its many variations. It is now often made with a thick, bready crust topped with a variety of ingredients.

pizza dough

Preparation time: 30 minutes
  + 1 hour 30 minutes proving time
Cooking time: nil
Makes two 30 cm (12 inch) pizza bases or
  one 42 cm (16½ inch) pizza base

1 teaspoon dried yeast
3 teaspoons caster (superfine) sugar
435 g (15¼ oz/3½ cups) white strong flour
60 ml (2 fl oz/¼ cup) olive oil

1 Place the yeast, sugar and 80 ml (2¾ fl oz/⅓ cup) warm water in a small bowl and stir well. Leave in a warm, draught-free place for 5 minutes, or until bubbles appear on the surface. The mixture should be frothy and slightly increased in volume. If your yeast doesn't foam, it is dead, so you will have to discard it and start again.

2 Sift the flour and ½ teaspoon salt into a large bowl and make a well in the centre. Add the yeast mixture, oil and 125 ml (4 fl oz/½ cup) warm water and mix together. Add a little more water if the dough is dry.

3 Gather the dough into a ball and turn out onto a lightly floured surface. Knead for 12 minutes, or until soft and elastic.

4 Place in a lightly oiled bowl and brush the top with oil. Cover with plastic wrap or a damp tea towel (dish towel) and leave in a warm, draught-free place for 1–1½ hours, until doubled in size. Knock back the dough. Divide the dough and gently knead on a lightly floured surface to the desired size and shape.

NOTE: To make a classic topping, using a half-quantity of pizza dough, roll out to a 30 cm (12 inch) circle. Spread 185 ml (6 fl oz/¾ cup) bottled tomato pasta sauce over the base. Top with 125 g (4½ oz) sliced Italian salami, cut into strips. Follow with 2 tablespoons chopped basil; 125 g (4½ oz) sliced small button mushrooms; 1 onion, cut into thin wedges; ½ green capsicum (pepper), sliced; and 12 pitted black olives. Place 6 anchovy fillets over the top and sprinkle with 150 g (5½ oz) grated mozzarella cheese and 30 g (1 oz) grated parmesan cheese. Bake in a 190°C (375°F/Gas 5) oven for 30 minutes.

potato and onion pizza

❋

Preparation time: 40 minutes
Cooking time: 45 minutes
Serves 4

2 teaspoons dried yeast
½ teaspoon sugar
185 g (6½ oz/1½ cups) white strong flour
150 g (5½ oz/1 cup) wholemeal (whole-wheat) plain (all-purpose) flour
1 tablespoon olive oil

TOPPING
1 large red capsicum (pepper)
1 potato
1 large onion, sliced
125 g (4½ oz) soft goat's cheese, crumbled
35 g (1¼ oz/¼ cup) capers
1 tablespoon dried oregano
1 teaspoon olive oil

1 Mix the yeast, sugar, a pinch of salt and 250 ml (9 fl oz/1 cup) warm water in a bowl. Leave in a warm, draught-free place for 10 minutes, or until bubbles appear on the surface. The mixture should be frothy and slightly increased in volume. If your yeast doesn't foam, it is dead, so you will have to discard it and start again.
2 Sift both flours into a bowl. Make a well in the centre, add the yeast mixture and mix to a firm dough. Knead on a lightly floured surface for 5 minutes, or until smooth. Place in a lightly oiled bowl, cover with plastic wrap or a damp tea towel (dish towel) and leave in a warm, draught-free place for 1–1½ hours, or until doubled in size.
3 Preheat the oven to 200°C (400°F/ Gas 6). Brush a 30 cm (12 inch) pizza tray with oil. Knock back the dough and knead for 2 minutes. Roll out to a 35 cm (14 inch) round. Put the dough on the tray and tuck the edge over to form a rim.
4 To make the topping, cut the capsicum into large flattish pieces and remove the membrane and seeds. Place, skin-side up, under a hot grill (broiler) until blackened. Cool in a plastic bag, then peel away the skin and cut the flesh into narrow strips.
5 Cut the potato into paper-thin slices and arrange over the base with the capsicum, onion and half the cheese. Sprinkle with the capers, oregano and 1 teaspoon cracked pepper and drizzle with oil. Brush the crust with oil and bake for 20 minutes. Add the remaining cheese and bake for 15–20 minutes, or until the crust has browned. Serve in wedges.

pissaladière

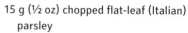

Preparation time: 50 minutes
Cooking time: 2 hours
Serves 8

2 teaspoons dried yeast
1 teaspoon caster (superfine) sugar
310 g (11 oz/2½ cups) white strong flour

2 tablespoons milk powder
1 tablespoon vegetable oil

TOMATO AND ONION TOPPING
80 ml (2½ fl oz/⅓ cup) olive oil
3–4 garlic cloves, finely chopped
6 onions, cut into thin rings
400 g (14 oz) tin chopped tomatoes
1 tablespoon tomato paste (concentrated
    purée)

15 g (½ oz) chopped flat-leaf (Italian)
    parsley
1 tablespoon chopped thyme
3 x 50 g (1¾ oz) tins anchovy fillets, drained
    and halved lengthways
36 small black olives

1 Lightly grease two 30 cm (12 inch)
pizza trays. Put the yeast, sugar and
250 ml (9 fl oz/1 cup) warm water in
a small bowl and stir well. Leave in a
warm, draught-free place for 10 minutes,
or until bubbles appear on the surface.
The mixture should be frothy and slightly
increased in volume. If your yeast doesn't
foam, it is dead, so you will have to
discard it and start again.
2 Sift 250 g (9 oz/2 cups) of the flour,
the milk powder and ½ teaspoon salt
into a large bowl and make a well in the
centre. Add the oil and yeast mixture
and mix thoroughly. Turn onto a lightly
floured surface and knead for 10 minutes,
gradually adding the remaining flour,
until smooth and elastic. Place the dough
in an oiled bowl and brush the surface
with oil. Cover with plastic wrap and
leave in a warm, draught-free place for
30 minutes, or until doubled in size.
3 Meanwhile, to make the topping, heat
the oil in a saucepan. Add the garlic and
onion and cook, covered, over low heat
for about 40 minutes, stirring frequently.
The onion should be softened but not
browned. Uncover and cook, stirring
frequently, for a further 30 minutes, or
until lightly golden. Take care not to burn.
Allow to cool.
4 Put the tomatoes in a saucepan and
cook over medium heat, stirring often, for
20 minutes, or until thick and reduced
to about 250 ml (9 fl oz/1 cup). Remove
from the heat and stir in the tomato paste
and herbs. Season to taste. Cool, then stir
into the onion mixture.
5 Preheat the oven to 220°C (425°F/
Gas 7). Knock back the dough, then turn
out onto a floured surface and knead for
2 minutes. Divide in half. Return one half
to the bowl and cover. Roll the other out
to a 30 cm (12 inch) circle and press into
a tray. Brush with olive oil. Spread half

the onion and tomato mixture evenly over the dough, leaving a small border. Arrange half the anchovy fillets over the top in a lattice pattern and place an olive in each square. Bake for 15–20 minutes, or until the dough is cooked through and lightly browned. Repeat with the rest of the dough and topping.

NOTE: If your oven can accommodate both pissaladière at once and you want to cook them together, the cooking time will be longer. Rotate the trays towards the end of cooking time.

yorkshire puddings

❋

Preparation time: **10 minutes**
    + 1 hour chilling time
Cooking time: **35 minutes**
Makes **6**

90 g (3¼ oz/¾ cup) plain (all-purpose) flour
125 ml (4 fl oz/½ cup) milk
2 eggs
30 g (1 oz) oil, ghee, dripping or lard, melted

1 Sift the flour and ½ teaspoon salt into a bowl, make a well in the centre and whisk in the milk. In a separate bowl, whisk the eggs until fluffy, then add them to the batter and mix well. Add 125 ml (4 fl oz/½ cup) water and whisk until large bubbles form. Cover with plastic wrap and refrigerate for 1 hour.
2 Preheat the oven to 220°C (425°F/ Gas 7). Put ½ teaspoon oil into six of the holes in a 12-hole 80 ml (2½ fl oz/ ⅓ cup) muffin tray. Heat the tray in the oven for 3–4 minutes, or until the oil is smoking. Beat the batter again until bubbles form and pour into each hole to three-quarters full. Bake for 20 minutes, then reduce the oven to 180°C (350°F/ Gas 4) and bake for 10–15 minutes more, or until puffed and golden. Serve immediately. Traditionally, these are served with roast beef and gravy.

yorkshire puddings

These first appeared on English tables in the 18th century when a batter made with dripping was cooked underneath the roasting joint (usually mutton) so that it would absorb the juices from the meat. This was called 'dripping pudding'. Later, a lighter version based on eggs, milk and flour and prepared in individual muffin tins was developed. Today it is served with a traditional roast. It is a cross between a soufflé and an American popover. Yorkshire puddings puff up when baked but can deflate rapidly and therefore should be served immediately.

sally lunn

One of the many tales of the origins of Sally Lunn has it that the name comes from an English baker in the late 18th century called Sally Lunn who had a bakery in Bath. Another more romantic variation of the story is that a well-known baker and musician bought the bakery and wrote a song about Sally Lunn and named the bun after her. It is popular not just in England and France, but the United States, especially in the south. Sally Lunn is a term used for a variety of yeast and soda breads and can be made as sweet large buns or teacakes.

sally lunn

✻ ✻ ✻

Preparation time: **35 minutes**
  + 2 hours 30 minutes proving time
Cooking time: **45 minutes**
Makes **1 bun**

2 teaspoons dried yeast
1 teaspoon caster (superfine) sugar
3 eggs, at room temperature
185 ml (6 fl oz/¾ cup) milk, warmed
115 g (4 oz/⅓ cup) honey
125 g (4½ oz) butter, melted
500 g (1 lb 2 oz/4 cups) plain (all-purpose) flour
1 tablespoon sugar, extra
1 tablespoon milk, extra

1 Grease a deep 25 cm (10 inch) round tin and line the base with baking paper. Put 60 ml (2 fl oz/¼ cup) warm water, the yeast and sugar in a small bowl and stir well. Leave in a warm, draught-free place for 10 minutes, or until bubbles appear on the surface. The mixture should be frothy and slightly increased in volume. If your yeast doesn't foam, it is dead, so discard it and start again.

2 Place the eggs, milk, honey, butter, ½ teaspoon salt, 250 g (9 oz/2 cups) of the flour and the yeast mixture in a large bowl. Using electric beaters, beat at medium speed for 5 minutes, then stir in enough of the remaining flour to make a thick batter. Cover loosely with plastic wrap and leave in a warm, draught-free place for 1–1½ hours, or until the batter is well risen. Stir the batter until the volume decreases and it is smooth.

3 Spoon the batter into the tin using a ladle or large spoon, then flatten the surface of the batter with lightly oiled hands. Cover with plastic wrap and leave to rise again for 1 hour, or until the batter reaches the top of the tin.

4 Preheat the oven to 180°C (350°F/ Gas 4). Bake for 35–40 minutes, or until a skewer inserted into the centre of the bread comes out clean. Brush with the combined extra sugar and milk, then return to the oven for 5 minutes. Turn out onto a wire rack and leave for 20 minutes. Slice and serve while still warm.

NOTE: Sally Lunn bread is a cake-like bread that is often served for afternoon tea. It is traditionally served in the following way. Leave the bread to cool, then slice it horizontally into three equal layers. Toast and butter each side, then reassemble into the original bun shape and slice for serving, as shown. It can also be sliced in the same way you usually slice bread. It keeps for up to 5 days in an airtight container and can be frozen for up to a month.

into a large bowl. Make a well in the centre and pour in the yeast mixture and beaten egg. Beat the mixture with a wooden spoon until well combined and the mixture forms a rough ball. Turn out onto a lightly floured surface and knead for 5 minutes, or until the dough is smooth and firm. Gradually incorporate small amounts of the butter into the dough. This will take about 10 minutes and the dough will be very sticky.

3 Sprinkle a clean work surface, your hands and the dough with a small amount of the remaining flour. Knead the dough lightly for 10 minutes, or until smooth and elastic. Place in a large buttered bowl and brush the surface with oil. Cover with plastic wrap and leave in a warm, draught-free place for 1½–2 hours, or until well risen. Knock back the dough and divide in half. Cover one half with plastic wrap and set aside. Divide the other half into six even-sized pieces. Remove a quarter of the dough from each piece. Mould the larger pieces into even rounds and place into the brioche moulds. Brush the surface with the combined egg yolk and cream glaze. Shape the small pieces into even-sized balls and place on top of each round. Push a floured wooden skewer through the centre of the top ball to the base of the round, then remove — this will secure the ball to the round. Brush again with the glaze, cover and leave in a warm, draught-free place for 45 minutes, or until well risen.

4 Meanwhile, place the remaining dough in the bread tin and brush with the glaze. Cover and leave in a warm place for 1 hour, or until well risen.

5 Preheat the oven to 210°C (415°F/ Gas 6–7). Bake the small brioche for 10 minutes, then reduce the oven to 180°C (350°F/Gas 4) and bake for a further 10 minutes, or until golden and cooked. Turn out immediately onto a wire rack to cool. Increase the oven to 210°C (415°F/Gas 6–7). Bake the medium loaf for 15 minutes. Reduce the oven to 180°C (350°F/Gas 4) and bake for a further 15 minutes, or until golden and cooked. Turn out onto a wire rack to cool.

brioche

✳ ✳ ✳

Preparation time: 1 hour + 3 hours proving time
Cooking time: 50 minutes
Makes 6 small and 1 medium brioche

2 teaspoons dried yeast
1 teaspoon caster (superfine) sugar
125 ml (4 fl oz/½ cup) warm milk
540 g (1 lb 3 oz/4¼ cups) (all-purpose) flour
2 tablespoons caster (superfine) sugar, extra
4 eggs, at room temperature, lightly beaten
175 g (6 oz) butter, softened
1 egg yolk, extra
1 tablespoon pouring (whipping) cream

1 Grease six small brioche moulds and a 11 x 21 cm (4¼ x 8¼ inch) loaf (bar) tin (if brioche moulds are not available, bake as two loaves). Put the yeast, sugar and warm milk in a small bowl and stir well. Leave in a warm, draught-free place for 10 minutes, or until bubbles appear on the surface. The mixture should be frothy and slightly increased in volume. If your yeast doesn't foam, it is dead, so you will have to discard it and start again.

2 Sift 500 g (1 lb 2 oz/4 cups) of the flour, 1 teaspoon salt and the extra sugar

hot cross buns

✹ ✹

Preparation time: **30 minutes**
  + 1 hour proving time
Cooking time: **25 minutes**
Makes **12 buns**

1 tablespoon dried yeast or 30 g (1 oz)
  fresh yeast
500 g (1 lb 2 oz/4 cups) white strong flour
2 tablespoons caster (superfine) sugar
1 teaspoon mixed (pumpkin pie) spice
1 teaspoon ground cinnamon
40 g (1½ oz) butter
150 g (5½ oz/1¼ cups) sultanas
  (golden raisins)

PASTE FOR CROSSES
30 g (1 oz/¼ cup) plain (all-purpose) flour
¼ teaspoon caster (superfine) sugar

GLAZE
1½ tablespoons caster (superfine) sugar
1 teaspoon powdered gelatine

1 Lightly grease a baking tray. Put the yeast, 2 teaspoons of the flour, 1 teaspoon of the sugar and 125 ml (4 fl oz/½ cup) warm water in a small bowl and stir well. Leave in a warm, draught-free place for 10 minutes, or until bubbles appear on the surface. The mixture should be frothy and slightly increased in volume. If your yeast doesn't foam, it is dead, so you will have to discard it and start again.
2 Sift the remaining flour and spices into a large bowl and stir in the sugar. Using your fingertips, rub in the butter. Stir in the sultanas. Make a well in the centre, stir in the yeast mixture and up to 185 ml (6 fl oz/¾ cup) water to make a soft dough. Turn the dough out onto a lightly floured surface and knead for 5 minutes, or until smooth, adding more flour if necessary to prevent sticking. Put in a large floured bowl, cover with plastic wrap or a damp tea towel (dish towel) and leave in a warm, draught-free place for 30–40 minutes, until doubled in size.
3 Preheat the oven to 200°C (400°F/ Gas 6). Turn the dough out onto a lightly floured surface and knead gently to deflate. Divide into 12 portions and roll into balls. Place on the tray, just touching each other, in a rectangle three rolls wide and four rolls long. Cover loosely with plastic wrap or a damp tea towel and leave in a warm, draught-free place for 20 minutes, until nearly doubled in size.
4 To make the crosses, mix the flour, sugar and 2½ tablespoons water into a paste. Spoon into a paper piping (icing) bag and pipe crosses on top of the buns. Bake for 20 minutes, or until golden brown. To make the glaze, put the sugar, gelatine and 1 tablespoon water in a small saucepan and stir over low heat until dissolved. Brush over the hot buns and leave to cool.

NOTE: These spiced, sweet, yeasted traditional Easter buns are heavily glazed and usually served warm or at room temperature. They are split open and buttered, or sometimes toasted. The dried fruit in these hot cross buns can be varied. Often, currants and chopped candied peel are used. The crosses are sometimes made with pastry instead of flour and water paste, or crosses can be scored into the dough prior to proving.

challah

✹ ✹ ✹

Preparation time: 1 hour + 2 hours 10 minutes
proving time
Cooking time: 1 hour 5 minutes
Makes 1 loaf

275 g (9¾ oz) boiling potatoes, cubed
2 teaspoons dried yeast
80 ml (2½ fl oz/⅓ cup) oil
2 large eggs
2 large egg yolks
2 tablespoons honey
550 g (1 lb 4 oz/4½ cups) white strong
flour
1 egg yolk, extra
sesame seeds or poppy seeds, to sprinkle

1 Boil the potato in 625 ml (21½ fl oz/
2½ cups) water for 10 minutes, or
until very soft. Drain well, reserving the
cooking liquid. Set aside for 5 minutes
to cool, then mash the potato until very
smooth. Grease and lightly flour a baking
tray. Put the yeast and 125 ml (4 fl oz/
½ cup) warm water in a small bowl and
stir well. Leave in a warm, draught-free
place for 10 minutes, or until bubbles
appear on the surface. The mixture
should be frothy and slightly increased in
volume. If your yeast doesn't foam, it is
dead, so discard it and start again.
2 Put the oil, eggs, egg yolks, honey,
1½ teaspoons salt, 125 ml (4 fl oz/
½ cup) reserved cooking liquid and the
potato in a large bowl and beat with a
wooden spoon until smooth. Leave to
cool. Add the yeast mixture and gradually
mix in 250 g (9 oz/2 cups) of the flour,
beating until smooth. Add another 185 g
(6½ oz/1½ cups) flour and mix until a
rough soft dough is formed. Place the
dough on a lightly floured work surface.
Knead for 10 minutes, or until the dough
is smooth. Incorporate the remaining
flour, as required, to keep the dough from
sticking. Place in an oiled bowl and brush
the surface with oil. Cover with plastic
wrap or a damp tea towel (dish towel)
and leave in a warm, draught-free place
for 1½ hours, or until doubled in size.

3 Turn the dough out onto a floured
work surface and knead for 4 minutes.
Divide the dough into two portions, a
one-third portion and a two-thirds
portion, then divide each portion into
three equal parts. Leave to rest for
10 minutes. Roll each part into ropes
about 35 cm (14 inches) long, with the
centre slightly thicker than the ends.
Braid the three thicker ropes, pinching
the ends together firmly. Place the braid
on the prepared tray. Whisk the extra egg
yolk and 1 tablespoon water and brush
some over the surface of the challah.
Repeat the process with the remaining
three ropes and place on top of the first
braid, making sure the ends of the braids
overlap. Secure tightly and brush the
surface with some of the egg glaze. Cover
with plastic wrap and leave in a warm,
draught-free place for 30 minutes, or
until doubled in size. Preheat the oven
to 180°C (350°F/Gas 4).
4 Brush the dough with the remaining
egg glaze and sprinkle evenly with sesame
seeds or poppy seeds. Bake the loaf for
50–55 minutes, or until golden brown.
Transfer to a wire rack to cool.

NOTE: No Shabbat (Jewish Sabbath)
dinner would be complete without a loaf
of this rich, braided bread.

greek easter bread

Preparation time: **35 minutes**
  + 1 hour 40 minutes proving time
Cooking time: **45 minutes**
Makes **1 loaf**

2 teaspoons dried yeast
125 ml (4 fl oz/½ cup) milk
60 g (2¼ oz) butter
55 g (2 oz/¼ cup) caster (superfine) sugar
1 teaspoon finely grated orange zest
375 g (13 oz/3 cups) white strong flour
1 teaspoon ground aniseed
1 egg, lightly beaten
2 dyed hard-boiled eggs (optional)

TOPPING
1 egg, lightly beaten
1 tablespoon milk
1 tablespoon sesame seeds
1 tablespoon chopped slivered almonds
1 tablespoon caster (superfine) sugar

1 Place the yeast and 2 tablespoons warm water in a small bowl and stir well. Leave in a warm, draught-free place for 10 minutes, or until bubbles appear on the surface. The mixture should be frothy and slightly increased in volume.
2 Combine the milk, butter, sugar, orange zest and ½ teaspoon salt in a small saucepan. Heat until the butter has melted and milk is just warm. Sift 310 g (11 oz/2½ cups) of the flour and the aniseed into a large bowl. Make a well in the centre, add the yeast and milk mixtures, then the egg. Gradually beat into the flour for 1 minute, until smooth.
3 Turn out onto a lightly floured surface. Knead for 10 minutes, incorporating the remaining flour, or until the dough is smooth and elastic. Place in an oiled bowl and brush the surface with oil. Cover with plastic wrap and leave in a warm place for 1 hour, or until well risen.
4 Lightly grease a baking tray. Knock back the dough (one punch with your fist) and knead for 1 minute. Divide the dough into three equal pieces. Roll each portion into a sausage 35 cm (14 inches) long.

Put the dough on the tray and sprinkle sesame seeds, almonds and sugar on top.

If you are using dyed eggs, press them into the dough after plaiting.

Plait the strands and fold the ends under. Place on the tray.

5 To make the topping, combine the egg and milk and brush over the dough. Sprinkle with the sesame seeds, almonds and sugar (if using dyed eggs, push them into the dough — see Note). Cover with lightly oiled plastic wrap and leave in a warm, draught-free place for 40 minutes, or until the dough is well risen.

6 Preheat the oven to 180°C (350°F/ Gas 4). Bake for 30–40 minutes, or until cooked. The bread should sound hollow when tapped on the base.

NOTE: Use Greek red dye, available in some Greek speciality food stores, which comes with instructions for dyeing eggs.

saffron buns

✴ ✴

Preparation time: 30 minutes
  + 2 hours proving time
Cooking time: 10 minutes
Makes 16

2 teaspoons dried yeast
500 ml (17 fl oz/2 cups) lukewarm milk
150 g (5½ oz) unsalted butter, chopped
½ teaspoon saffron threads
875 g (1 lb 15 oz/7 cups) white strong flour
160 g (5½ oz/⅔ cup) sugar
160 g (5½ oz/1 cup) raisins
2 eggs, lightly beaten

1 Combine the yeast with 125 ml (4 fl oz/½ cup) lukewarm milk in a small bowl. Set aside for 5 minutes, or until foamy. Melt the butter in a small saucepan, add the saffron and remaining milk and stir over low heat until warm. Remove from the heat and cover.

2 Sift the flour into a large bowl, stir in the frothy yeast, 1 teaspoon salt, sugar and half the raisins, then make a well in the centre. Add the just-warm saffron milk mixture and half of the egg. Mix with a flat-bladed knife, using a cutting action, until the mixture comes together to form a soft dough.

saffron

This is the most expensive spice in the world. It comes from the dried stigma of a crocus plant species. The word comes from the Middle East and can be traced as far back as Phoenician times. Saffron has been used for centuries for colouring and flavouring food. It is well known for its use in savoury dishes, especially rice dishes such as paella and risotto, but is also used to add colour and a slightly bitter flavour to yeasted breads and cakes. Saffron threads can be bought in small containers from speciality food stores. Keep in an airtight container in a cool, dark place, as saffron threads lose their colour and flavour if exposed to light.

3 Turn the dough out onto a lightly floured work surface and knead for 5–7 minutes, or until smooth. Place the dough in a large, lightly oiled bowl, cover with plastic wrap or a damp tea towel (dish towel), and leave in a warm, draught-free place for 1–1½ hours or until doubled in size.

4 Turn out onto a lightly floured surface and knead for 5 minutes. Cut into 16 even portions. Roll each portion into a sausage shape about 20 cm (8 inches) long and then form each into an 'S' shape. Place on a greased baking tray. Cover and set aside in a warm, draught-free place for 30 minutes, or until doubled in size. Preheat the oven to 200°C (400°F/Gas 6).

5 Brush the buns with the remaining beaten egg and decorate with the remaining raisins, placing them gently into the 'S' shape and being careful not to deflate the buns. Bake for 10 minutes, or until the tops are browned and the buns feel hollow when tapped on the base. Transfer to a wire rack to cool. Serve warm or cold, plain or buttered.

individual panettone

✷✷

Preparation time: 30 minutes + 1 hour soaking
   and 1 hour 40 minutes proving time
Cooking time: 35 minutes
Makes 8

95 g (3¼ oz/½ cup) chopped dried apricots
75 g (2¾ oz/½ cup) currants
80 g (2¾ oz/½ cup) sultanas (golden
   raisins)
125 ml (4 fl oz/½ cup) Marsala
2 teaspoons dried yeast
185 ml (6 fl oz/¾ cup) milk, warmed
125 g (4½ oz/½ cup) caster (superfine) sugar
180 g (6¼ oz) butter, softened
2 teaspoons natural vanilla extract
3 eggs
2 egg yolks
500 g (1 lb 2 oz/4 cups) white strong flour
1 teaspoon ground aniseed
icing (confectioners') sugar, to dust

1 Combine the fruit and Marsala in a
bowl, cover with plastic wrap and stand
for 1 hour, or until most of the liquid is
absorbed. Put the yeast, warm milk and
1 teaspoon of the sugar in a bowl, mix
well and leave in a warm, draught-free
place for about 10 minutes, or until
bubbles appear on the surface. The
mixture should be frothy and slightly
increased in volume. If your yeast doesn't
foam, it is dead, so you will have to
discard it and start again.

2 Place the butter, vanilla and the
remaining sugar in a bowl and beat using
electric beaters until light and fluffy. Add
the eggs and yolks one at a time, beating
well after each addition.

3 Sift the flour and aniseed into a bowl,
make a well in the centre and add the
yeast mixture, butter mixture and fruit
mixture. Mix with a flat-bladed knife, until
the mixture forms a soft, sticky dough.
Cover with plastic wrap or a damp tea
towel (dish towel) and leave in a warm,
draught-free place for 40 minutes, or until
the dough has doubled in size.

4 Lightly oil the base and sides of eight
125 ml (4 fl oz/½ cup) soufflé dishes. Cut
a strip of brown paper long enough to fit
around the inside of each dish and tall
enough to come 10 cm (4 inches) above
the edge. Fold down a cuff about 2 cm
(¾ inch) deep along the length of each
strip. Make diagonal cuts up to the fold
line on each strip, about 1 cm (½ inch)
apart. Fit the strips around the inside of
the dishes, pressing the cuts so they sit
flat around the bottom edge of the dish.
Cut circles of brown paper using the dish
as a guide, place in the base of each dish,
and grease the paper.

5 Turn the dough out onto a floured
surface and knead for 3 minutes, or until
smooth. You will need more flour, up to
60 g (2¼ oz/½ cup) — the dough should
be soft but not sticky. Divide into eight
equal portions and press into the dishes.
Cover with plastic wrap or a damp tea
towel and leave in a warm, draught-free
place for 1 hour, or until doubled in size.

6 Preheat the oven to 200°C (400°F/
Gas 6). Bake for 30–35 minutes, or until
golden brown and cooked through when
tested with a skewer. Remove from the
soufflé dishes, leaving the paper attached.
Dust with icing sugar, if desired. Serve
warm or cold.

NOTE: If your panettone has gone stale
and dried too much, you can still eat it.
It is good for toasting or can be used to
make bread and butter pudding.

stollen

✹✹

Preparation time: 30 minutes + 2 hours
   45 minutes proving time
Cooking time: 40 minutes
Makes 1 loaf

80 ml (2½ fl oz/⅓ cup) lukewarm milk
2 teaspoons sugar
1 teaspoon dried yeast
125 g (4½ oz) butter, softened
90 g (3¼ oz/⅓ cup) caster (superfine)
   sugar
1 egg
2 teaspoons natural vanilla extract
½ teaspoon ground cinnamon
375 g (13 oz/3 cups) white strong flour
80 g (2¾ oz/½ cup) raisins
75 g (2¾ oz/½ cup) currants
95 g (3¼ oz/½ cup) mixed peel (mixed
   candied citrus peel)
60 g (2¼ oz/½ cup) slivered almonds
30 g (1 oz) butter, melted
icing (confectioners') sugar, to dust

1 Put the milk, sugar, yeast and 80 ml (2½ fl oz/⅓ cup) warm water in a small bowl and mix well. Leave in a warm, draught-free place for 10 minutes, or until bubbles appear on the surface. The mixture should be frothy and slightly increased in volume. If your yeast doesn't foam, it is dead, so you will have to discard it and start again.

2 Beat the butter and sugar using electric beaters until light and creamy, then beat in the egg and vanilla. Add the yeast mixture, cinnamon and almost all the flour and mix to a soft dough, adding more flour if necessary. Turn out onto a lightly floured surface and knead for 10 minutes, or until the dough is smooth and elastic. Place in a lightly oiled bowl, cover with plastic wrap or a damp tea towel (dish towel) and leave in a warm, draught-free place for 1 hour 45 minutes or until doubled in size.

3 Knock back the dough (one punch with your fist) and press it out to a thickness of about 1.5 cm (⅝ inch). Sprinkle the fruit and nuts over the dough, then gather up and knead for a few minutes to mix the fruit and nuts evenly through the dough.

4 Lightly grease a baking tray. Shape the dough into an oval about 18 cm (7 inches) wide and 30 cm (12 inches) long. Fold in half lengthways, then press down to flatten slightly, with the fold slightly off centre on top of the loaf. Place on the tray, cover with plastic wrap and leave in a warm, draught-free place for 1 hour, or until doubled in size. Preheat the oven to 180°C (350°F/Gas 4).

5 Bake the dough for 40 minutes, or until golden. As soon as it comes out of the oven, brush with the melted butter, allowing each brushing to be absorbed until you have used all the butter. Cool on a wire rack. Dust with icing sugar.

index

Page numbers in *italics* refer to photographs. Page numbers in **bold** type refer to margin notes.